# dancing with strangers

*a memoir*

## mel watkins

*simon & schuster*

Simon & Schuster
Rockefeller Center
1230 Avenue of the Americas
New York, NY 10020

Designed by Jeanette Olender
Manufactured in the United States of America

1  2  3  4  5  6  7  8  9  10

Library of Congress Cataloging-in-Publication Data
Watkins, Mel.
Dancing with strangers: a memoir/Mel Watkins.
p cm.
1. Watkins, Mel—Childhood and youth.
2. Afro-Americans—Ohio—Youngstown—Biography.
3. Afro-Americans—Ohio—Youngstown—Social life and customs.
4. Youngstown (Ohio)—Biography   5. Youngstown (Ohio)—Race
relations.   6. Watkins family.   I. Title.
F499.Y8W38   1998
977.1'3900496073'0092—dc21        97-37631
[B]                                 CIP
ISBN 0-684-80864-1

## *acknowledgments*

Special thanks to my sisters, Doris and Cherrie, my brother-in-law, Leroy, my sister-in-law, Julia, and their friends for prodding my memory about family and the early days in Youngstown; to the gang of old- and not-so-old-timers who gather at Roller's Restaurant to swap tales about black folks in and around the Mahoning Valley each Saturday morning; to Professor Alfred Bright for aiding in the recall of our adolescent adventures; and to Pat Watkins, George Davis, and Walt Shepperd for helping to revive memories and sentiments stoked at Syracuse and Colgate universities.

for my sisters,
Doris and Cherrie

*Remember the dream was yours,*
*And let it guide your way.*

Stephanie Tyrell, Joe Sample, and Steve Tyrell
from "Remember the Dream"

# miss aggie's tale

"They call him Lobo," my grandmother whispered, "but his real name was Dancer. Used to be a slave."

Miss Aggie—that's what we called her—told me about Dancer during her last year, as she lay in our upstairs bedroom and her body slowly bowed to various ailments that, since her stroke, had plagued her and, near the end, reduced her robust frame to a frail stick figure. Jet black hair pulled back in a bun, high cheekbones jutting against withered chocolate skin, splintered lips pursed and barely moving, she cradled her cracked teacup (an heirloom, she said) against her bosom and spun out tales passed down from her parents, grandparents, and others. Ghost stories in which phantasmal "haints" either dissolved into disembodied specters or reared themselves as hooded, white-robed marauders; folktales about Anansi, the West African spider-trickster, or Coyote, the Native American shaman, that reflected her mixed African and Indian ancestry; bona fide tales of slaves and sharecroppers (courageous or craven) and masters (barbarous or benign); and allegorical tales like "Dancer" that, real or imagined, relayed more truth and wisdom than my four-year-old mind could possibly fathom.

I filled her cup with a dark herbal brew that continually warmed on the kitchen stove (she insisted it would sustain her), and as I sat spellbound, she filled my head with sagas, legends, flashes of the spirit. They soared into my child's mind and settled uneasily. Many, unused, faded and sank beyond recall; others I tried to cast out, only to discover later that they had merely retreated to the unconscious. Some, like "Dancer," were put aside, for a time ignored—but not forgotten. Later, they resurfaced unexpectedly, just showed up like those remote, vagrant relatives who sometimes appear at our doorsteps and insistently reacquaint themselves, reaffirm their kinship, and despite our hesitant reception, force us to revisit the past. Much later, I realized that in some ways they did for me what Miss Aggie's herbal brew finally could not do for her.

"Not long after that child walked he showed what he could do," she told me. "Seemed like he had rubber for bones and wings on his feet. First, them white folks didn't take too much notice. They come down to the meetin's on Sunday and watch him strut his stuff, though. He was a bitty mite, so they took to callin' him Low-Boy, then, shortened that to Lobo. So little it was hard to see him out there among all them colored folks, prancing round barefoot, doin' the walk around, the cakewalk, and such as that. Then, they discover that child can do the *men-u-et* and all them s'iety steps just as good as he did the cake and the jig—better than most of them. They took his mamma out the fields and put both of them up in the main house. Used to have Dancer show off whenever they had a great ball. Dressed as fine as he wanna be. Wasn't no nigra women on the plantation could do them dances, so sometime they allowed him to dance with one of them visiting ladies from the North. He just dance pretty as you want to, never said nothin' and seem to be humble as they pleased. Had privileges and eats and clothes like no slave ever had, my father told me—some nobody dared talk about. He might laugh and beat his chest with the colored folks. But when he danced in the main house he put on that innocent smile a his, and whenever they'd stare real hard like he was havin' too much fun, he drop his eyes like you drop a hot poker. Wouldn't miss a beat, though, and, quicker than a wink, he was dancin' and smilin' again.

"But, see, Dancer was thinkin' somethin' else even whilst he smilin' and puttin' them white folks on. Didn't matter what *they* say or thought, child knowed he weren't nobody's property—and didn't 'tend lettin' them think it for long. Then, sho'nough, just about time he was stretchin' into manhood, they woke up and found him gone. Some say he was out ridin' one a his master's finest horses and just kept on goin' till he reach the North. Some say it was one them Northern ladies he danced with made her husband get him a ticket on that underground railroad. And some say one night he just upped and danced on off, spread them wings on his feet and sailed right on up there to follow the North Star. Nobody know for sure. But wasn't no doubt 'bout him being gone. Took his mamma and his baby sister, too, and ain't none of them felt no shackles since that night.

" 'Course now, some say it's a sin to be dancin' and carryin' on—the Lord don't look favorable on no backsliders and midnight prancers. Still, my grandpa use to say, 'The path have the deepest footprints ain't the only road to heaven.' And seems to me, it's better to come up on the Lord dancin', head held high, than walkin', eyes all down at your feet. That way you less likely to trip over somethin' tryin' to block your path.

"Then there's them say never was no Dancer. But don't you let that fool you, son. Them's the same folks always mistakin' fact for truth."

She smiled and paused, eyes scanning my face for a reaction, before continuing. " 'Sides, ain't one of them never 'counted for where Bojangles's daddy come from."

## III

My grandmother spoke that way—riddles within riddles, arcane allusions to old days and older ways that, at the outset, to my restless mind, seemed little more than dusty, aimless meandering. Unwelcome reminders of a far distant past that smacked of horseless carriages, blistering hot cotton fields, and shuffling, dirt-poor, slow-talking, country-store-porch-rocking Negroes obsessed with folksy, old-timey ruminations that seemed no more useful in a Northern industrial town in the late 1940s than that elusive "forty acres and a mule" that some old folks still talked about. Took me near twenty years to begin seeing how sly and artful, how sage and perceptive, she'd been all along.

Nearly another decade passed before I fully appreciated that, as she'd sometimes said, "Two and two ain't always four"—in fact,

could easily be twenty-two or, if the folks doing the math were imag-
inatively divisive enough, even one. That's when I began considering
the real implications of Miss Aggie's story. Saw the parable as I *think*
she intended and started relating it to my own experiences. Mind
you, I say "think" because, by that time, I also realized that, while
not nearly as dangerous, parables and allegories can be near about
as tricky, elusive, and recondite as a slick politician's campaign ora-
tory. Don't even have to go that way, since we've all met those people
who insist on saying *this* to actually say *that* or whatever else they
might have on their minds—with whom, unless you eliminate the
nonsense and pretense, tune into the context as well as the subtext,
you'll most likely miss the real sense. Take those dusky plantation
vassals who bamboozled owners into thinking they had an otherworldly Promised Land on their minds when they rhapsodized
about flying away home to Jesus.

Anyway, it was sometime during the mid-eighties, while sitting at
my desk in the Sunday Book Review section of the *New York Times*
and gazing out over the rooftop of Sardi's restaurant toward the line
of Broadway theater marquees along Forty-fourth Street, that the
real connection was made. Ironic that Miss Aggie's folktale leaped
to mind in those rarefied surroundings. A place where, at least when
I became the first black editor in that department, during the sixties, most all Negro folk wisdom except that spoon-fed by Joel
Chandler Harris's fictional Uncle Remus was dismissed out of hand.
An environment so contrary that a portable phonograph brought in
for a party in the editor's office halted, sputtered, then absolutely refused to play after a Beatles album was replaced with Ray Charles—
the ominous sign did not go unnoticed and several of my colleagues
joined me in stifled laughter. Destiny, you see. *Should have known
that Ray Charles's low-down reflections and inflections—even though
they might have introduced a taste of hip-shaking, soul-searching reality—wouldn't easily fly in the somewhat stuffy confines of editor
Francis Brown's mahogany-and-leather-appointed, first-edition-bound
sanctuary.*

Still, I couldn't shake the perception of how traditionally American was Miss Aggie's Dancer allegory. Talk about rugged individualism or Horatio Alger and pulling yourself up by your own
bootstraps—old Dancer was bootless when he started. Even more
striking was that, although I'd come to enjoy the tale, had some

fuzzy sense of its intention, I hadn't directly related it to myself. Had not grasped that Miss Aggie was wading into some deep waters concerning the fact that what *was* still *is* or, at least, *might well be* and will, most likely, *be again*. Not, mind you, that tremendous advances had not been made between Dancer's nineteenth-century experience and my mid-twentieth-century upbringing in America's heartland. But despite the progress, most Negroes—not to mention Italians, Poles, Irishmen, Asians, Catholics, Jews, and Wasps, as well as all the motley combinations straddling the crevices—were still strutting to someone else's tune, even as they sought to introduce their own individual steps into an American choreography inspired not only by its well-advertised love of Mom, baseball, and apple pie but also by its less heralded infatuation with avarice, bluster, and race.

Same old same old, as we used to crack. But for all that, it still ain't really *all that*. Just part of the deal—what we all, in one way or another, had to confront and, in various different ways, still do.

But suddenly, recognizing the similarities between the circumstances of Dancer's escape from bondage and my own growing up in the Ohio heartland during the forties and fifties, I began thinking of Miss Aggie as a kind of soothsayer. I no longer saw the Dancer story as the old-fashioned, if entertaining, rambling of a beloved matriarch. Instead, it reared as a divination, an eerily illuminating guide for jitterbugging through the snares and pitfalls of an American landscape that, for all its opportunities and whatever else it may be, is thoroughly littered with racial scarecrows, decoys, and bugbears. Saw it finally as a reflection of how—for Ohio steel-town Negroes in the fifties and sixties just as for beleaguered plantation nigras toiling in the antebellum South or, for that matter, most everyone in the nineties world of attitude and platitude, whether they're Afro- or some other variety of ethno-centric—our likenesses far outweigh our differences. And how it just may all come down to a simple street rhyme such as *"Nothin' to it but for you to do it."*

Anyway, I began to look at Dancer's *gittin' ovah* as an allegory—one that remains, for me, just as illuminating now as it was that day at the *Times Book Review* or during the fifties or even way back in the day when it did, *possibly* did, or *did not* happen. Saw him as a kind of elusive, unsung hero. Not of the mythic stature of, say, George Washington, Frederick Douglass, Abe Lincoln, FDR, or Malcolm and Martin, but still vastly more significant than most of our current idols. Particularly those celebrities who, as Robert Penn Warren has pointed out, are too often simply "known for being known" rather than being known for doing something. Something, that is, that you might proudly disclose to your mamma or grandmother or anyone else with the good sense to know right from wrong, def from wack.

Now, I guess I've said all this to say that, perhaps, this hero stuff—fractured and flawed and unlikely as the designation's representatives most often are—is the perfect place to begin a tale of ordinary folks in America's heartland some fifty years ago. A tale that, while not as agile or fragile as Miss Aggie's parable, may still reveal something about Buckeyes and democracy, dodging booby traps and bogeymen, sliding through and *gittin' ovah,* or even feinting and juking and creating your own moves while dancing through America's polyrhythmic procession. Might even suggest why Miss Aggie or anyone else would seriously consider peering back over their shoulder to catch a glimpse of Bojangles's daddy or any of a vast assortment of shifty hobgoblins and spooks that, although they preceded and more or less defined us, have been frivolously abandoned or ignored.

# 1

# heroes
# and
# immigrants

"Heroes ain't born," a wit once quipped, "they're cornered."

True enough, but even at that, they're rare. I discovered that at a very early age, when—like Lash LaRue, Tim McCoy, Roy Rogers, or another of those valiant B-movie Western stars—my father came dashing to my rescue. It happened before I understood what he was about, before I really knew who he was. In fact, unless one counts those Saturday afternoon picture show idols, I didn't actually know what a hero was. If I had, I might have grown up viewing him with the reverence that I and most of my friends felt for heavyweight champ Joe Louis or, perhaps, the bemused admiration many of us had for old Ramrod Jackson, a local hero. Weather permitting, Jackson apparently spent most of his days perched on a wooden crate outside the liquor store at Westlake crossing, where Federal Street, the town's main drag, crossed the railroad tracks before slicing through the newly built housing project. But according to legend and some savvy storytellers, one steamy summer day Jackson set his pint of Thunderbird down without spilling a drop and left his crate long enough to amble over and help pull a family of four from a car that had stalled on the railroad tracks, just before a freight train reduced it to scrap metal. Afterward, Jackson returned to his perch and, although his heroic act was never repeated, became a part of local street lore.

Although he commanded respect, my father was neither a world boxing champion nor a local celebrity of excess magnitude. And, since I was only five years old, even I didn't fully realize what had happened when he saved my young life.

What I felt at the time was helpless and scared—more of my father's anticipated response to my innocent but heedless act than of the near disaster that I'd caused.

He had parked his old battered Model T Ford—the kind with an external crank starter and running boards along the sides—in front of his aunt's house and left me in the backseat. Now, Aunt Whitney's home was on Harry Street, a cobblestone road that might have been conceived by an engineer who longed to design theme parks and roller coasters. It was only one block long, and once you turned off Wilson Avenue to enter, it dipped precariously on a near sixty-degree angle and ended at a dirt cul-de-sac where, with some difficulty, one could turn an automobile around and renegotiate the steep hill. On a dead drop twenty or so feet below the turnabout were railroad tracks that followed the winding banks of the Mahoning River, a dumping ground for the city's raw sewage as well as the industrial waste from the steel mills and factories that seemed to stretch endlessly along the other side of the river.

As usual, my father had warned me to stay put and not to touch anything in the car. But on that hot summer day, left alone for longer than I thought necessary, out of curiosity or boredom or, perhaps, out of some outburst of juvenile defiance, I decided to climb into the front seat. Somehow, in playing with either the gearshift or the hand brake, I unleashed the car. The front wheels were turned on an acute angle toward the curb so, instead of quickly picking up speed, it began its descent slowly. First it rolled sluggishly onto the lawn of the house next door to my aunt's, crushing shrubbery and flowers, before lurching back toward the road and picking up speed.

That's when I began yelling and trying to scramble out of the partially opened passenger-side window.

I've never been sure whether it was my outcry, the clamor of the next-door neighbor who watched the scene from her porch, or mere chance, but just as the car began accelerating my father appeared at the front door of his aunt's house. Seconds later, he was sprinting toward the moving car. He leaped onto the running board and, while yelling at me to keep me from jumping out, tried to apply the hand brake. The car kept rolling—in slow motion, it seemed to me, and in stark contrast to my own frantic thrashing against the window. I was terrified. Then, just before we reached the bottom of the hill, my father pitched himself through the open driver's-side window. He pumped the brake pedal furiously and, just as the car reached the dirt turnabout, sharply twisted the steering wheel to the left. The car swerved and we came to a skidding halt. When the dust settled, the Model T sat facing the upgrade with its boxlike rear end resting about three feet from the slipshod chain, wood fortification, and attached sign that warned drivers of the twenty-foot drop.

My father pulled me back through the passenger-side window, where I had hung during the entire descent. He hugged me, then breathed deeply before shaking his head and pushing me away. By this time my aunt and several other people had rushed down the hill to see if everyone was all right. My father stepped outside and, as he checked the car for damages, assured them that we were okay. When they left, he turned and stared at me as I cowered next to the door, still trembling. Although he was angry (in fact, his teeth were clenched in rage), his eyes reflected more intense concern for me than I'd ever seen or would see again.

"Don't *ever* do that no mo', boy," he said haltingly. "You understand me?"

He didn't have to repeat that warning.

We drove back to our own house in silence. When he told me to go upstairs and drove off, I thought I had miraculously escaped the punishment that I fully expected. No such luck; nothing was quite that simple with my father. When he returned the next day, he gave me one of the worst whippings I ever received. Later, as I sat in an upstairs bedroom nursing my welts, I still wondered if it was me or his Model T that had inspired the heroic dash and rescue.

My father was a hero, and already, I was a blossoming cynic.

His name was Pittman but no one called him that. A few, like my mother, called him Pitt. Mrs. Mitchell, who lived across the street from us when we moved to Woodland Avenue, for reasons unknown to me, always called my father Cheyenne. But most everyone else

called him Tennessee, which, when I was old enough to realize that
he was named after a state, impressed me nearly as much as his
daring rescue.

What did you have to do, to accomplish, to be addressed like
that? What kind of reputation did a man have to build, before he
was considered imposing or estimable enough to be named after a
state, even if it was a Southern state? (Of course, it later occurred to
me that, instead of a compliment, "Tennessee" might have been a
put-down meant to ridicule his country origins. But I quickly dismissed that thought since no one ever laughed at my father, at least
not to his face.)

In one sense, it was easy to see why he commanded so much respect. Although he was a slight man—about five feet eight and less
than 160 pounds—he was wiry and carried himself like a Zulu war-
rior. His broad, rough features were sheathed in skin the color of
polished ebony and punctuated by piercing green eyes that gave
him a distant, exotic look that could switch from warmth and affection to icy intimidation in an instant.

There was an air of mystery about him that was heightened by his
insistent silence. As enigmatic and elusive as the delta blues that
flourished in his namesake state, he seldom offered up anything
about his past, and even when directly questioned, he was evasive.
If pressed, he'd react with a wry grin or cold, deadly stare that usually terminated the conversation. Despite his secretiveness, tales filtered down; others spoke in hushed voices or, sometimes, in fear.
But they began filling in the past. What they finally revealed, to
paraphrase the old James Brown song, was quite simply that "Papa
*Didn't* Take No Mess": *Don't take Papa light/ Cause when Papa gets
uptight,/ He knows he's right, You got yo'self a fight.*

As it turned out, that's one of the reasons that I grew up in Ohio
instead of Memphis.

It seems that in 1939, shortly after I'd been conceived, my mother
summoned my father at his job and told him that the man who lived
next door had reprimanded and struck one of my twin brothers.
When Tennessee came home, the man was still there and the situation intensified. Words were exchanged, and push, as they say, came
to shove. My father nearly always carried at least one gun, and on
this occasion, he fired several shots as the man made a hasty retreat.
He missed but chased the man down and proceeded to pistol-whip

him. The neighbor barely survived and my father escaped immediate imprisonment only because the influential white family for
whom my mother worked intervened. Before the case was settled,
Tennessee left for Ohio.

Actually, the original destination was Detroit, and my oldest sister, Cherrie, traveled with him. They rode as far as Youngstown with
another family who, for their own reasons, had determined that the
North might be more hospitable than Memphis, which had been
ruled with an iron fist by the hard-line segregationist and former
mayor Edward Hull Crump since 1909. When my father found
work, he decided to stay in Ohio. A few months later, he sent for the
rest of the family.

I, of course, don't remember the trip. But when I was ten years
old, one of our cousins came up and, bent with laughter, vividly described just how we looked the day we arrived in Ohio.

"Say yall was some real country niggers. Looked like refugees
from one a them slapstick Hollywood picture," he snickered, before
launching into a long, detailed description.

By that age, I was well aware of how melodramatic and eccentric
my family could be, so his comments didn't come as a total surprise.
Still, his razzing was relentless. He savored every moment, pausing
to regain his composure only after some particularly farcical tidbit
doubled him over. As he told it, when my mother stepped off the bus
with me in one arm and a paper grocery bag stuffed with diapers,
clothes, bottles, and other sundries including scraps of uneaten
food and leftover chicken bones tucked under the other, she looked
to all the world like comedienne Moms Mabley.

Now I'm sure my mother wasn't wearing anything like the signature gingham dress and clodhoppers that Moms Mabley wore on-
stage. But—tired, hot, sweating, and disheveled—she may well have
enacted the role of the weary, overburdened parent that the comedienne affected. She could do that. Moreover, my three brothers and
my sister Doris had already piled off the bus. Huddled together just
inside the arrival gate, surrounded by a trunk and an assortment of
boxes and paper bags that held nearly all of our worldly possessions, they must have enhanced the picture of a family of poor
sharecroppers. With me in tow and a gang of unruly urchins at her
feet, my mother might well have been mistaken for one of those beleaguered black women who, accompanied by a gaggle of wide-eyed

Buckwheat-looking ragamuffins, stumbled through the old *Our Gang* comedies.

Of course, I've always pictured that scene differently. I imagined our arrival in that hot, steamy Greyhound bus terminal as having more in common with poor refugees of a different sort. Aside from the admittedly whimsical appearance we presented as we stood there waiting for my father to pick us up, it seems to me that we more closely resembled those weary, awestricken European immigrants who crowded into Ellis Island waiting rooms before arriving on the shores of New York City to look for a new life in America. But being less than half a year old at the time, I was unconcerned with how we looked, how we may have mirrored some historical trend. My attention was focused solely on my mother's bosom.

If I'd been older, less orally fixated, or more historically inclined, I might have realized that neither the timing nor the manner of our arrival was unusual. We were simply part of a mass exodus of African Americans from the Old South, and in a larger sense, of blacks and whites from rural to urban America. It seems, however, that black folks had more urgent reasons for escaping the agrarian South than most.

Fed up with repressive Jim Crow laws in areas where they were mostly restricted to work as tenant farmers or to dwindling menial jobs as servants, bootblacks, and migrant workers, they left the South in droves during the 1920s. Most headed for Northeastern urban centers like Washington, Philadelphia, and New York, as well as such large Midwestern cities as Chicago, Detroit, and Cleveland; some even ventured to the West Coast and settled in Los Angeles and San Francisco.

The first massive migration to the Youngstown area began during World War I, when steel mill recruiters were sent south to persuade rural blacks to come north and fill jobs vacated by conscripted servicemen. The agents promised high salaries and ideal living conditions, enticing prospective laborers with photos of black families living in large, expensive homes. The pitch worked. Youngstown's Negro population doubled during the 1920s as nearly eight thousand blacks arrived. Although the surge subsided during the Depression, a steady flow of Southern blacks continued migrating to the area during the thirties. By the end of the decade, area steel mills had begun gearing up production again, and accordingly, black migration picked up.

We arrived in Youngstown in the summer of 1940 as part of that second large wave of Southern black emigrants.

Steel mill recruiters, of course, had exaggerated wildly; the ideal working and living conditions that they promised, like visions of gold in the streets that some European immigrants entertained, were mere fantasies. It was not the paradise my father described when he decided we would settle there.

Fanciful photos of beautiful homes notwithstanding, blacks were herded into restricted areas in the city's most undesirable areas when they arrived. And although its targets were usually foreigners, Catholics, and Jews, the Ku Klux Klan was active in the area. By the 1920s, a Memorial Day Klan Konklave with fiery crosses and white hooded robes could attract over twenty-five thousand supporters and spectators to nearby Canfield, and the same year, Klan members were welcomed when they presented a Bible and a silk American flag to assembled students at South High, a school that I would later attend. They did not go away.

The city founders boasted of one of America's largest and most beautiful natural municipal parks, and during the early 1940s, local steel mills produced 10 percent of the nation's steel; but the mills that provided the area's economic base also spewed forth a cloud of soot and debris, which settled and left some neighborhoods coated with grime and saturated with a rancid, sulfuric stench.

Inside the mills, even after the United Steel Workers of America gained a foothold, in 1942, and eliminated some of the worst injustices, black workers were routinely paid less than whites. They were also regularly shunted to such so-called nigger sections as the coke ovens with their nearly unbearable heat and oppressive smoke, or the chipping department, where constant drilling and pounding of air hammers would rock the brain as well as the body.

Still, there was work. And after the Japanese attack on Pearl Harbor, in 1941, and America's increasing involvement in the Second World War, blacks and women were even more urgently needed to fill the jobs of departed soldiers. In some ways, Youngstown must have seemed like Canaan to my family, as it apparently did to many of those that followed. And others did follow—many of them. By the

1950s blacks accounted for almost 20 percent of its near-170,000 population.

As for me, I had been uprooted before taking my first step. My family had made a move that drastically transformed my life. Unlike my brothers and sisters, who were reared in Memphis and steeped in an urban Old South tradition and the down-home rhythms of Beale Street, I would grow up in a less soulful Northern steel town that led one to expect more opportunities and a less rigid application of the color line.

In the forties and fifties, of course, America's heartland seldom offered either the mean-streets drama and random violence depicted in Claude Brown's *Manchild in the Promised Land* or the overtly oppressive backdrop of stifling Jim Crow laws and lynch mobs that haunt many memoirs of blacks who came of age in the South. Instead, to grow up in Ohio was to confront a congenial Midwestern atmosphere and surface tranquillity that insistently suggested all was right with the world. Everyone was promised a bright future. Well, nearly everyone. Things were not quite so clear-cut if you happened to be black or, in some situations, Jewish, Asian, or female. The smiling faces and surface cordiality often masked a less hospitable spirit, and problems could arise, particularly if you were not inclined to stay in your predetermined place amid all the serenity.

Still, there was the promise of something greater. That promise set the tone for the next eighteen years of my life.

### III

To this day I'm not certain how we all fit into Aunt Whitney's house, which was the first home I knew in Youngstown. My father took us directly there after picking us up at the bus depot. I am sure that there is no way his aunt could have been prepared when my eight-year-old brother, McKay, my older, twin brothers, Herbert and Al, my teenage sister Doris, and my mother, Katie, with me in tow, piled out of my father's car and invaded her modest home.

It was a narrow, two-bedroom clapboard dwelling. Inside, the house was immaculate—the type kept by many of those staid, religious, working-class black folks who, once across the Mason-Dixon Line, struggled to insulate themselves from a white world, which in the South had so relentlessly imposed itself. Her home was a sanc-

tuary; the outside world and most white intruders were nearly always vigorously denied. Even salesmen and the insurance man who
came each week to collect ten-cent premiums for a policy that allegedly covered burial costs were stopped at the front door.

The small living room was filled with inexpensive overstuffed
furniture, which was wrapped in plastic. Atop the plastic covers,
delicate, lacelike doilies were carefully placed on the arms and
backs of every couch and chair. Coffee tables and shaky dime-store
étagères were crowded with glass or ceramic knickknacks of nearly
every conceivable type—from farm animals to Aunt Jemima and
Sambo figures. Although I didn't share my aunt's aversion to the
white world, I was surprised by the likenesses of Mary Magdalene
and Jesus Christ. As confusing was the framed photograph of a
smiling Franklin Delano Roosevelt and a faded print of Jesus on
the cross, which hung on one wall next to a photo of a stern Booker
T. Washington. When I was a little older, FDR's photo did not seem
so out of place. Word, at least in the black community, was that he
was definitely passing: "No doubt about it. Man got some tar in
'em. You know ain' no *real* white man gon do nothin' to help us."
Later, I discovered that the sentiment was not confined to the black
community; others, most notably conservative Republicans, had
come to the same conclusion. But before I'd been introduced to the
Baptist church, for the life of me, I couldn't figure out why Aunt
Whitney had a picture of a dead white man nailed to a cross hanging on her wall when live ones were denied access.

We children, of course, were forbidden to touch or sit on anything
in that room. And when McKay, the youngest of my brothers, or I
erred, forgot that edict, we were immediately reprimanded and
punished.

The dining room was similarly off-limits to us. In fact, except for
Sundays, when everyone gathered there for a ceremonious afternoon meal, the room was merely a passageway from the living
room to the kitchen, where nearly all indoor activities occurred. No
one disturbed the six chairs and carefully arranged wooden dining
room table, which was covered by a linen tablecloth and translucent
plastic covering on which sat two unlit candles and a bowl filled
with artificial fruit.

In the evening, under the cover of darkness, the rigid orderliness
was relaxed as we all found places to sleep. The kitchen and dining

room were transformed into an impromptu campsite as foldaway beds were opened and makeshift pallets were prepared for my sisters and brothers. Aunt Whitney retired to an upstairs bedroom with her husband, Tom. I slept with my parents in the other bedroom. The next morning, as if by magic, the house was always returned to its cloistered, pristine state.

For me, it was as eerie and foreboding as the parlor of Amos Linton's funeral home, where for reasons I can no longer recall, my parents had taken me one afternoon. It was dark, silent, stifling, and saturated with a musty, camphorlike odor that, to this day, I associate with old age and death.

Aunt Whitney contributed to the overall sense of gloominess. A prim, stern woman, she always swathed herself in high-collared, jet black dresses that matched her complexion and gave her thin, straight frame a menacing, ghostly aura. Moving stealthily about the house, she seemed to be engrossed in some unspoken, personal vigil that weighed on her even more than our presence there. I seldom remember her smiling and, except for a weekly trek to the Baptist church on the corner, she rarely ventured beyond her own front porch or backyard.

When I was old enough to walk and allowed to follow her, I began to discover that the world was neither as dull and predictable nor as safe as I had come to expect.

In back of the house was a field that stretched about two hundred yards to Shehy Street, which ran parallel to Harry. Apparently unclaimed or, at least, unused by its owners, the property was partially cleared and had become a kind of squatters' garden patch. Many of the families who lived on Harry and Shehy had carved out small vegetable gardens on the slanted turf; some had even built rickety chicken coops. During the summer it was a veritable open-air market. As the war effort escalated in the early forties and products (from cigarettes, shoes, and gasoline to canned vegetables, butter, and meat) were added to the list of items included in the nation's rationing program, those gardens filled many of our neighbors' near-empty stomachs.

My father's aunt rarely set foot in that field, and while we lived at her house, neither did I. Sometimes she would sit on the back porch and shout instructions to her husband, Tom, who was charged with the down-and-dirty task of tilling their plot of tomatoes, collard and turnip greens, lettuce, and onions or, occasionally, of preparing for a Sunday feast of fried chicken by wringing the neck of one or two of the hens they kept in their coop. I was allowed at those times to sit by her side. Despite cringing and grasping her bony fingers, I was hypnotized by the sight of those lifeless animals flailing in the dirt for what seemed like hours after they had been killed.

About two years after we arrived, my family packed up and moved across the field to Shehy Street. It was another two-bedroom frame house, but it was not nearly as substantial as Aunt Whitney's home. And although our new house was only a few hundred yards away, that slight move introduced me to a vastly different environment.

# 2

## madman
## on the hill

Harry was an enclosed road and its sharp incline kept most transient traffic away. Although the homes were modest, all but one was well kept. That one, which set at the bottom of the hill near the dirt turnabout, was little more than a dilapidated wooden shack. Several of the windows were covered over with cardboard and planks, and because its structure was askew, it seemed to hang over the edge of the drop above the railroad tracks. The old man who lived there apparently cleaned the tracks for the rail company, but according to rumors among the adults, he was some sort of reclusive madman who was best left alone. "Yes, Lawd, used to be a good man," Aunt Whitney explained, "then he left the church. Started drinking and foolin' round with them loose women."

I seldom saw him and gladly observed the warnings of the old folks. The other home owners were not as bizarre or neglectful of their property. All of them, black and white, had seemingly determined to resist the blight surrounding them. There was a distinct residential air about the street.

Shehy was entirely different. There were only four houses on our block, all on one side of the street, and the one at the bottom of the hill had been abandoned—for good reason, I suspect, since the others, including our own, were nearly as ramshackle as the madman's shack. Although the street also dipped to a dead end just above the railroad tracks, it was an active block. Across the street, a scrap yard and an adjacent gas station were busy throughout the day. And two doors from my house, at the corner of Wilson Avenue, was a general store and pool hall that had become a neighborhood gathering place.

Across Wilson Avenue was the Ritz Bar, a cabaret that, at the time, catered to whites only but after the war became a black-and-tan bar. When I was allowed to stay up after dark and sit on our front porch, I'd peer up the hill and try to imagine what caused the gales of laughter or the clamor of occasional brawls that broke out and pierced the night. Or I'd listen to the gay, bouncy sounds of big-band and country music that drifted down the hill and skipped lightly through my mind. They seemed to come from a world totally removed from the corner pool hall and my own home, where heavier, bluesy tunes surged from either the jukebox or my sister's record player, throbbing and pulsating throughout my body. Separate even from my mother's church, where gospel music swelled up and nearly burst the walls. The source of that difference remained a mystery, however, since, while we lived on Shehy, I was never permitted to cross Wilson Avenue alone and explore its source.

At the time, I wasn't even allowed to go beyond the front part of the corner store, since my mother considered the pool room and the private room in back a gateway to hell and damnation. On those occasions when I did venture inside to buy candy or soda pop, however, I would linger as long as possible. I watched the men who gathered outside on the porch or sat inside at the shoeshine stand and listened as they jived, swapped stories, and told bawdy jokes that I definitely was not supposed to hear.

"Say you went out wit' ole Lucy, dat bowlegged gal up on Himrod, my man. Yeah, she sho' is fine, and you know what dey say, *De blacker de berry, de sweeter de juice.* And judgin' from her color, she must be real sweet. Fact is, if I was you, I'd watch out, fo' you knows it you gon come down wit the di'betes. And ain nothin' they can do 'bout that, 'cept chop off sumpthin' you don't wants to lose."

Usually I sat inconspicuously near the door listening to the old men lying, but whenever I could, I'd inch toward the entrance to the pool hall, where my brothers sometimes drank beer and played eight ball, or I'd try to peer into the extreme back room, into which my father would often disappear. Later, I discovered that it was a gambling parlor, where games of cooncan, tonk, and craps were played nearly twenty-four hours a day.

By this time I'd acquired the nickname Pepper, the result, I'm told, of having noticed my father's graying hair and shouting out, "Here come my pepper-haired daddy." From that day on Tennessee and practically everyone else called me Pepper. I was only three or four years old but I became something of a mascot in that funky joint. I was the kid with the funny name, but it worked for me. I hung around whenever I could, doing errands and collecting the small change the men handed me. Despite my mother's admonition, I was drawn to the scene. It stood in colorful contrast to the doggedly routine life led by my aunt Whitney's husband, the deacons, and most of the dour, sanctified men who filled the pews of the church my mother took me to on Sundays. For me, it was a welcomed option and I was thrilled to silently observe and absorb as much as I could.

The graying older men with their guarded, penetrating glances, deliberate movements, and rural wit were particularly intriguing. They'd sip homemade whiskey from Dixie cups as they laughingly prodded one another with clever gibes and spun out exotic tales about the South. And although they were much less tolerant of me, I was also fascinated by the upstart young hustlers with their glistening conked hair and razor-sharp raps.

Most were just anonymous faces, but there were some who looked out for me as if I were their own kin. There was Sammy, the cantankerous old Italian who worked the cash register and settled or ended any disputes that arose with a baseball bat that he kept behind the counter next to the Hershey bars. He not only made sure that no one bothered me but also saw to it that no one reneged on their promise to reward me when I came to get cigarettes or a soda for them. Red, so named because of his freckled face, light complexion, and near-auburn-colored hair, was a friend of my father's, but unlike Tennessee, he spent nearly as much time in the store or on the front porch rapping as he did gambling in back. Then there were my brother Al's running buddies, Jitt and Little Jitt, brothers whose rowdy antics and boasting could be heard a block away, and Snag, whose missing front tooth and lean, loose-jointed frame per-

fectly amplified his cocky, wisecracking demeanor and kept everyone in stitches.

They, along with my father and brothers, must have understood
that my being there was a necessary experience, a kind of rite of
passage, since they usually either winked at or encouraged my presence. "C'mon here, Pep," Jitt would shout, "wantcha to see how I
run the table on this here chump."

It was a world filled with excitement, loud, riotous characters,
and laughter that was as distinct from the insistent sobriety of Aunt
Whitney's home as night from day. Yet, as I discovered years later,
despite its enticement and surface allure, it masked pitfalls that
were as dangerous as the hill on which her house set. That lifestyle
was as confining and restrictive as Harry Street, and to enter heed-
lessly was to rush headlong down a steep incline toward a dead end.
Surviving the descent was a feat in itself. But even if you did, as the
madman evidenced, it was a long, hard road that conceded few
turns. No retreat.

At the time, however, I was permitted only to hover at its edges.
Still, for a child, Shehy had many other attractions. Both my
mother and father worked long hours in local plants, so during the
day I was either sent to stay with my father's aunt or left under the
supervision of my brother McKay, who was only eleven or twelve,
one of my sisters, or an occasional teenage baby-sitter. Usually they
allowed me to spend the day playing with Myron, the son of an employee of Herman's scrap yard.

He was a year or so older than I and came to work with his father
nearly every day. One afternoon, he simply walked across the street
and introduced himself; since he was the only other child of my age
in the neighborhood, we struck up a friendship. We spent most of
our time exploring the mysteries of the deserted house at the bottom of the hill, rummaging through the endless piles of rubble and
debris collected by his father (used tires, junked cars, discarded
household appliances, pipes, and scrap metal of every conceivable
type) in search of some hidden treasure, or, much to my neighbors'
dismay, racing through the field that separated Shehy from Harry
Street.

It was a carefree time and I enthusiastically embraced it, tasting
and touching everything I could. At that age, my neighborhood—
the world that I knew—seemed vast and wondrous; in truth, it was

severely limited. Except for occasional auto trips to my parents' jobs or to one of several outdoor markets where they bought food, visits to the barber where my father took me for our biweekly haircuts, and the frantic doom-and-gloom ritual of Reverend Rose's get-down Mt. Carmel Baptist Church, where my mother dutifully took me whenever she was not working on a Sunday, my world was outlined by Harry and Shehy streets, the railroad tracks at the bottom of the hill, and Wilson Avenue. Other than the passing vista seen through the windows of my father's car, I knew practically nothing about Youngstown and, obviously, even less about life. Still, I was testing my own capacity to deal with the small part to which I'd been exposed. From my four-year-old, knothole view, most everything seemed to work flawlessly. Grown-ups appeared to have everything under control.

Obviously, I was very young and very naive, but, as my grandmother was fond of saying and I would later learn to appreciate, "A mole ain't never gon see what his neighbor's up to."

As it turned out, the scrap dealer's son played an important part in my unraveling that strange proverb. In a way, he was my Huck Finn. From the moment we met, I was taken with his confidence and sense of entitlement. Myron projected an aura of self-assurance that was missing even among the young adults I'd met at the corner store. It surfaced in the insolence he displayed with his father—an immigrant, who although aggressive and successful in business, deferred to or encouraged his son's boldness—as well as in the fearless attitude he showed as we played in the neighborhood. Even the cockiest of the Young Turks who hung out at the poolroom, I'd noticed, occasionally tempered their boasting with a wary glance or an uncertain note in their voices. With all their bravado, they seemed aware of some larger, silent, and unseen authority or threat. Not so with Myron; he was cocksure and seemingly undaunted by any outside restraints.

But lest you misunderstand me, let me reiterate that the thought of talking back to my parents never even crossed my mind. I'd landed on my butt too many times for simply allowing a questioning expression to flash across my face to contemplate any such madness. Nor, I should add, did I consider the possibility that Myron might simply have been a spoiled, unruly brat or weigh the influence of race when comparing his behavior to that of the black men around me. I did, however, eagerly join him in a series of adventures, many of which ended with me nursing welts inflicted by my father's belt or the switches that my mother sent me out to retrieve from the nearest tree.

We regularly raced through the garden plots in back of my house or, despite warnings to the contrary, occasionally poached other people's tomatoes or fruit. Myron even convinced me to overcome my fear and, under cover of dusk, spy on the Harry Street madman's shack. (Far from being the monster we'd been led to expect, we discovered that he was simply a lonely drunk who, behind his boarded-up windows, gulped rye whiskey from the bottle as he tearfully mumbled to himself.) And as we grew bolder in our playful escapades, so my sense of the certainty and order of the adult world faded.

Our adventurous spree was ended on a chilly autumn day about six months after we met. Determined to play outside despite temperatures that had dropped near freezing, we decided to build a campfire in the empty lot next to the abandoned house at the bottom of the hill. It took less than five minutes for the wind to sweep some of the burning newspapers and twigs under the old house. Although we stomped and poured dirt over the flames, the dried, rotting beams that supported the porch began simmering, then burst into flames. It seemed only seconds before the entire house was on fire. Play had turned to disaster, and when it was obvious that the fire was completely out of control, we turned and ran—Myron back to the scrap yard, I to the safety of my house. My parents were not at home, and initially, I watched from our porch as the fire engines arrived. But the dried leaves covering the ground had started a brushfire that threatened all the houses on the block, so the firemen were forced to evacuate nearby houses; soon I was huddled in the midst of the crowd that had gathered at the top of the hill to watch the blaze. It took over two hours to put out the fire and secure nearby homes.

Some, I'm sure, suspected that we were the culprits, but no one had actually seen us near the house. And although Myron became a rare visitor on the block and my father glared at me as if I were a criminal for weeks afterwards, neither the scrap dealer's son nor I was ever punished.

Much of the freedom, irresponsibility, and recklessness of those days ended, however, a few months after my fourth birthday. As she put me to bed one evening, my mother told me that my grand-mother had had a stroke. The next day my parents drove to her home, in Tunica, Mississippi, and brought Miss Aggie back to live with us.

I had met her only once, when my parents took me and my brother McKay to spend a week in Mississippi a year earlier. In fact, all I remember about that trip to this day is the unremitting heat, the indelible image of a dirt road near her home, which was lined on either side by vast fields of cotton, and my grandmother's insis-tent warning that neither I nor my brother, under any circum-stances, sass any white person who spoke to us. I suppose it was that incident that caused me to wipe most of that trip from my mind. No one had ever spoken to me so urgently about anything. Nor had anyone ever suggested that I should fear white people or, for that matter, anyone else except the so-called madman of Harry Street. (No one had to tell me to fear and exercise caution around Tennessee.) I hardly knew her, but when she first arrived, more than anything else she frightened me.

Still, she was unable to get around or even walk to the bathroom without help, so I was often asked to take care of her or, at least, stay with her during the day. No one else was available, since my brothers and sisters all worked or went to school, and my parents were usually working. Initially, I resented the responsibility, but af-ter expressing my feelings about it either too often or too emphati-cally and being escorted to the basement to be persuaded otherwise by my father, I learned to live with it.

Later, I began to thrive on it.

From almost the moment she arrived, Miss Aggie made me her confidant. Perhaps it was that near-desperate focus on the past that overtakes old folks when they sense that death is near, or maybe it was my youthful curiosity, or the simple fact that I was a captive au-dience, but even when there were others in the house she would constantly call me to her bedside.

"Come on over here, boy," she'd rasp. "Somebody gon have to talk some sense in yo' head." And when I'd pulled a chair near the bed, she would grasp my hand and begin talking. She seldom offered up details about her own past, mind you. Oh, she would sometimes mention her husband, Thomas, who had died a few years earlier, or the Chandlers, the white family for whom she worked most of her life. But that was only in passing, as were her comments about such day-to-day household concerns as my sisters' whereabouts, my brother McKay's brash back-talking and disobedience, or the arguments that had increasingly begun to erupt between my mother and father. Mostly she told stories, and if they had any vague connection to her personal life, it was so well disguised that I could never tell. Even when she referred to real events, such as the weekly blackouts that left the city in total darkness at night—a precautionary exercise in anticipation of Japanese or Nazi air attacks, which lasted until the end of the war—she spoke impersonally, in parables, as if she were merely echoing some remote, disembodied voice.

"Darkness ain' gon help none," she told me one night as she sat up in bed and a lone candle cast flickering shards of light across her face. "Fact is, some things get mo' clear when it's dark. Them folks better stop all this fightin' and killin'. They can turn out the lights and try and hide the fire, but what they gon do 'bout the stench of the smoke?"

Of course, I had no idea of what she was talking about. I thought about it for weeks but the riddle was beyond me, even though my own covert experience with fire and smoke was still fresh in my mind. Still, she had gotten my full attention. At first, it was just the way she put words together, the sense of mystery and hidden meaning that hovered about the picture images she created. Despite being mystified, I was intent. And occasionally, some sense of what she'd meant filtered through to me. At least, I sometimes thought it did.

Once, she interrupted me while I was rattling on about wanting to be grown up, by saying: "You know, boy, what separates children from us grown people is secrets. Child don't have no secrets. They world is clear and bright as a sunny day in springtime. You'll know when you gettin' grown 'cause that's when you gon have to start hidin' things. . . . from other folks well as from yo'self. Don't be in no hurry. Soon enough that spring day gon start turnin' gray and gloomy and befo' you know it you gon have a head full a clouds and confusion. Secrets pile up and weigh you down like a heavy load, child. That's why old folks is like me, all gray and bent over. Do without it as long as you can."

I guess that was the beginning, the point at which I realized I'd started to lose my childhood innocence. Myron and I had never told anyone about the burning of the old house at the corner. And whether she knew it (which I strongly suspected was true) or not, Miss Aggie's remarks had set off a flash of recognition that forced me to attempt associating my behavior with something beyond my own wants and needs. Not that I was tempted to put down my burden and confess; memories of the flash of my father's belt buckle outweighed my vague awareness of how burdensome a secret might be. Still, for the first time, I felt that I'd partially decoded one of my grandmother's proverbs and had some inkling of what she was really saying.

That wasn't the last time Miss Aggie's tales magically took form for me—moving from murky indirection to reveal some insight that startled and baffled me. The thing is, most of the time I wasn't even aware of it.

You see, I was most interested in slave tales like "Dancer" and animal tales like "The Tortoise and the Hare" or Br'er Rabbit's adventures with the Tar Baby and the briar patch. I was mesmerized by those stories, completely caught up in the action, the surprise endings. I listened and savored them without ever consciously considering or understanding their underlying meaning. Of course, I was being tricked just as surely as was Br'er Fox when he threw Br'er Rabbit back into the briar patch. Miss Aggie had found a means of keeping me by her side and, at the same time, surreptitiously imparting a far more complex vision of the world than I would have otherwise imagined.

If, indeed, that was her intent, it worked perfectly; there was never a more willing dupe. Miss Aggie lived with us for less than a year, but during the last six months, I spent most of my waking hours by her side.

Much later, I realized that the time spent with my grandmother had subtly reshaped my sense of the world around me. Until she arrived, like most children my age, I accepted the authority of adults and the outside world without question. In fact, as I'd later discover, in the Midwest during the forties and fifties few adults actually challenged the ruling powers—even when they had serious reservations about them. Despite World War II and lingering effects of the Depression, most Midwesterners set store by government and religious authority. There was scattered resistance to both FDR's New

Deal and the United States' entry into the war, but in general, conformity and a belief in traditional values and the sanctity of officialdom reigned in Ohio and the rest of the country's heartland.

Those were the fabled "good old days," and Americans both imagined and struggled to present themselves as a just, idealistic community in which wrongdoing would be quickly unearthed and punished and the good would ultimately triumph. Even black Americans, who, as I would soon learn, had more to complain about than most groups, had a deep-seated faith in traditional religion and an as yet unshaken belief that the nation's democratic principles would soon be extended equally to them.

In this setting, impressions of the world initially came in manageable, ordered handfuls that could be fingered, assessed, and easily assimilated; children were expected to digest them as presented. My parents' word was law. I didn't question them or hesitate when told to do something. Moreover, unless I was specifically advised to stay away from them, as in the case of the Harry Street madman, I heeded my neighbors' commands. There were few faster ways of getting an ass whipping than sassing a neighbor or ignoring a warning from one of the dignified, churchly types who sometimes visited on Sundays. Along with one's neighbors, parents, and teachers, Hollywood films and a few newspapers and radio stations defined the world in more or less homogeneous terms.

For me, the seeming orderliness was awesome and overwhelming. My impression was derived from the most commonplace observations: the way my father would always rise at dawn to go to work, for instance, no matter how out of sorts he was the night before; the tacit agreement that ensured that motorists stop at red lights, then simultaneously start again on green; the seeming infallibility of numbers, which, since I was just beginning to count, had assumed a special intrigue for me; how everyone seemed to know the words of whatever hymn Reverend Rose asked them to sing; the near-absolute punctuality of the twelve-thirty train and the whistle that announced its arrival as it passed our house each afternoon en route to the B & O Railroad terminal, which was a few blocks away. Everyday reality and adults' apparent knowledge of and control over it—not to mention me—seemed irrepressible.

Myron and Miss Aggie, however, had begun to awaken a suspicion, if not yet a full-blown awareness, of some chinks in the facade.

I was beginning to suspect that everything was not necessarily what it seemed. Much later, that suspicion would lead me to attempt untangling one of Miss Aggie's more cryptic proverbs—the one that she seemed to take most delight in issuing and repeatedly came back to: "Don't be no fool, son. Go round here mistakin' fact for truth. It ain't always so."

# 3

## arrivals
## and
## departures

During the fall of 1944, we left Shehy, moving from the east side of Youngstown to the more fashionable south side. The most prestigious area was still the north side, where, during the 1930s and 1940s, most of the city's wealthiest families resided and the mere presence of Negroes was discouraged unless they were summoned to cook, clean house, or perform some other domestic or manual chore. But the south side, with its expansive municipal park, was a close second.

Our new neighborhood, of course, was well into a transitional phase when we arrived. Decades before video rental emporiums dotted the landscape, blockbusters were not in the entertainment business; real estate agents had discovered that they could turn a quick profit by bringing poor or minority families into middle-class white neighborhoods, inflaming residents' fears with tales of decreased property values, then selling houses at inflated prices to other poor or minority buyers. By the time we arrived, working-class black and white families, many newly arrived from the South, were rapidly replacing the old-line residents on our block. Our arrival undoubtedly accelerated the process.

In fact, when neighbors saw our family of eight arrive with our meager possessions piled into the back of a borrowed pickup truck, I'm sure some immediately decided to join the exodus. If they didn't consider it on that first day, the thought may have arisen during the spring of the following year when my parents erected a makeshift chicken coop in one of our garages. It wasn't the first on the street but it speeded up the block's countrification. Our neighbors' reactions and the unsettled nature of the neighborhood aside, we moved in without incident. Later, I would happily discover that our house was only two blocks from Mill Creek Park and the well-kept recreational facilities that within a few years would become my home away from home.

Our escape from Shehy was aided by a stroke of luck. Tennessee had hit the numbers, big . . . an event that in many black communities was tantamount to prospectors striking it rich during the old gold-rush days or winning the lottery today.

Tennessee, like many black men during the pre-civil-rights era, was augmenting the salary from his regular job at Republic Steel with what old-timers called a hustle—a scam or secondary source of income that in many instances was necessary to survive or get over. It was a tradition that grew partly out of the general distrust with which blacks viewed mainstream society and white authority, and partly out of the need to supplement paychecks that in most instances were considerably lower than those taken home by white workers doing exactly the same job. Many of Youngstown's black residents had grown up in the South, where they had been victimized themselves or had witnessed friends and relatives being bilked out of property and wages by employers and banks—on occasion even by the courts. And as the least hired and most often fired even in Youngstown's thriving steel industry, they were not inclined to depend entirely on the security of a job. Hard times had a way of rearing up even amidst an apparent feast, the old folks whispered, and if asked, they'd tell you straight out that the most you could expect from white folks was trickery and a whole lotta wish-I-coulds.

"Don't go down there tryin' to deal wit 'em, 'less you got a ace up yo' sleeve, boy."

No, you were well advised to have something to fall back on, and a hustle, whether extralegal or simply a second job, was considered indispensable.

The practice was not confined to laborers or menial workers such as servants and domestics (who in lieu of adequate wages regularly liberated food and household goods from employers who, aware of the wage inequity, condoned the thievery) but extended even to black professionals, lawyers and doctors who sometimes made less than steelworkers and had to take unskilled labor jobs to get by. Some insist, for example, that during the forties and fifties one of the reasons that none of the four or five Negroes hired by the Youngstown police force were ever promoted to positions as officers was that, once they established hustles in the black communities to which they were inevitably assigned, such advancements were unprofitable.

Even the best hustle could go awry, however; and some were uncovered in strange ways. Nearly every Negro in Youngstown knew the story of the black waiter who, after working at the prestigious, private, and highly segregated Youngstown Club for years, built a luxurious new house for himself. He proudly invited his boss to the housewarming. Minutes after arriving at the party, his boss took one look around and exploded. "No way this boy could've paid for this on the money I pay him," he reportedly said. "He must be stealing." The waiter was fired on the spot.

As far as I know, Tennessee's first hustle in Youngstown was working part-time as a numbers runner—collecting bets and turning the wagers over to the local mobsters who ran the policy operation, or bug bank, as it was sometimes called. It may have been his connection with the racketeers that assured that—unlike some others, who after a big hit were informed that they were mistaken about the number they *thought* they had played—he collected immediately. With his winnings ($600) and the generous aid of my brother Al, who had worked and saved over a thousand dollars in savings bonds after quitting school and going to work in the steel mills, my father made the down payment on the Woodland Avenue property. On it stood two identical wood-frame houses, which were separated by a narrow cement driveway. My parents rented one house; the other would remain my home until I graduated from high school and left for New York and college.

It was an exciting time for the entire family, particularly my mother, who hated the shabby Shehy house. But before I'd even begun to explore my new surroundings, a much more critical change occurred.

In December 1944, a week before Christmas, Miss Aggie died.

It took nearly a year for me to forgive her; I'm not sure I ever got over it. I simply could not believe that she had gone.

There was no warning, no dramatics or hysteria. It was early evening, and as usual, she was sitting up in her bed, smiling and talking to me—caught up in the flight of her own words, her own tales. Then, suddenly, she stopped speaking. Her lips froze and a seemingly calm expression settled on her face. Her eyes blinked and fluttered, then closed. A second later, her head rolled gently to one side.

It seemed as though she just lay back and relaxed, as if she had been startled by some unexpected thought or vision, then drifted off in a comforting reverie. I thought she had fallen asleep. But she had been holding my hand, and within minutes her hand stiffened and a chill coursed to the tips of her fingers. Almost instantly, she broke out in small hivelike pimples and the color drained from her skin. At the same time a ghostly, pale gray mask enveloped her face. Death, I discovered, does not announce itself; it descends silently, like a chameleon.

I squeezed her hand, shook it, but there was no response. She did not move.

I sat there for what seemed like an eternity, hoping and praying that she was all right, that it was just a deep sleep. It was as if I was paralyzed; I had never been more frightened, even when Tennessee had loomed over me with his belt. It seemed as though the chill that had moved down her fingers had crept inside me, rooted itself there, piercing and frigid. Finally I realized that she wasn't just sleeping, it was something else. I dropped her hand, stood up, and began backing out of the room. Something was wrong, terribly wrong. And although I had no idea what it was, I thought it was my fault. Somehow, I had failed Miss Aggie when she needed me most.

I turned and ran from the room, screaming, "Mamma, mamma, Miss Aggie sick—Miss Aggie sick." I stumbled down the stairs and raced into the kitchen, where my mother was starting to cook dinner. "Miss Aggie sick, she real sick," I cried. "Somebody help her— she's goin' away. Help her, mamma, please."

At first they ignored me. My father and brother Herbert were sitting in the living room listening to the radio, but they didn't move. And even though I was pulling at the hem of her dress, my mother didn't respond until she looked down, saw the dread in my eyes. Then she pushed me aside and ran upstairs. Moments later, I heard her scream. "Pitt, Pitt, call a doctor quick!"

The next few minutes, hours, were a blur.

My father rushed into the kitchen and picked up the telephone. My brother followed him, brushing past me as he ran upstairs. I crouched in a corner at the bottom of the stairs, petrified.

Before I knew what had happened, the house was filled. Mrs. Clinton, who rented our house next door, appeared first. Then Mrs. Mitchell, who lived across the street, and someone from down the block. Soon the doctor arrived and went upstairs. And somewhere during this time my sisters and brother Al returned. Before long, the house was packed with family members and a crowd of grim-faced, teary-eyed strangers, who stood in small clutches whispering to one another while they somberly shook their heads. From time to time, one of them would approach my mother and attempt comforting her: "Sister Katie, don't you worry none, it's gon be all right. You'll see, the Lord works in mysterious ways, but he don't never burden us with no mo' suffering than we can stand."

I don't remember exactly when, but sometime during the evening an ambulance must have arrived to take Miss Aggie away.

All the while, I was kept in the living room sitting next to Mrs. Clinton. Whenever a piercing wail or the muffled sound of someone moaning, "Lawd, Lawd, oh my Lawd," drifted from upstairs, she or another adult would turn to me, assuring me, "Don't you fret, chile, she gon be all right."

They lied, of course. Miss Aggie wasn't all right.

I never saw her again.

I wasn't told when the funeral took place, for my own good, someone later explained, and for months no one mentioned Miss Aggie's absence in my presence. When I asked about her, my mother would just say, "She done passed," or, "She's gone on to a better place, son. But don't you worry, she's still with us."

For a time, I imagined or, at least, hoped that Miss Aggie was okay—that, like Dancer, she had just upped and flown away. I convinced myself that her disappearance was only temporary, that she'd magically return for me and we'd sail off into that fantasy land that she had conjured up in her stories. I sensed that my parents and their friends were being evasive, but I didn't fully comprehend what had happened until much later. The notion of death never reared itself. As far as I knew, that was something that happened only to scrawny, limp-necked chickens who exhausted themselves in a savage struggle after their necks had been wrung.

I did quickly realize, however, how dependent I'd been on my grandmother, how much I relished the time spent with her, and how much I missed the tales she had spun out for me. I'd been drawn into a strange twilight zone where reality was shaped more by my imagination than the outside world. While she was with us, I seldom went outside to play or to do any of the things other four- or five-year-old children did. Miss Aggie had guided me into a fantasy world where the day-to-day struggles and mundane problems, as well as the rewards, of the outside world were excluded.

During the year she lived with us, she was much closer to me than my mother or anyone else in our family. It was not just that her hands and bosom provided the warmth and nurturing that I needed but also that her tales and bigger-than-life characters had exploded like fireworks in my mind, expanding my imagination and opening up new areas that my curiosity struggled to fill. Although young and very naive, I sensed that she had given me something that no one else could have offered. Her absence left me in a daze.

I felt not only alone and abandoned but also guilty and, yes, more than a little scared.

I desperately missed the maternal cocoon she had so ingeniously woven, and without her prodding and stoking my curiosity, lapsed into a kind of enervated stupor; for months I was intimidated by the thought of beginning to survey our strange new neighborhood. On Shehy, my interest in the world outside my own household had been whetted by Myron and the buzz of activity at the pool hall. My grandmother had drawn me toward an opposite but equally strong attraction—an inner world of fantasy and imagination. In her absence, although our new house suddenly seemed cold and empty, its walls became a fenced enclosure to me; I hid behind them as if they were a fortress.

For months, I spent nearly all my time indoors. I stuck as close to my mother's side as possible, partly to assuage the guilt that I felt and partly out of anxiety and the hope of replacing the companionship and warmth that had been snatched away. My mother, however, had almost no time for me.

It wasn't that she intentionally ignored me or any of her children. In fact, as I'd discover firsthand when I reached my teens, my mother (whom my father called Little Sister and everyone else but her children called Sister Katie) was usually excessively protective of her brood. When my brother Herbert was hit by a car at age seven, his head was split open, leaving him with injuries so grave that a priest was prompted to perform the last rites before an ambulance arrived. He spent nearly six weeks on the critical list in a Memphis hospital room and my mother refused to leave his side during the entire stay. Her faith in his recovery never wavered, and despite the doctor's dire prognosis, Herbert survived. He sustained some minor physical and mental handicaps, but although he lived with our parents throughout his adulthood, he managed to work and live a more or less normal life. My mother usually showered the rest of us with the same devotion and care whenever we were truly in need.

During World War II, however, women were an integral part of the labor force. Local plants were still geared up for maximum productivity, and my mother, along with thousands of other women, was desperately needed on the assembly line. She was logging long hours at the Ravenna Arsenal, a plant that manufactured shells. With the shortage of gasoline due to rationing, car pools were common, and most days, either in the afternoon or in the evening, it seemed that a coworker would pick her up for the drive to nearby Ravenna. I was left in the care of my brothers and sisters or, when no one else was available, our next-door neighbor Mrs. Clinton.

When she was at home, however, I literally clung to her apron strings. I was continually underfoot. Trailed her like a shadow. I tried helping her with housecleaning, even with baking and cooking. I tagged along when she labored over an old-fashioned, metal-ribbed scrubbing board washing clothes and, after forcing them through a hand-cranked wringer, hung them to dry in the backyard. And every time I sensed that she was going somewhere in the family car, I'd scamper into the backseat and claim a spot near the window in hopes that she'd take me along.

The most relaxed times with her, however, were when we gathered in the dining room and listened to the radio. My brother Herbert usually joined us and sometimes my sisters or even my father would sit around the table with us. Although it was the golden age of Hollywood films and I'd been taken downtown to one of the movie houses on a few special occasions, radio was by far the most popular and accessible form of entertainment, particularly among poor families. It was my favorite because the evenings spent sitting around our old RCA radio were practically the only times our family did anything together.

Occasionally, even Tennessee would join us. On those days, since it was his favorite show, we would inevitably listen to the staccato clicking of the telegraph keys as Walter Winchell opened his popular *Jergen's Journal* news show with the familiar "Good evening, Mr. and Mrs. North and South America, and all the ships at sea. Let's go to press. Flash!" Then, if he didn't launch into a blistering attack on communist infiltrators or lash out at the new president, Harry Truman, he would serve up some juicy item about New York's café society or, perhaps, a famous Hollywood star. That gossip and his seemingly intimate knowledge of the lives of everyone in America, along with his apparently unbridled patriotism, made him the most popular and influential broadcast journalist of his time. I was, of course, completely lost once he began his rapid-fire outpouring of news and gossip, but the opening theatrics always excited me.

My father, however, rarely joined us. In fact, since my parents worked odd hours with constantly rotating shifts, it was unusual for all of us to gather for any activity. There was no set time for anything, including meals, which made for a kind of frenetic, first-come-first-served atmosphere in which everyone fended for themselves and the quickest fared best. As the youngest, I didn't always do well with this arrangement but my sisters looked out for me and I generally got my fair share. The jovial, well-organized households and wholesome family gatherings portrayed on radio shows like *The Adventures of Ozzie and Harriet* and, a few years later, *Father Knows Best* bore little resemblance to our unruly daily routine.

Perhaps for that reason, I was always drawn to more raucous comedy programs like *The Jack Benny Show* (with Eddie Anderson as Rochester), *Amos 'n' Andy*, *Fibber McGee and Molly*, *The Great Gildersleeve*, or *The Baby Snooks Show*. For one thing, the behavior of brash, colorful, frequently scheming characters such as Gildersleeve, George "Kingfish" Stevens, McGee, and Fanny Brice as the irreverent seven-year-old Snooks seemed more natural to me than the sanitized folks who peopled Ozzie and Harriet Nelson's home. A few of those shows also had black characters who, at least on the surface, resembled people I'd actually met. At the time, I had no idea that many of the actors portraying those characters—Andy Brown, Kingfish, and even Beulah—were, in fact, white men.

Comedy aside, the programs that most fascinated me were action and horror shows such as *Boston Blackie, Gang Busters, Captain Midnight, The Lone Ranger, The Green Hornet, Inner Sanctum Mysteries*, and *The Shadow*. After all, Captain Midnight was introduced as a "mysterious pilot who, whenever trouble started in any part of the world, was certain to come diving furiously from the night sky"; the Green Hornet, with his faithful valet, Kato, came buzzing onto the airways with "The Flight of the Bumblebee" as background music and the promise that he hunted "the biggest of all game, public enemies that try to destroy America"; the Shadow, a mysterious loner with the ability to "cloud men's minds" and disappear at will, began each show with an eerie laugh and that still-familiar question, "Who knows what evil lurks . . . in the hearts of men? The Shadow *knoooooows!*"

And after a scary organ intro, Raymond, the host of the *Inner Sanctum Mysteries*, would slowly turn the knob, open the fabled squeaking door, and welcome his listeners: "Good evening, friends. This is your host, inviting you through the gory portals of the squeaking door." Then, anticipating the morbid humor of HBO's Cryptkeeper by half a century, his laughter would roll fiendishly, then subside as he introduced the night's tale with a seemingly off-hand remark such as, "Now, if your scalpels are sharpened and ready, we'll proceed with the business of the evening." The actors who appeared on those shows were always convincing (much later, I discovered that they included many of the best character actors of the time—Boris Karloff, Raymond Massey, Claude Rains, and Peter Lorre, to name a few), and those macabre tales usually frightened me so much that I was reluctant to turn off the lights before going to bed on Tuesday nights.

Still, despite their often heavy-handed, superpatriotic overtones, on the surface those shows (particularly *The Shadow*) seemed to echo the cryptic, double-edged messages and magical possibilities that I'd sensed in Miss Aggie's tales; naturally, I was intrigued by them. Moreover, they were as believable as supposedly more realistic programs in which properly polite parents and their cute (if sometime mischievous) children lived harmoniously in model middle-class neighborhoods. I had driven through those residential enclaves with my parents by this time and, nose pressed against the windowpane, looked for signs of real-life counterparts to the Nelsons beyond the manicured lawns and imposing facades of the homes. Those mythical radio folks were, after all, models that suggested how the ideal family should act, and I'm sure that in the back of my mind I'd begun to compare the disarray and chaos of our household to the order and routine of theirs.

At the time, however, I had not met anyone even vaguely resembling the Nelsons and did not even when I worked up the nerve to begin exploring our block.

As one of the main thoroughfares on Youngstown's south side, Woodland Avenue was a heavily trafficked street. It was part of the municipal bus route that connected the downtown area to Idora Park, an amusement and recreational center that attracted visitors from central and eastern Ohio as well as Pennsylvania. It was also one of the most commercialized streets in what was primarily a residential area. Perhaps because it was an area in transition, a number of small businesses had sprung up on our block. There were grocery stores at the corners on each end of the block, and across the street from one was a dry cleaner's and shoe repair shop.

Of the twenty-five homes on our block at least fourteen were occupied by relatively new arrivals—more than one-third of whom were black. By the time we arrived, a kind of class system had already emerged; although there was some fraternization between newcomers of both races, the old-guard residents mostly kept to themselves and avoided contact with any of the new arrivals. And since there were only one or two children my age among the newcomers, my first year on Woodland was spent either alone or in the company of adults. I had plenty of time to observe my new surroundings without much interruption.

A few lots had expansive, three- or four-bedroom homes that might have been featured in *Better Homes and Gardens*; at that time they were still owned by old-guard residents. Most houses were, like ours, more modest two-bedroom structures.

Overall, it was a safe, tight-knit block where most families kept a keen eye on their neighbors' property and children. During the summer, some adult was always sitting on one or another of the surrounding front porches, apparently scrutinizing everything that went on. They seemed to know my whereabouts at all times, as I found out whenever I ventured beyond the corner in my parents' absence. When they returned, they seemed to immediately know exactly what I'd done. It was restrictive but comforting and often rewarding, as when Mrs. Clinton insisted that I have a piece of freshly baked apple pie or Mrs. Mitchell walked across the street to offer a piece of fruit from her backyard.

The block had one large multiple dwelling, which housed more families than I was ever able to count. I remember only one person who lived there—a kid about three years younger than I who moved in five years after we did. And he was memorable primarily because of his family's peculiar medicinal remedies. During the winter, whenever the child came down with a cold, his mother forced him to drink his own urine. They should have kept it to themselves, of course, since everyone thought they were crazy. The child became known as Wee-wee for obvious reasons, and needless to say, the ribbing began the moment he so much as sneezed. (No one dreamed that, by the mid-1990s, some legitimate doctors would be prescribing that cure.)

Despite some unique characters and strange households, on the whole, the yards were kept neat, clean, and uncluttered. There was, however, one glaring exception. In fact, the most unkempt lot on the block bordered our property, so it was not difficult to understand why the previous owners had hastened to sell two houses in perfect condition for what my father referred to as a steal.

Adjacent to the house that my family rented to the Clintons was a huge lot with a large, ramshackle house in front and a cottage, which in better times, with its original owners, was probably a guest home, in back. By the time we arrived the front lawn had already been turned into a dumping ground for the rusting, twisted frames of what seemed like a small fleet of misused autos and a collection of discarded appliances, kitchen sinks, bathtubs, and engines that had been ripped from auto bodies and plundered for parts. The property looked more like the Shehy junk yard, or trailer parks that we had passed on our way to the country to purchase meat from the slaughterhouse, than most of the lots that surrounded it. The young couple who lived there had a son who was about my age, but we rarely spoke to each other even when we passed on the sidewalk or played in our respective backyards. I never knew the names of anyone in the family except the young child, Buster. So I called them the Busters. They were from West Virginia. Hillbillies, my mother warned me; not to be trusted and certainly not to be messed with.

"Goddamn white trash," my father said, "they ain' never goin' be nothin' but trouble."

Their warnings, of course, only heightened my curiosity about those odd people with their sharp, high-pitched twangs (harsher and far more irritating, I felt, than the slow, syrupy drawl with which my family spoke), raucous country music, bib overalls, and—their own eminent poverty notwithstanding—seeming disdain for nearly all of their "colored" neighbors. During that first spring, when the weather permitted I sat on our back porch and surreptitiously watched them cooking out or cavorting in their yard as Grand Ole Opry tunes barked from their radio, or tried to catch a glimpse of the older woman (a relative of theirs, I suppose) who lived in the small house in the rear. She was, by most accounts, a little loony and seldom ventured outside the cottage. On rare occasions when she did, the couple and their son treated her like a leper. Inevitably, she would skulk back inside, to remain unseen for days.

It wasn't very adventurous, but spying on our next-door neighbors marked the break in my self-imposed hibernation. It was a first step toward overcoming the grief caused by Miss Aggie's sudden departure. I had almost no direct interaction with the hillbilly couple, but snooping on them not only reawakened my interest in the world outside our home but also became an amusing pastime.

In fact, a few years later, one encounter between the Busters and my family sparked an incident that we laughed about until I was well into my teens. For some reason (a city council zoning ordinance, I believe), the chicken coops that a few families had maintained (the Busters included) were all razed. The Busters, however, kept a rooster as a pet. He wandered freely about their yard and, more often than wanted, boldly strode onto neighboring property. A feathered, strutting, feces-dropping alarm cock, he had become the block's central nuisance. His early morning wake-up calls irritated everyone in our newly gentrified, chicken-free neighborhood.

At the time, my brother Al, his wife, Julia, and their tenants, Esther and Jimmy, were living in our house next door. One morning, after the Busters' rooster had awakened our family, he made the mistake of wandering onto the porch of my brother's house. I heard about this only after the fact, but apparently fed up with the cackling transient, Al crept to the door and snatched him inside. There was, I'm told, a raucous feather-strewing imbroglio before the rooster was subdued, safely stuffed into a sack, and ensconced in the cellar.

The question then was what to do with him. And since my brother's favorite food was chicken, Esther, always something of an instigator, easily sold them on the idea of roasted rooster. In order to avoid detection, they decided to take the rooster to a friend's house on the other side of town, where they'd kill and clean him, then bring him back to be cooked. The plan unfolded without a hitch, and later that evening, the Busters' rooster had been transformed into a roasted dinner. When my sister-in-law Julia arrived home from work, the table was set with the somewhat scrawny but not unappetizing bird placed on a platter at its center. It was Julia who kept the rooster from becoming part of the food chain. The idea of eating someone's pet, even one as despised as the Busters' rooster, did not set well with her. Reluctantly, Esther stuffed the fowl into a paper bag; they decided to wait until nightfall before disposing of it.

Buster's mother came by to ask if anyone had seen the rooster that evening. And while Al, Esther, and Jimmy rolled with laughter in the background, Julia bit her tongue and swore that the bird hadn't been seen. Later the Busters' rooster was put to rest at the town incinerator.

For a few weeks afterward, I and most everyone else wondered about the rooster's strange disappearance. I'd even begun missing his cackling wake-up calls. After Esther admitted what had happened, however, I couldn't look at the Busters without a guilty grin.

There was nothing amusing about the neighbor on the other side of our property. For one thing, he lived next door to the house we occupied, so it was difficult to avoid him. His driveway was separated from our house by less than a foot, and from the moment we moved in it was evident that the proximity was not to his liking. During the first month after our arrival, he and my father had several shouting matches that I feared might turn violent. He made it clear that he didn't want any of us to set foot on his property; in turn, my father warned him never to even look wrong at anyone in our family. Once they drew their individual lines in the sand, things quieted down. And even though we looked directly across his driveway and lawn to the side entrance of his house when we sat at our dining room table, I seldom saw our neighbor during that first winter.

In the spring, however, he reappeared, more ill tempered and nasty than ever. I quickly discovered that he lived alone, except for his dog, a vicious, muddy brown mongrel whose sole purpose, it seemed, was to intimidate everyone who approached the yard. He was part German shepherd and, as far as I was concerned, part demon. (I distinctly remember my mother saying, "That goddamn dog came straight from hell!") His name was actually Spade, an irony that escaped me since, at the time, I was unaware of the racial connotation.

Our neighbor kept the animal chained outside most of the time, even during the winter, and its loud barking and wailing remained a source of friction between him and my parents. Not coincidentally, the dog's chain was just long enough for him to reach the edge of the only open space between our property—an area at the rear of our house where the thick weeds and shrubbery separating our backyards had been removed, presumably so the previous owners of our home could enter our backyard through his driveway, which was much wider and therefore more accessible for automobiles. That courtesy was never extended to us.

During the summer, he spent hours sitting outside on a lawn chair guzzling beer or iced tea. By that time, I had come to think of him simply as Red, partly because my father never mentioned him without calling him a redneck bastard and partly because of his appearance. Of course, I never called him Red to his face. In fact, I never spoke to him at all; I avoided him at all costs, which meant that I was always keenly aware of him.

What I noticed most was his neck, which during the summer was lit up with a flame-red glow that I would later associate with steamed lobsters. Quite simply, the man had the reddest neck I'd ever seen or have seen since then.

He was no taller than my father but he must have weighed close to 250 pounds. His gut hung walruslike over his belt when he sat outside in shorts and the flab of his upper arms and thighs hung down like the stomach of a hog ready for slaughter. The scowl that was etched on his face whenever he peered toward our house or watched me playing in my backyard was as menacing as anything I'd heard on *Inner Sanctum*. Years later it occurred to me that a forebear of the infamous Selma police commissioner Bull Conner might have donned Bermuda shorts and taken up residence next door.

With Red and his demon dog, Spade, scrutinizing my every move, playing in my own backyard became an eerie test of my resolve to get out and explore the neighborhood.

The inevitable clash occurred during our first summer on Woodland. I'd been warned of Red's feelings about the sanctity of his property. So, when the Spalding ball that I bounced off our garage door accidentally rolled into his yard, I had to make a decision: I could have left it there and said nothing; told my father and almost certainly have been punished (Tennessee had explicitly warned, "Don't mess with that fool next door. I don't wanna have to kill him."); or tried retrieving the ball myself. Since the ball was at least ten yards beyond the reach of the demon dog, and Red was nowhere in sight that afternoon, I decided to take matters into my own hands.

As usual, Spade was lying near the open space between our houses, his gaze following my every move. Sitting on his haunches with his head resting on his front paws, he looked almost harmless. Only his eyes and the guttural growl that occasionally punctuated his breathing belied the calm outward demeanor. When I stooped down and crawled through the bushes separating our yards, however, he reared up immediately and lurched toward the back of the yard. Although his chain kept him safely away from me, his loud barking and frantic struggle to escape his bonds quickly attracted his master's attention. Seconds after I found the ball and began creeping back toward my own yard, Red appeared and started walking toward the rear of his yard to see what was causing the disturbance.

I'd made it back to the thick underbrush near the edge of my own yard by the time Red reached his backyard. Puzzled by Spade's agitation and anger, he scanned the yard for a few minutes, then picked up a rake and began poking around in the bushes. Huddled underneath the cover of the dense shrubbery and wild dandelions I remained perfectly still, frozen with fear. Even so, sweat was pouring from my face so heavily I thought Red would surely hear it dripping onto the dirt. Several times, the rake's prongs missed me by no more than a few inches and I flinched, but Red didn't notice me. Cursing under his breath, he moved along the length of shrubs that separated our yards, still poking and prodding the underbrush. Finally, satisfied that there was no one there, he angrily threw the rake aside and stomped off toward Spade.

"What the hell's wrong with you, mutt?" he shouted. "Shut up, gawddam it!"

Spade didn't stop barking and straining to get to the back of the yard until Red kicked him viciously and, still cursing, stormed off toward his house. When I crawled back over to my own yard, Spade lay yelping and cringing near the empty lawn chair. Still, his eyes followed my every move. If he could have freed himself, he would have torn me apart.

I never told my parents about the encounter with our neighbor and his dog, but it left an indelible impression. Although I was still shaking after the narrow escape, something about being that close to the edge of discovery and possible disaster excited me. The rush of adrenaline I felt that day was new to me, but during the next three or four years, I found that it was as alluring as a drug.

There were, however, no further confrontations with our next-door neighbor. Within a year of our arrival, Red had packed up his dog and his possessions and departed.

4

# elementary woes

The bad blood that existed between my family and our next-door neighbor notwithstanding, racial distinctions didn't play a big part in my life until after I began attending elementary school. Perhaps because the situation was so explosive, no racial epithets were exchanged between my father and Red, even when they argued. Although I'm sure that when he was out of earshot our neighbor didn't censor himself as readily, a condescending "you people" was the most direct insult I ever heard him utter. Similarly, while my father never called Red out of his name when they quarreled, conversations in our own home led me to believe that his real name was Honky. That was unusual, however; tight lipped and stoic, Tennessee rarely referred to anyone's race. And while my mother vacillated between suspicious criticism and ingratiating admiration of whites, she was always an equal-opportunity critic; Negroes received just as much abuse.

The so-called N-word was commonly used inside our house. But it was nearly always used to point out some individual's rowdy or inappropriate behavior—as in, "Ain't that just like a nigger?" or, "That nigger done lost his mind." I grew up thinking of it as defining

the kind of loud, unruly behavior that my parents disapproved of—
at least when someone outside our household was the culprit.

I didn't identify with the word on a personal level until a few years
later when I was walking through an all-white neighborhood while
returning home from Little League baseball practice. When a three-
or four-year-old, curly-haired blond child skipped out onto her lawn
flashing a cherubic smile and looking like Shirley Temple, I responded with my best Bill Robinson grin. After all, I'd seen the
movie *The Little Colonel* along with *Lucky Ghosts* with Mantan
Moreland and *Harlem Rides the Range* with Herb Jeffries on a triple
bill at the Regent Theater, an East Federal picture show that offered
its almost exclusively Negro clientele a steady diet of 1940s race
films. And on that day I felt as cheerful and nearly as light on my
feet as I imagined Bojangles had been in the movie. My grin disappeared, however, when she began shouting, "Nigger! Nigger! Nigger!" as if excitedly confirming the sighting of an alien.

Since she was pointing in my direction, I immediately turned and
looked to see who might be standing behind me. There was, of
course, no one there. Still, since I'd been on my best behavior—definitely not acting rowdy or unruly—the intended accusation came
as a complete surprise. I couldn't believe that she had actually mistaken me for a nigger!

For several minutes, I stood there totally bewildered. My reaction
must have shocked both the child and her mother, something like
having a familiar pet suddenly refuse to respond to a name it had
been trained to accept. The girl had initially approached me with a
playful confidence that had no hint of malice; instead, she radiated
an assurance that may have been derived from her pride in confirming a reality passed on to her by her parents. But my lack of response had apparently shaken her, and within minutes her
confident grin shifted to bafflement, then fear. She took one step
backward, raised her fists to her eyes, and started to cry. So I found
myself standing on the sidewalk in a white working-class enclave
with my rubber-spiked Little League shoes and Rawlings baseball
glove slung over my shoulder while a dimpled Shirley Temple look-
alike stood in front of me cowering and screeching. The moment
the child began balling, her frantic mother raced out to the front
yard. I realized later that, in the mother's mind, the child was being

threatened by a truly dangerous species—a nigger that didn't know who he was.

Mumbling faint apologies as she stumbled away, she dragged the child back toward their house.

I was dumbfounded, too much in shock to either move or make out what she was saying. So I watched them for a few minutes, then turned and *walked* away. That, of course, was a mistake, a transgression that, in more threatening circumstances, might have cost me dearly. Anyone less naive than I would have known that, if you're black and someone begins yelling "Nigger" in a white neighborhood, a hasty departure is the recommended response.

Arriving home safely, I asked my brother McKay about the incident. He nearly fell off the front porch steps laughing before assuring me that, yes, as far as whitey was concerned I was definitely a nigger. I was not entirely convinced that McKay was correct, but it did occur to me that, if my mere presence could incite that kind of uproar, being a Negro was a powerful, if not necessarily advantageous, attribute.

Before that incident, however, I'd had little reason to even consider my identity in racial, or black-and-white, terms. In part, this derived from the peculiar makeup of our family. As I've said, my father was as dark as a new-moon night; his African ancestry was never questioned. On the other hand, strangers very often assumed that my mother was white—an error that, as I later discovered, almost brought her marriage to an early end. In fact, she might have easily pretended to be white; there were rumors that some on the paternal side of her family had, fading into that substantial group of pragmatists who escaped the black world through silence, subterfuge, and pretense. My mother refused that option, if not consciously, certainly in a de facto sense by choosing to marry my father and identify with Miss Aggie's African and Native American heritage rather than the Irish heritage of her biological father.

Due to the disparity in my parents' appearance, however, my three brothers, two sisters, and I were a motley brood who reflected nearly all of the wide pool of contrasting physical features at our disposal. My sister Doris was nearly as light complexioned as my mother; my brother McKay was only a shade lighter than my father but had my mother's near-straight black hair. The rest of us were tan to brown skinned with a mixture of features that might have been found anywhere from Nigeria to the Netherlands.

The diverse makeup of our family forced us to embrace a kind of Rainbow Coalition long before Jesse Jackson coined or, at least adopted, the term as a descriptive sound bite for his political constituency during the 1980s. McKay was the only family member who seemed fixated on race differences, and during my early childhood I saw very little of him. My experience assured that I grew up generally insulated from the outside world's notions about the importance of skin color and physical differences. That came later. For the first five or six years of my life, I was merely part of a colorful array of individuals who, I assumed, were all equally important.

Things began changing when I started first grade at Ulysses S. Grant Elementary School in the fall of 1946. The strange attitudes that I encountered at school, along with the chaos that seemed suddenly to have descended on our household, was not only confusing but also seemed to accelerate my plunge into a tailspin from which I only narrowly escaped.

For one thing, during our first few years on Woodland it felt as if we were living in a boardinghouse rather than a home. People moved in and out so quickly that from one week to the next I didn't know who would show up in the kitchen for breakfast or where I'd be sleeping.

When we arrived, the only member of the immediate family who did not live with us was my brother McKay, who was in the Boys Industrial School in Mansfield, Ohio. Even when he was released a few years later, he didn't remain at home long. He disappeared within a few weeks; later we learned that although he had not reached the required age, he'd managed to join the army by forging Tennessee's signature on a permissions document.

Still, the house was filled; Miss Aggie, my parents, two sisters, twin brothers, and I all lived together. During that time, the dining and living rooms as well as the basement served as bedrooms at night.

Within the next few years, both my sisters started their own families. Doris married Leroy Wallace and moved to his parents' house during the winter of 1945. About two years later, they moved back into the Woodland house with their two young children and stayed for a few months before buying their own home. Cherrie married

Leroy's brother, Billy, in 1948; she moved out at that point but returned the next year, and they stayed until they bought their own home on Woodland in 1950.

My brother Al left to join the air force in December of 1945. He was discharged in 1947 and stayed with us for more than a year before marrying. Afterward, he and his wife, Julia, moved into the adjacent house, which the Clintons had rented since our arrival. McKay, whom I hardly knew, made a dramatic return in 1949, bringing a new and unique brand of chaos into the household. After he again departed, my parents took in a boarder.

For more than a year a quiet, mysterious man that I knew only as Robert rented a room in our house. He was the first college-educated Negro that I'd ever met and I was intrigued by the way he spoke and carried himself. Occasionally he had a guest, a hefty white woman who, as I remember, had a noticeable growth of hair on her upper lip. She frightened me; but Robert was always generous and polite, even though he was more serious than anyone I'd met and seemed obsessed with labor unions and workers' rights.

Still, I was shocked when I discovered that my parents had asked him to leave because rumors had begun to circulate about his being involved with the "Red infiltrators" that Senator McCarthy and Walter Winchell passionately vilified. Other than Miss Aggie's often puzzling allusions, it was the first hint I had that some concerned, seemingly thoughtful people, particularly black ones, had serious reservations about the way the country was being run.

Our extended-family household arrangement was apparently not unusual for Southern black families who migrated to the North during the post-Depression years, and for a child my age, it had some advantages.

In addition to our boarder, Robert, who first exposed me to a critical if misguided view of what he called "American imperialism," my new brothers-in-law opened up new experiences for me. Cherrie's husband, Billy, besides being a skilled plasterer, had an uncanny ear for music and seemed to know every show tune written. Couldn't sing a lick, but he recited the lyrics of Gershwin and Kern tunes as if he had penned them himself. On Sunday evenings between eight and nine o'clock he took center stage when the family gathered and listened to *Stop the Music,* a quiz show hosted by Bert Parks that randomly called and asked listeners to identify the song being played. Although we were never called, Billy's unerring ability to name the tunes correctly amazed me. Doris's husband, Leroy, was a member of the Sons of Harmony, a gospel group that appeared on the same programs as such legends as the Soul Stirrers with Sam Cooke and the Five Blind Boys with Ray Charles. The Sons of Harmony often practiced at our house, and on those occasions I'd sit clapping my hands along with them as they breezed through rollicking versions of "How I Got Over" and other gospel songs.

Holiday barbecues in the backyard offered platefuls of succulent ribs or chicken that I'd watched my mother select at Ginster's East Federal Street market, where, holding my nose to ward off the barnyard odor, I moved cautiously over the sawdust-covered floor as live fowl strutted and squawked inside wire cages and an array of cleanly plucked birds—with wrinkled pink carcasses resting in pails of water—hung from hooks attached to the ceiling. Our sizzling barbecue was always accompanied by potato salad laced with boiled eggs and hot sauce; by colorful concoctions of tomatoes, green peppers, and whole-kernel corn that I'd helped strip from the cob, all taken directly from the garden; and by the savory, if arm-wearying, hand-churned, homemade ice cream whose sugary aftertaste kept the festivities at a gleeful fever pitch. At most Sunday dinners I was greeted with the rich aromas of inexpensive but expertly prepared fried chicken feasts, pots of greens or butter beans, hot corn bread, and the freshly baked peach and apple cobblers or banana puddings whose warm fruit filling I surreptitiously plundered before the others returned from church. At those gatherings the Woodland Avenue house rocked joyfully with the intermingling of disparate voices, diverse personalities. Despite the close quarters, the sounds of laughter and music and the near-tangible optimism of my sisters' newly formed unions created a sense of unity that seemed capable of withstanding any outside influence.

Still, it did not make for the most stable living arrangements.

In the midst of this overflowing, constantly shifting household, my parents had started going through one of their most serious marital crises. The verbal sparring that I'd heard on Shehy had intensified; now there were angry shouting matches that occasionally became violent.

One reason for the increase in tension was that about a year after we arrived on Woodland, Tennessee lost his job at Republic Steel. He had been fired when he got into a fight with another employee, and since jobs that had been readily available during the war were being swept up by returning white soldiers, he remained unemployed for nearly a year. When he did find work, it was a lower-paying job with the sanitation department. A proud man whose appearance and natty attire were always important, he never came to terms with his role as a garbage collector.

During the same time, my mother, who had also been laid off from her job, at the Ravenna Arsenal, had begun doing housework for well-to-do white families on the north side of town.

Many of their arguments seemed to revolve around either money or Tennessee's objections to my mother's spending more time caring for other people's homes than she did taking care of her own.

His objections, of course, were either intentional fabrications or a result of his frustration at being unemployed and dependent on my mother. He was still earning some money as a collector for the policy racket and had begun gambling heavily in an attempt to pull his weight, but the effort often went in vain since what was gained one day was routinely lost the next. He began drinking more and, always high strung, became even more edgy and irritable. During that time, when he was at home everyone braced for the outbursts that more and more frequently erupted without warning or provocation.

My mother was most often the target of his frustration and rage. When he was drunk, the slightest misstep—an overcooked egg, a stale piece of corn bread, too much noise when he was attempting to sleep—would lead to an outbreak of cursing and threats. Usually it ended there. My mother might mumble something under her breath or react with a cold stare that let him know he had gone far enough, but most often she'd avoid pushing the issue. Still, although she was a petite woman, she was no shrinking violet. If the verbal abuse continued, she would react. And when she did, she would not be controlled. Once involved, she would match him curse for curse, threat for threat; no matter how much he tried to intimidate or subdue her, she would not back up one inch.

I rarely saw him hit her. Instead, they faced off, taunting, then shoving, grappling, and tussling while curses flew like projectiles. Their bodies straining against each other, she would fling harmless blows against his chest until he grabbed her arms and held fast, flaunting his strength and power. Breaking away, she would clutch at anything nearby—a pot, brick, plate, or knife—lashing out or, if she could step back, hurling it at him. He'd duck and shield himself, then push forward to again grab and restrain her.

As I looked up at them from my waist-high view, it was like an eerie, slapstick dance, comic, in a sense, but nonetheless frightening—only an instant away, it seemed to me, from disaster, maiming, or death. But pleas to stop went unheeded, drowned out by their thundering imprecations.

"Mamma . . . Daddy! Stop it. Please Stop!"

"Boy, shut up and get yo' ass outta here! Put that pot down, woman . . . put it down, I say!"

"I'll kill you, nigger. Get your hands off me. Come in here drunk, smellin' like that black ho!"

"Stop! Please, stop."

A few times I tried to jump in, protect my mother. It only inflamed the situation. He swiped me away like an annoying insect. "Don't you hit that boy," my mother would snap.

"Tell *yo'* chile to get outta here befo' I have to hurt him," he'd yell.

Typically, the encounters ended with him storming out of the house and her crying and screaming, "Go on back to that dirty bitch. You don't have to ever bring your ass back here again."

Afterward, there were sometimes bruises and cuts, but they were only superficial flesh wounds in a war where the lasting lesions were psychological. When the police were called, he refused to leave or try to avoid them. Few things were more important than the sanctity of his home, and he was fiercely protective of it. Intruders, no matter what outside authority they may have represented, were unwelcome; their mere presence was an affront and challenge. There was no pretense about his feelings.

The police would arrive with guns drawn, knowing they had stepped into a minefield; the stare-down that ensued was as intense as the fray that had preceded it. Tennessee wore his defiance like armor. He showed no contrition—even on those occasions when they unceremoniously cuffed him and forced him into a patrol car.

Most often I was the only one in the house when the confrontations occurred—perhaps because my parents didn't want their older children to bear witness or feared that the brawls would escalate if they were present. In fact, my brother McKay, who was eight years older, had once tried to intervene and restrain Tennessee; he was sent fleeing from the house when my father drew his pistol and fired at him, miraculously only perforating the screen door and availing the house to mosquitoes for nearly a year. That incident, I'm certain, hastened McKay's departure and influenced his decision to deviously enter the army.

Violence and chaos at home were not restricted to encounters between my parents, however; with a dozen or so people sometimes crowded into a two-bedroom house, there were bound to be other antagonisms and run-ins. At times it seemed to me that arguments and quarrels erupted with the explosiveness of the fireworks that lit up the Idora Park ball field on the Fourth of July.

There were the expected domestic disputes between my sisters and their spouses; scuffles also occasionally broke out between one of my brothers and one of my new brothers-in-law. In that tense, overcrowded atmosphere a game of checkers or stickball could be instantaneously transformed into a heated verbal exchange and test of manhood, then a shoving match or scuffle. A disagreement over which radio program should be tuned in or whose turn it was to use the bathroom might easily become a shouting match, then escalate into an angry confrontation in which a nearby bottle, pencil, baseball bat, or gun (and there were always several available) became a potential deadly weapon.

In addition, during his unemployed period, Tennessee had taken to giving gambling parties where tonk, poker, and cooncan games were played and a cut, or percentage of each pot, was taken out for the house. The parties provided some desperately needed income during a very lean period. We all pitched in on those nights; my job was to sell soda pop and hot dogs. It was an upbeat, carnival atmosphere in which the down-home blues tunes of Muddy Waters, B. B. King, and Sonny Boy Williamson (my father's favorite artists) blasting from the record player could barely be heard over the buzz of the jive talk and wolfin' that filled the air. With gambling and drinking involved, disputes inevitably arose. I saw shots fired on at least one occasion and witnessed several people being escorted out drunk and bloodied after a brawl.

Although I wasn't exposed to the avalanche of fictionalized TV carnage that my daughter would experience and there were no drive-by shootings or drug shoot-outs on the streets to numb my senses, by the time I was nine, domestic violence and in-house brawls were familiar sights. When I entered the public school system, at age six, those experiences were part of the baggage I carried. And although I learned quickly and got on relatively well with most of my classmates, my first few years in school were a disaster.

Grant elementary school was only a block and a half away from our house, and after my mother accompanied me the first day, I was on my own. The first hurdle was adjusting to spending each day with a large group of children my own age—two-thirds of whom were white. Up until then I'd spent very little time with anyone even nearing my own age. There was, of course, Myron on Shehy and, after we moved, Sonny (or Huck, as we came to call him), the ten-year-old son of Mr. and Mrs. Hicks, the black couple who moved next door to us when Red and his dog departed. For a month or so there was also the five-year-old daughter of a poor Polish family who lived behind the grocery store at the corner of our block; that friendship had quickly dissolved when her mother discovered that doctor and house were among the games we played. In school, however, I was suddenly surrounded by a diverse group of kids my age.

From our house on Woodland, Grant was one block down the hill that sloped toward the Mahoning River and the valley occupied by downtown Youngstown. One of the largest elementary schools in town, it had previously been a junior high school, and the building and adjacent ball fields and playground were spread over an area the size of a city block. Its several hundred students came from diverse neighborhoods and widely varying ethnic and economic backgrounds. The school's immediate vicinity was the transitional area that included my block on Woodland Avenue; farther down the hill the neighborhood was nearly all black. Up the hill and south of Woodland was the beginning of the suburban area that stretched to the city limits; it was nearly all white.

From the first day at school, I seemed to have hooked up with the wrong crowd. Most of the black children that I met in my first-grade class and on the playground during recess were from working-class families who, like mine, were from the South. They not only spoke with variations of the same Southern dialect that I did but also mirrored many of the same rural attitudes and mannerisms that I had picked up from my parents. I naturally gravitated toward them, and joining with a few working-class white kids with a similar fondness for disorder, we soon formed our own small but vocal band of troublemakers. Although we were rarely malicious or intentionally destructive, we were boisterous and loud; our antic behavior irritated teachers, generally disrupted classes or any other organized activities (forcing some teachers to spend as much time on discipline as on instruction), and tabbed us all as miscreants who were immediately suspect whenever something went wrong.

Initially, I was far from being a leader in our crowd; in fact, I was little more than a peripheral attendant, a hanger-on in a gang of innocent but rowdy youngsters starved for attention and hell-bent on grabbing the spotlight, no matter what the cost. For most of us, neither the scorn of our teachers nor the embarrassment of occasionally being yanked out of class and taken to the principal's office to be chastised with Mr. Conners's imposing wooden paddle dampened our misplaced enthusiasm. I, for one, seemed to grow bolder during that first year and, by the middle of my second year, had convinced most teachers that I was irredeemable, a lost cause.

Mrs. Smith—the dour, straitlaced, and extremely corpulent woman who was unfortunate enough to have had me assigned to her second-grade class—probably thought of me as some kind of ill-bred terror or thug. I quickly became her primary adversary and the chief obstacle to the order she vainly sought to establish in her classroom.

The soul of propriety, she conducted that classroom as if she were a British subject under the reign of Queen Victoria. Once, having slipped and fallen, exposing both her dignity and the ample circumference of her garters to the wanton gazes of the passing hoi polloi, she spent an entire morning fuming about public nuisances and condemning the barbarians who had spit on the sidewalk, leaving the saliva into which she had stepped before unceremoniously sprawling. No incivility, however slight, escaped her, and no one responsible for a rude, discourteous, or crude remark or act avoided her scorn and rebuke. I was among her favorite targets—deservedly so, I might add, because, since the previous year, I'd become one of the chief instigators in our band of juvenile upstarts.

Even more seriously, outside of school, I had become a fledgling petty thief, following the path that had led my brother McKay to reform school.

Since Tennessee was still unemployed, there was little or no money for anything except bare necessities in our household. Sometimes even they were not available. During the worst of times—when his luck went sour at gambling during the winter, for example, and there was nothing available from the garden—we were fortunate to have even ketchup or mayonnaise to put on stale bread and make sandwiches. If there was no bread, we made do by snacking on a box of Argo cornstarch. During better times, although I'd come to hate the frequent servings of chicken, I relished the spareribs, neck bones, okra, collard greens, chitlins, and other soul food dishes that my mother prepared. Still, on many days the cafeteria's standard, bland meals were the best food I had during my first few years at Grant; occasionally they were the only ones.

Having quickly learned to read, I had also developed a taste for books. Not the established masterpieces of, say, Dickens, Melville, Twain, or Frederick Douglass, of course; there was no tradition of reading those authors in our family and certainly no signs of any of their works around our living room table. The only book I'd seen in our house was the Bible, which I was disinclined to pick up.

I was hooked on comic books, and before long, I'd begun haunting the magazine section of a nearby soda fountain. I'd read as many comics and gory magazines as I could before the owner kicked me out; whenever I felt I could get away with it, I'd slide one or two under my shirt and into my waistband before I left.

By the winter after I began school, I'd also become friends with Huck, my next-door neighbor. Soon we'd devised a solution to the recurrent problem of holiday neglect by Santa Claus.

"Santa can't make it to everybody's house, son," my mother had said the previous winter. "Maybe we'll see him next year." I listened but I was not an overly patient child.

Huck and I simply walked downtown to Federal Street, bought shopping bags for a nickel, then toured the major stores. We "shopped" at Woolworth's and McCrory's as well as McKelvey's and Strouss-Hirshberg's, the town's largest two department stores. Taking turns acting as lookouts or as distractions for suspicious salesclerks, one or the other would sample those items we felt Santa might have left if he'd been able to find our houses. Usually we left with our shopping bags nearly filled. Our bounty, of course, had to be small and inconspicuous enough so that it could be hidden away from our parents.

Either destiny was on our side or the angels were looking over our shoulders, despite my ineptitude at shoplifting and thievery, we were never actually caught. On my own, however, I did have some close calls. Once, as I attempted casually exiting the soda fountain with copies of *Archie* and *Superman* comics tucked under my belt, the owner pulled me aside and said, "Look, I know you've got some comic books under your shirt, but I'd have to call the police and search you to prove it. You don't seem like a bad kid, so I'm warning you, it's the last time you'll get away with it."

Although that close encounter didn't stop my pilfering, it did force me to scout the neighborhood for another magazine vendor whose racks were equally accessible.

During that same time, my behavior in school was getting me into more and more trouble. Although I sailed through the required schoolwork with minimal effort, I was one of a few kids in my class who had begun to think of themselves as class cutups or jokesters. We tried to top one another with witty responses to Mrs. Smith's instructions or inquiries and nearly fell over ourselves trying to outdo one another with pranks when she stepped out of the room or turned her back. Spitballs or the soft brown nuts taken from thorny buckeye tree husks were regularly fired across the room. In winter, when we returned from lunch, snowballs were hurled or clumps of freezing snow dropped down the backs of girls' dresses. Near the end of the school year, one of my disruptive cohorts was kicked out of class after a seven-year-old girl unknowingly drank from a thermos bottle into which he had poured ink. I survived until the end of the year only because of my good grades and, despite Mrs. Smith's personal dislike of me, her sense of my potential.

At one point, the principal did warn my parents that I was headed for trouble, but I convinced them that I was just bored with the schoolwork. "I'll do better, Mom," I insisted; "wait, you'll see."

Actually, I wasn't quite sure what was driving me closer to the edge in school, and if I did, I would have probably been too ashamed and afraid of embarrassing my parents to mention it.

Although the clues were there from the beginning, it wasn't until much later that I realized what was fueling the frantic need for attention. From the time I entered school, I'd noticed that teachers did not treat all students alike. It was not just racial; poor white kids fared no better than I. The special attention was generally aimed at those well-dressed, well-mannered white children who, I imagined, lived behind the curtains of the sprawling suburban homes in which my mother sometimes worked and that I had occasionally driven by with my family. When dealing with those kids, Mrs. Smith would temper both the sullen turn of her eyebrows and the harsh edge of her voice. A near-cheerful expression would momentarily brighten her face and a more subdued, almost deferential tone would soften her speech. Like my first-grade teacher, Mrs. Smith both spent more time with and showered more encouragement on her favorite pupils; those chosen were almost always white and middle class.

It was more out of ego and simple jealousy than any conscious sense of social inequity, but I felt I deserved the same treatment and I was determined to get it. It just so happened that I chose some bizarre and unusual ways of doing so.

During the winter of my second year at Grant, I found an old silver-plated pocket watch in a trunk that my mother had brought down from the attic. I'm not sure what possessed me, but somehow I became obsessed with it. It wasn't expensive and it no longer kept time, but I latched on to that ornate, antique timepiece and began carrying it with me. I'm not exactly sure how it started, but someone must have noticed it, complimented me, and asked what time it was. At any rate, I began pretending that the watch was actually working. I had a fairly good internal sense of time, and with the aid of external indicators such as the large hallway clocks in school or steel mill whistles that sounded on the hour, it was easy to periodically take it out and reset it to something approximating the right time. After a few weeks I was firmly locked into pretense and the watch had become a kind of symbol of the affluence I wished I had.

In retrospect, I'm certain that many of my classmates realized that the watch wasn't really keeping time; after all, I was in and out of my pocket every ten minutes or so just to keep up appearances. Still, they either ignored that fact or went along with the hoax, and as childish as the pretense was, it worked. Whether it was recognition of my flair for acting or the watch itself, for a few months the sham was instrumental in attracting attention that I desperately needed.

It backfired when I got into an argument with a second-grader from another class on the playground. He was an Irish kid with whom I'd had some shouting matches before while playing dodge-ball. On this occasion, when he felt he'd been hit too hard, he decided to lash out verbally. I'm not sure if it was the embarrassment I felt when he accused me of being a fool and carrying an "old, useless, hand-me-down watch" or the tone he used when he called me a "dumb black jerk," but something snapped, and I was on him practically before he finished the sentence.

The actual fight lasted less than two minutes. Truth is, we rushed at each other and I tackled him. As we rolled around on the ground trying to throw punches, I slipped to the side and, gripping his neck between my cocked arm and upper body, began squeezing as tightly as I could. A crowd had gathered around us and I could hear them yelling for me to hit him, but all I could do was hold him in the hammerlock and tighten my grip. I was totally out of control. Later I realized that I might have choked him to death if one of the teachers monitoring the playground hadn't rushed over and tried to stop the scuffle.

Seeing the Irish kid's face turning purple as he gasped for breath, the teacher screamed for me to loosen my grip and tried pulling my arms away. It didn't work.

Desperate, now, he grabbed me by the shoulders and dragged me toward the entrance to the school. He dragged me and I dragged the Irish kid by his neck. The jeering, hooting faces of the students who surrounded us flashed before me as our bodies scraped along the asphalt surface of the school yard. But it wasn't until we were lying on the cool marble floor of the school lobby and two other teachers arrived that someone was able to pry my hands from his neck.

Afterward, I was ushered to the principal's office, where I was again introduced to Mr. Conners's paddle. I was also suspended from school for a week.

Mrs. Smith, of course, was delighted. Presumably, during my absence, she reestablished some control and her class reverted back to its normal orderliness.

The incident was advantageous to me also, since it provided me with a certain dubious celebrity, particularly among my more macho cohorts. I even came to think of it as a milestone. It was, after all, the first of a mere handful of fights that I'd ever have, and although there would be some later standoffs and draws, it was the only one I ever won.

As for Mrs. Smith, she had decided not to tolerate any of my smart-aleck antics, which meant that we were set on a collision course.

Actually, sensing Mrs. Smith's resolve, I managed to avoid any direct confrontation with her during the first few weeks after I returned. But that spring, just before school was to let out for summer vacation, she busted me for the final time.

During my first year at Grant, I'd discovered that I had some talent for drawing, that is, producing reasonable facsimiles of things I saw in simple line sketches. And during the following summer, my next-door neighbor Huck had shown me some French postcards with photos of men and women in various stages of undress and intimate coupling. Although I wasn't overly endowed with either artistic talent or, apparently, good judgment, at age seven, I was blessed with some aggressive entrepreneurial instincts. By December I was combining my modest representational gift and my exposure to the forbidden delights of French pornography to produce a four-panel cartoon each week. For a nickel, I allowed classmates to view it; later, I sold it to my best customer for a quarter. I had chosen one of the most popular and straitlaced cowboy stars of the era, Roy Rogers, as my subject. And each week I would produce an episode that depicted Roy, Dale Evans, and sometimes even Trigger interacting in some compromising, highly imaginative positions.

At that age, of course, I knew almost nothing about sex. In fact, I was so naive about the subject that two years later, when two girls teased me about my sexual inexperience, I had no idea what the term "hard-on" meant. Yes, I'd drawn them and even had them by that time, but given the general level of prudishness in Midwestern America at the time, no one had advised me of what that tumescent state was called. Still, the drawings, which owed much of their claim to any anatomical validity to the French postcards, were notable mostly because of their exaggerated coarseness. Their graphic nature always startled the prudish seven-year-olds who accidentally stumbled onto them or, despite their strict upbringing, became curious enough to seek them out.

Finally it was one of this group who was responsible for my downfall.

While I was showing the latest drawings to three guys shortly before the start of class one morning, one of the most prim and proper little girls in our class approached without us seeing her. She took one look at the crude cartoon and let out a scream that had to echo throughout the entire school. Instantly Mrs. Smith and a male teacher ran into the room. There was no chance to hide or destroy the evidence, particularly since the little girl was by then crying and pointing directly at me.

Mrs. Smith took one look at the drawing, handed it to the other teacher, then peered down at me with a look of contempt and loathing that was frightening. I felt that if she could have crushed me, destroyed me, she would have done so without hesitation. Instead, she hoisted herself to her maximum height and walked away.

"Take that trash to Mr. Conners," she disdainfully told the other teacher. The principal immediately informed me that I was expelled and need not return to Grant for the final two weeks.

When the school term ended, my mother was called in and told that I had flunked second grade. At the time, my primary concern was that a profitable enterprise had been brought to an abrupt halt.

# 5

## money wit' a hat on

Although I'm almost certain that he never consciously considered it, in his own enigmatic way, my father probably did more than anyone else to help me overcome my early childhood incorrigibility. Not that he seemed overly concerned with school or, for that matter, the grades I received. Those considerations were left to my mother; and after discovering that I'd have to repeat second grade, she made her position abundantly clear.

"Boy, don't you know we got enough fools out here already! That what you wanna be, another dumb nigger runnin' round beggin' somebody else to do somethin' you oughtta do fo' yo'self? I thought you was different—had some damn sense. But look like you goin' end up exactly like your brother.

"Yeah, I know he's a sweet child and I see you lookin' up to him like he was some kind of picture show star. But look where he is, locked up out there in Mansfield with a bunch of hoodlums. That where you wanna be? 'Cause that's sho'nough where you headed. Now you listen to me, boy. I ain' goin' whup you this time, but if you come in here next year with any more of these unsatisfactories and whatnot on your report card, I'm goin' beat some sense into yo' head. Understand me?"

Of course, I quickly nodded in agreement. But it wasn't my mother's warnings or advice that finally nudged me off the wayward path that I'd chosen. She was right about my admiration for my brother's brash assertiveness. And without the influence she wielded because of her respect for education I may have never overcome my fascination with the outlaw posture that he had come to represent. But during those preteen years, what I sought was an outlet, some way of expressing and channeling the aggression and energy that was welling up inside me.

At the time, however, black mothers were not prone to accommodate or encourage that part of their male children's personalities. Since slavery, one of the black woman's foremost concerns had been nurturing and protecting her children from the always present threat of violence from an outside world that most often demanded acquiescence—at least, the appearance of it. Just as they instinctively advised their daughters to stay far afield of predatory white males who assumed that black girls were always in heat, they shielded their sons from potentially deadly encounters with outside authorities by teaching them to moderate their aggressiveness, coaxed them to curtail or dampen that pubescent surge of bravado and willfulness that among most other ethnic groups was prized and applauded. That motherly impulse—profoundly loving and well intentioned as it was—nearly always collided head-on with the natural instincts of their sons. As mothers struggled to rein them in and harness their aggressiveness, inexperience and native eagerness pushed them toward a recklessness that their parents had usually long since abandoned. I was no exception.

On my mother's part, the protective instinct surfaced in varying forms, ranging from subtle persuasion to the most forceful and humiliating lessons in obedience.

She would sometimes coddle and entreat, never with quite the same warmth that Miss Aggie had showered on me, but as I later discovered, my grandmother's behavior toward me was not typical. Miss Aggie had been a stern and, on occasion, even cruel disciplinarian herself, according to my sister Doris. On one occasion as a child, she and my brother Al were punished so severely that they were driven to flee Miss Aggie's Tunica home, traipsing along solitary railroad tracks for miles before a farmer found them, contacted my parents in Memphis, and arranged for their return home by bus.

That I never saw this severe, more despotic side of Miss Aggie's personality, I suppose, is as much a testament to her condition when she lived with us as it is to the unfathomable mystery of women.

Similarly, my mother could reveal a softness and vulnerability that had become rare for her, a nearly seductive femininity that mesmerized me and, I imagine, must have blinded my father as a teenager. Over twenty years later, however, with an increasingly intense combativeness defining their relationship, it had practically disappeared. Still, when she chose, she could charm and sway the most hardened heart.

"Don't worry none, son," she'd say, patting my head as we stood in the kitchen, "ain' nothin' wrong with learning how to preserve some fruit. You know how much you like to eat it come winter. You can go out and play ball later. Right now, go on out there and pick some mo' peaches for yo' mamma. Them boys look like trouble anyhow. You don't need to be playin' with them." Or, "I know how much you'd like to listen to *Captain Midnight*, son, but don't you think you oughtta study some? You know, we ain't read the Bible in some time; c'mon here and sit with me while we read."

Her rage was just as commanding and, often, embarrassing for me. Once, at age nine, when I was late getting home to perform some chore that she'd left word for me to do, she marched down to the Grant school yard and, in the middle of an inning, pulled me off of the baseball field. She was carrying a peach tree branch, which she euphemistically called a switch. With twenty or so neighborhood kids watching and laughing, she literally whipped me back up the hill to Woodland Avenue, then down the block to our house. Mind you, she didn't hurry and I wasn't permitted to run. "Don't you dare try to run from me," she shouted when I sped up. "Don't make me run after you, I'll tear your little butt to pieces."

So I skipped, hopped, tap-danced—anything to attempt avoiding the swish and cut of that branch, to get off the street and indoors quickly, out of sight of the other neighbors and the two or three young ballplayers who followed us, pointing, jeering, and laughing from a safe distance. My mother, of course, paid no attention to the laughter. Instead, she kept up a running monologue, scolding and reprimanding me all the way back to the house and punctuating her remarks with quick flicks of the switch.

"Didn't I tell you to wash them damn dishes!" Then, her arm

pumping like a whip-wielding lion tamer's, *swish* and the burning sting of sapling branch against arm or jean-covered legs or outstretched hands. *Swish.* "And what about cleaning up the basement!" *Swish.* "When I tell you to have your ass home"—*swish*—"I mean be there"—*swish*—"on time!" *Swish.* "Do you understand me?" *Swish . . . swish.*

My ego, of course, was bruised much more than my body, which I'm sure was her intention.

It was several days before I worked up enough nerve to return to the playground, and even then, I remained a laughingstock for weeks. "Hey, Pepper, you sure you wanna play, man? I heard yo' mamma was comin' down here to whip yo' ass again. Ha-ha-ha."

I'm sure that in my mother's view, discipline and gentle persuasion both worked toward the same end—keeping me close to home, away from the constant threats she saw in the streets. Both tacks were aimed at urging me to curb my aggression, assume a safe, passive approach.

Had she been preparing me for a game, a sports event, she might well have been a defensive coach. Throughout my childhood, she tutored, drilled me in a strategy of survival by avoidance that in many black communities and families was as deep rooted and sacred as the word of the Lord. It was a passive, risk-free approach that was totally at odds with my youthful enthusiasm. What she underestimated was my need to express and test myself, take the offense and challenge adversaries head-on.

Although he never talked to me about it, Tennessee, like most black fathers, understood that urge. He had, no doubt, faced a similar challenge. In fact, growing up in the South during a more repressive era, he probably encountered even more resistance.

He was born to Dave and Anne Watkins on June 6, 1902. The offspring of former slaves, his parents were sharecroppers who worked a farm in Montpelier, a small town located about fifty miles south of Tupelo in eastern Mississippi. Within two years of my father's birth, Anne died in her sleep of unspecified causes. Dave Watkins was hard pressed to make ends meet, so, as children, my father and his sister, Percy, were called on to help work the cotton fields alongside him. When Dave Watkins died in 1912, the children were sent to live with his father on a nearby farm.

Restless and ambitious even as an adolescent, my father soon tired of the drudgery of farmwork and sharecropping. At age thirteen, he left Montpelier and set out on his own. His sister, who remained, eventually married John Malcolm and moved to Falcon, Mississippi, where they purchased land and opened a successful country store.

My father moved west to Mississippi's Delta region, where he worked odd jobs in and around such towns as Clarksdale, Yazoo City, Greenwood, and Tunica—an area where, some insist, the blues were born. Indeed, it was the home of the gritty down-and-dirty sound of the bottleneck guitar and the plaintive, droning voices of bluesmen such as Bukka White, John Lee Hooker, and Son House. As a young man, at the end of the workday, my father would sometimes visit the sharecroppers' shacks, backwoods juke joints, and roustabout honky-tonks where Delta bluesmen played and honed their craft. He drank, gambled, and rubbed shoulders with folks that the black sociologist Charles S. Johnson later described as the "vagabonds," "outcasts," "bad niggers," "outlaws," and "renegades" who made up the "underworld" of the rural South.

Like the itinerant bluesmen whose songs eventually made the area legendary, he quickly learned the limits of Southern hospitality as it related to expressions of black manhood. Mississippi, under the auspices of the notorious Sen. Theodore Bilbo, had a well-deserved reputation as one of the most repressive states in the South. During the early twentieth century, the senator had vigorously urged that all Negroes be immediately repatriated to Africa. Determined to demonstrate how appealing the idea of returning to their homeland could be to those who insisted on residing in the Magnolia State, he engineered the passage of the nation's toughest black codes and Jim Crow laws.

Bilbo sanctioned harassment of Negroes by all manner of whites, from average citizens to law enforcement officers and the Ku Klux Klan. In his state, blatant defiance of voting and legal rights, segregated public accommodations, and in many communities, rigid curfews were day-to-day realities for the Negro community. In small hamlets as well as larger cities, when eleven o'clock approached, Negroes could be seen scrambling to get either indoors or out of town. If caught without a pass issued by local white authorities, they were subject to penalties ranging from a punitive ass whipping to jail or forced labor on a cotton plantation owned by one of the local whites.

These restrictions notwithstanding, Bilbo had about as much success convincing Negroes to return to Africa as did Marcus Garvey, the Jamaican-born black nationalist leader who in 1916 began promoting a similar scheme.

Given my father's reluctance to abide by outside authority or to back down from an altercation or fight, he undoubtedly ran afoul of Bilbo's statutes on numerous occasions. But he almost never talked about his personal experiences during that period. I could only assume that it was his usual reticence or that the memories were too painful, too traumatic for him to share with his children, particularly a son, his youngest, who was struggling to come to terms with his own manhood nearly a half century later. Still, he once revealed that he had witnessed a man being dragged off to be lynched. "I ain' seen nothin' near 'bout bad as that in my life," he said. "Mississippi was a mighty hard pull. Wasn't no place fo' the timid. But I wasn't no more than a fool youngster. I didn't know no better."

The one personal incident that he mentioned occurred late in the 1920s, after he had met my mother in Tunica. He had gone to a mill right outside of town to look for work when a group of white men cornered him. "I didn't think I was goin' make it," he said. "They came up on me befo' I could get back to the car I was drivin'. Belong to a cut buddy of mine from Memphis and I had my pistol hid in there. Anyway, they commence to firing at my feet, laughin' and yellin', 'Dance, black boy! C'mon now, dance some for us. Don't be lyin', we know yall dances. Yuh runnin' round here with that half-white woman, yuh must be a entertainer or somethin'." Afterward, they let him go. He laughed about it that day, but the memory of that embarrassing confrontation apparently lingered with him for the rest of his life.

Small wonder that the legendary bluesman Robert Johnson, a Son House protégé whose music, among other things, often expressed the subjective torment of the Delta blues experience, would later sing:

> The blues is a low down shakin' chill . . .
> a low down shakin' chill.

You ain't never had 'em, I hope you never will . . .
Blues is a low down achin' heart disease
like consumption, killin' me by degrees.

"Mississippi didn't give up nothin' but hard times and sad rhymes to black folks," Tennessee told me the summer after I'd failed second grade. "You can thank Jesus and two or three other white folks that we got outta there befo' you was born. May not look like much, may not even be all that. But up here, least you got a chance to make somethin' out yo'self. Don't be a damn fool. Put some use to it."

After that conversation, his attitude toward me shifted dramatically.

Whereas previously he had mostly ignored me, leaving my care to Miss Aggie, my sisters, and my mother, he began taking a more active role. During the next few years, even as I sometimes dragged my feet, he ushered me into his life, introducing me to a world I had often wondered about during his frequent absences.

"Where do Daddy go?" I'd once asked my mother.

"That's somethin' you don't need to know about," she'd snapped. "That bastard's out there runnin' around with the rest of them devils—gamblin' and doin' whatever he please while we sittin' here with near nothin' to eat. I don't ever want to catch you out there runnin' the street, you hear me?"

Of course, I couldn't wait until I was old enough to get out and find out what "runnin' the street" was all about. It sounded like fun to me. Meanwhile, Tennessee was introducing me to an adult world shaped by male camaraderie and bravado. More often than not, unless he was off on a weekend gambling binge or (according to my mother) a rendezvous with one of the "black heifers" who increasingly occupied his time, he took me with him.

Sometimes they were no more than short trips to the garage to have his car repaired or to pick up or deliver my brother Herbert at his job at Tamarkin Trucking, where he worked moving produce from huge trailer trucks onto the loading docks.

When I accompanied him to the homes of the numerous "clients" whose policy wagers he collected, the trips could take more time as those visits often turned into extended rounds of gambling. "You just set right there, boy. I'm goin' show you how to pick a turkey clean . . . ha-ha-ha. See, Mr. Jones here is what we call money wit' a

hat on . . . ha-ha." The laughter, loud banter, and feverishly competitive card games sometimes lasted until the phone rang and my
mother demanded that he get me home either to eat or to rest for
school the next day.

When he was winning at cards, however, Tennessee forgot everything except the card count in the current hand. So, despite her entreaties, I'd sometimes find myself sleeping on a stranger's couch
until near dawn. My father would wake me and, if it had been a successful night, leave our host with a parting remark such as, "Now,
don't be no stranger. You know where to find me if you get ahold
some mo' money. And don' worry none 'bout transportation. Fact,
you just call. I be glad to send a taxi over here to pick you up."

When we returned, my mother was furious, of course, but those
evenings were always exciting to me. I never complained.

My favorite trips with Tennessee occurred when we went to
Campbell, the township that bordered Youngstown's southeast
boundaries. For one thing, the drive there often took us along Wilson Avenue, pass Shehy and my old neighborhood. More important,
going to Campbell meant that we were headed either for Joseph
"Sandy" Naples's restaurant, where Tennessee dropped off the money and policy slips he'd collected, or to Oates's barbershop, where
we had our hair cut every week.

My interest in accompanying Tennessee to the Center Sandwich
Shoppe was primarily monetary. Not that the dapper Naples wasn't
affable enough. In fact, whenever my father and I entered the sandwich shop, he usually greeted us warmly. Although my father always seemed more tentative and reserved than usual when they
met, they'd joke like old friends before retiring to a back room to
complete their business. Before they left, Naples would always offer
me a bottle of orange pop and, most often, slip a dollar bill into my
hand and whisper, "Don't tell Tennessee. That's just for you."

As a nine- or ten-year-old kid, I was definitely impressed—as was
nearly everyone else, or so it seemed. Known for his tailored silk
suits and expensive Italian shoes as well as for flashy cars and the
wad of $100 bills he always carried, Naples had become a kind of
folk hero. Not only did everyday people, like my father, admire him,
but his influence also extended to politicians and the local police,
who could often be found sipping coffee at the sandwich shop. In
fact, some claimed that despite a loudly ballyhooed crackdown on

vice and gambling in the late forties, Naples's operations went virtually untouched because he had some high city officials in his pocket. In much the same way that such mobsters as Joey Gallo and John Gotti later parlayed style and rakish charm into national celebrity status, Sandy Naples became a local luminary in the Youngstown area.

Naples was, in truth, a career criminal who had fought and clawed his way to the top of Youngstown's rackets circles. He was as ruthless as he was charming, a fact that I was unaware of when Tennessee initially took me to the sandwich shop. Of course, I wouldn't have turned down the money and refreshments even had I known. But I would have been much more anxious while I was there.

As it turned out, Naples's violent past caught up with him. In 1949 he was wounded by an unidentified gunman who walked into the Center Sandwich Shoppe and opened fire. A few years later, his home was bombed and seriously damaged, and in 1960, during my sophomore year at college, he and his girlfriend were gunned down and killed on the front porch of her home.

When Naples was shot, my mother and a group of black well-wishers gathered at South Side Hospital. "We was all cryin' for Sandy," she told me later.

A white nurse noticed them and supposedly said, "All them niggers standing out there like they lost a relative. What they crying about?"

"We cryin' 'cause he done more for us than any a you ever done," my mother snapped.

Sandy Naples's violent death was not that unusual for Youngstown during the fifties and sixties. Organized crime was firmly entrenched in the community, and gangland violence had become so endemic that, in 1959, newly elected mayor Frank R. Franko called on the governor of Ohio for assistance. Nearly seventy bombings were reported in the district between 1951 and 1960, some occurring in broad daylight on Federal Street in the central downtown shopping district. The exploits of and struggle for control of the rackets between gangland figures such as Sandy Naples, Vince DeNiro, Joseph "the Wolf" DeCarlo, John B. Burnich, and Charles "Cadillac Charlie" Cavallaro regularly commanded front-page coverage in the local newspaper, the *Youngstown Vindicator*. By the 1960s, journalists across the country were referring to

Youngstown as Bombtown, U.S.A., and locals were sardonically calling car bombings "Youngstown tune-ups."

During the early fifties, even Edward DeBartolo, now Youngstown's wealthiest resident, was a bomb target. The reclusive senior DeBartolo (Mr. D, as Youngstown insiders called him) is now owner and director of a multibillion-dollar construction and real estate developing corporation, which includes among its holdings the Pittsburgh Penguins and the San Francisco 49ers. In the forties, however, the company struggled, and former employees insist that salary checks regularly bounced at local restaurants. Then, just after the company was transformed by his pioneering construction of suburban shopping malls and became a rapidly expanding concern, it apparently attracted the wrong kind of attention, and properties belonging to him, his relatives, and several associates were the targets of unsolved bombings. As late as the mid-1990s, security guards were still posted in front of DeBartolo's home in suburban Boardman—where he had built one of the nation's first shopping malls.

Still, while gangland exploits left an indelible mark on Youngstown's national reputation from the forties to the sixties, they rarely spilled over into the black community. Despite the apparent admiration that many blacks had for Sandy Naples and some of his cohorts, none became important players in the rackets. Much as in city politics, blacks in organized crime were restricted to token or marginal roles as gofers or, like my father, runners or pickup men. The mob's influence touched everyone's life indirectly, but except for casual interaction with a few high school classmates who drove expensive late-model cars and were rumored to be related to mobsters, and my brief encounters with Naples, it never entered my personal life.

I didn't need money as an inducement to anticipate the weekly trips Tennessee and I took to the barbershop, which was run by the stately Governor Oates. (He wasn't an elected official, of course. That was his name, and it struck me as strange until years later when I discovered that Southern blacks often named their children King, Princess, Major, or even Mister in order to bedevil whites who insisted on addressing them by their first names.) The barbershop was always packed, and sometimes Tennessee left me there while he went out to "see a man about a horse," as he put it. I didn't mind the wait. I'd been going to have my hair cut there since just before we moved to the south side, when Governor Oates or one of the other barbers had to place a wooden board across the arms of the chair so I sat high enough for them to reach my head. As at the Shehy pool-room, I'd become a kind of mascot. Someone would always buy candy or a soda for me, and over the years I'd come to appreciate the lively give-and-take and outrageous tales served up by the more flamboyant characters and the best of the storytellers and liars.

My favorite was a dark-skinned, craggy-faced older man whom everyone called Pines, a name that I later learned came from a familiar street jingle: "Tall like pine, / Black like crow./ Talk more shit, / Than a radio." He rarely failed to live up to the name, keeping the overflowing gallery of customers in stitches whenever he took center stage, which he usually did. He was a master at storytelling and signifying—or snapping, as it's called today—and few even attempted competing with his quick wit.

The atmosphere was always lighthearted and sportive as customers kidded one another and swapped stories about their jobs or embarrassing situations that they or an acquaintance had gotten into. One might, for example, have heard of Lindbergh, who acquired his name in an unusual manner. He had been visiting the wife of a steelworker while the husband was working the night shift. For some reason, the mills closed down one evening and the husband came home unexpectedly. Needing a quick exit from a second-story bedroom, he took flight and leaped through the window. From that day forward, he answered to the name of America's best-known aviator.

Amid all the foolery and wisecracking, Pines would occasionally get serious, or as close to it as the situation allowed. "*Eisen-hour* ain' worth but a minute," he once snapped during a more or less sober political discussion, "and *Tru-man* ain' nothin' but a liar. Neither one of 'em goin' invite yall to they party." On another occasion, during a discussion of slavery and its aftermath, he stopped the rambling conversation with: "Yeah, they set yall free ah right. Promised to give you ten acres and a mule, but didn't give you a damn thing. 'Sink or swim,' that's what they told you. Now, you know white folks knew most a them niggers couldn't swim a lick.

That weren't no accident, boy. If you don't believe me, go down to one a them *public* swimming pools now and see if they let you ass in there."

Sitting beside Tennessee, listening to the tall tales, colorful harangues, and infectious laughter that filled Governor Oates's cramped barbershop—even though I'm certain I didn't understand half of what was being said—gave me a sense of fellowship and belonging, perhaps even a kind of tribal identity that I'd been missing. I was much more comfortable there than I was in Mrs. Smith's classroom, where I was being bombarded with ideas, concepts, and a view of the world that still seemed foreign and totally unconnected to the life I knew at home.

As much as I enjoyed and benefited from accompanying my father on those excursions, it was the time he spent with me at home that most altered my childhood.

A few weeks after I learned that I'd be repeating second grade, I broke my arm. For most of the summer I was unable to join my friends to play ball or hang out at the playground. In fact, much of the time I was stuck in the house.

During that time my father began amusing himself by playing checkers and cards with me. Initially, I approached those sessions eagerly, but my youthful zeal and confidence were quickly stonewalled. Tennessee was furiously competitive, and when he introduced me to these games, there was no attempt to curb his aggression and will to win.

Although I'd just discovered checkers and had never played any card game except solitaire before, *he* approached those sessions with the same intensity, the same swaggering combativeness that I'd seen him display when challenging another gambler. As I sat across from him at our dining room table, it often seemed that he viewed me much as he would a hostile stranger trying to take his last dime in a game of cooncan. When he reared back in his chair, the wry smile and disdainful look he assumed when I watched him gambling with one of his numbers clients would descend over his face like a menacing mask. He prodded and bullied, baited and ridiculed my incompetence. Even though there was no wager, nothing tangible at stake, at least nothing I could discern, it seemed that I'd become little more in his eyes than another of the suckers he dismissed as "money wit' a hat on."

I stood no chance, of course, and initially he toyed with me, easily won every game.

When I inevitably lost, he'd call my mother or one of my brothers or whoever was nearby and laughingly gloat over his victory. The teasing was relentless. "Boy, you cain' play no checkers. You better get in there and help yo' mamma wit' the food . . . do somethin' you good at. Ha, ha-ha. Go on now, get on up from here." Embarrassed, sometimes nearly in tears, I'd often boldly insist on playing another game, which only resulted in another loss and an even louder round of taunting and ribbing.

My mother would sometimes intercede, saying, "Pitt, why don't you let that boy alone? You know he can't beat you." When she did, although I was ashamed that she had to step in and defend me, I'd take the opportunity to slip away and regroup—try to figure out what was going on. Why was my father tearing into me, attacking me over nothing more than a game? At those times, I hated him or came damn close to it.

These episodes, mind you, occurred during the time that he was also taking me with him on jaunts around town during which he treated me in an entirely different manner. Perplexed and more than a little confused, I began thinking of Tennessee as a kind of Dr. Jekyll and Mr. Hyde.

Not that his aggressively goading me while we played checkers or cards was the only indication of the contradiction. Hyde surfaced on many other occasions. The loud confrontations and shoving matches with my mother continued, and when he had been drinking, he could be a holy terror. More than a few times I saw him come home either intoxicated or bloodied and disheveled from a brawl. We had all learned to keep out of his way whenever his car roared up the driveway as if he were at the Canfield Raceway and the smell of gin preceded him through the doorway. Most times my mother, brothers, and I did exactly that. But if someone slipped up, didn't cut him enough slack, the consequences could be as bizarre as they were grave.

One afternoon while I was lying in an upstairs bedroom reading a comic book, Tennessee returned in one of his stoically silent inebriated states, which usually meant that he not only had been drinking but also had lost at cards. Although there were no best times, these were the worst of times to cross him. My brother Herbert happened to have gone into the bathroom just before Tennessee stomped into the house and was unaware of his return or his condition. When he entered, my father didn't say a word to anyone; he came directly upstairs and, seeing that someone was in the bathroom, shouted, "Hurry up in there. I got to use the toilet."

"Okay," my brother replied, "I'll be right out."

I heard my father turn and go back downstairs. Then, a few minutes later, he called out again, "Damn it, boy, I told you I had to get into that bathroom. You better get yo' ass outta there, now!"

The tone of voice should have been a tip-off, but for some reason Herbert had underestimated the degree of Tennessee's frustration and anger. "I told you I'm comin' out," Herbert yelled. "You . . . you, goin' have to wait."

A moment later, Tennessee stomped up the stairs again. This time he didn't say a word. The next thing I heard was the deafening sound of his pistol as he fired four shots through the bathroom door. The explosive, crackling sound of the revolver, the thud of bullets piercing wood, and the sharp, crashing sound of tile and glass merged with my brother's scream and echoed throughout the hallway. Herbert immediately bolted from the bathroom. "Are you crazy?" he screamed. "I told you, I was comin' out!"

I looked out of the bedroom door just in time to see him, pants still gathered around his ankles, scramble pass my father and lunge down the stairs. At the same time, my mother was rushing upstairs, screaming, "What happened? Lord have mercy, what's goin' on?" Amidst the chaos, Tennessee walked calmly into the bathroom and locked the splintered door behind him.

As I said earlier, Tennessee was an unpredictable and extremely complex man.

That, along with his insistence that I challenge him at the game board or card table, is probably why I never completely gave up or gave in to his relentless dogging. I did consider it. For a short time at the beginning of the summer, I sometimes avoided my father for days—either retreating to an upstairs bedroom or going outside whenever he came home. He quickly caught on to that ploy and, confronting me one day when I was hiding out upstairs, renewed the challenge: "What, you scared, boy? I hurt yo' damn feelings, huh? Ha, ha-ha. Well, you can sit up here hidin' out if you want, but if you had any gumption you'd come on downstairs and take this whipping like a man." Reluctantly, I followed him downstairs.

As the summer wore on, however, I gradually learned the strategy of both games. And before September, when I returned to school, I was competing on a near-equal level with my father. By the next year he could not come close to beating me at checkers, and only the luck of the draw determined who would win at cards.

What surprised me is that once the tables were turned, when he was consistently losing, he would still happily call folks over and tell them who had won. "You got me that time," he'd laugh, "Sister Katie, come on in here and look. This boy might be all right after all." That he called attention to my victory, of course, was totally unexpected. My resolve to beat him was inspired by revenge, getting even, and it would have been infinitely more sweet if losing had depressed him as much as it had me, if it had at least dampened his spirits.

Winning did not clear up my confusion.

It was months after our reversal of fortunes before I began to realize why it was so easy for him to celebrate what I thought of as *my* victories. He won, I came to believe, each time I did—something that only a parent, an extremely close friend, or a lover can do. My father, I'd discovered, was not only unpredictable but also much more cunning and resourceful than I'd given him credit for as a child.

Although I never directly confronted him with my suspicions, I was convinced that Tennessee had engineered the drama that had roused me from apathy and ignited my desire to beat him. He apparently thought I was too passive, too much influenced by Miss Aggie's dreamlike reveries and outlandish tales and, therefore, too involved with abstractions and unworldly fantasies with which he could never come to terms. After all, at age thirteen, he had been forced to fend for himself. Confront the ugly, often deadly reality of Southern racism alone. Meeting the real world full-face, getting over by challenging it aggressively, was for him the only legitimate way to survive. Fantasy and dreams were playthings, baubles and dalliances that only children, women, and the idle rich could afford.

To him, I must have seemed too comfortably ensnared in what he saw as a delicately woven web of tenderness and concern. Or perhaps he felt that I was becoming too gentle or too sensitive to compete and survive in the harsh, cutthroat world into which he was leading me. Apparently, he decided to snap me out of it, force me to face a reality he presumed I'd someday have to confront.

If my mother was tutoring me in the ways of defense and protection, Tennessee was schooling me in offense, attack. And miraculously, I had passed the first test without ever being aware that there was an exam.

My father had awakened a dormant competitive sense that, once ignited, shaped much of the rest of my life. Perhaps, most important, it immediately provided the outlet for self-expression that I'd been missing. I'd improved so much at cards that Tennessee had begun asking me to sit in for him when he decided to get up and rest or play at another table. Small successes such as becoming citywide checkers champion whetted my appetite and led to more confidence and a further testing of my abilities in sports. I became nearly obsessed with softball, which we played on the Grant school playground in the summer, then with hardball and the newly organized Little League.

During the summer before I reached the fourth grade, my name had appeared in the sports section of the *Vindicator* several times— in box scores as well as in headlines and the body of the stories. I'd had a successful year and so had our team, Steel City Chevrolet; even the older kids began to recognize and acknowledge me. Although I was only ten years old, I'd earned a certain respect at the ballpark and, in pickup games, I was often chosen before kids three or four years older.

I never thought about it then, but as I became more deeply involved in sports, my behavior in and outside the classroom changed radically. I'd had no further problems with teachers after I left Mrs. Smith's class; in fact, Mr. Abromovitz, my fourth-grade teacher, was impressed enough with my work and the apparent turnaround in my behavior that he later suggested that I skip the fifth grade and be passed along to the sixth, where I belonged. Outside school, I had curbed my habit of simply taking things that I wanted if I couldn't afford them. Not eliminated the habit, mind you, just checked it.

It wasn't completely stopped until an unusually warm spring day when I was eleven years old.

I was sitting on the front porch with my father when a Pepsi delivery truck stopped at the food store at the corner. When Tennessee got up to go into the house, I ran down to the unattended truck, lifted two bottles of pop from its open racks, and sprinted back to our porch. I'd always tried to carefully conceal my pilfering from my father, even though in the back of my mind I felt his picking up the numbers was just as illegal as my stealing. I'm not sure what got into me that day, but when my father came back, I offered him a pop. It was not a wise decision.

"Where'd you get that pop, son?" he asked.

"I . . . uh, I bought it at the store."

"But you didn't have no money a minute ago."

"Yeah, but . . ."

"Don't lie to me, boy. Did you steal these damn pops? *Did you?*"

"Well, yeah, Dad . . . but I thought—"

" 'Thought' my ass! Get up from here, take these bottles back, and if you get caught, I hope they take you downtown. You hear me? Get the hell up and do it! Now!"

Tennessee stood and watched me sneak back to the delivery truck and replace the bottles. Luckily, the driver was still inside the store and no one saw me. When I returned, sweating, scared, and shaken, my father looked at me disgustedly and said, "And I thought you had some sense, boy. Say one thang, you sho' had me fooled."

He shook his head, then walked away. Tennessee didn't speak to me again for more than a week.

That encounter brought an end to my days of ripping off toys, comic books, and soda pops.

# 6

## cat bones
## and
## crosses

I heard the sound of glass crashing onto the packed dirt in our back-yard just as I turned to walk up the driveway that separated the Woodland Avenue houses. It was a few weeks after the Pepsi incident and I had just finished playing a softball game at the Volney Rogers Field ballpark. When I reached our back porch, I saw that the yard was littered with pots and pans, utensils, shattered glasses and plates. Kitchenware of every description was still flying out of the window, which had been broken, presumably when the first plate or glass was tossed.

From within came the sound of my mother humming, a soft, gut-tural rendering of one of her favorite hymns, "Nearer My God to Thee," that was regularly punctuated by stinging condemnations of my father, delivered under her breath, and further embroidered with soulful, high-pitched moans. Falsetto wails that Al Greene might have envied. "Dirty so-and-so . . . uhhh umm-hummm. *Ah-hhh Lawd* . . . uhh umm-hummm . . . bring his ass in here with that whiskey on his breath . . . uh-hummmm um-hum. I'm not goin' take it. I'll show him . . . damn his soul."

I rushed inside and saw my brother Herbert standing in the kitchen doorway, helplessly looking on. "Mamma, what's wrong with you? Why you got to do that?" he asked. She ignored both of us, never breaking stride as, one by one she plucked items from cabinet shelves and flung them through the window. I did not interfere. By this time I knew better. I paused only for a moment, catching her eye briefly, then averting mine and quickly going upstairs. Later, after nearly everything that was not bolted down had been tossed outside, my mother called me and told me to clean up the mess. "I don't want to see one speck a glass left out in that yard. And get some cardboard and close up this window."

My parents' marriage was in trouble. The stare-downs and heated run-ins had escalated, and there was talk of divorce. Each had pulled me aside, faulting the other, coaxing, schooling me on what to say in court should it be necessary. But while Tennessee became more distant and stoic as the tension mounted, my mother's emotions were undraped, bared for observation. One moment needful and demonstratively loving, the next, destructive and filled with rage as she yielded to the stress. Her eyes and shifting moods also transformed me, made me—chameleonlike—most often simply a manchild to be nurtured and protected, then, inexplicably, an adversary, little more than the diminutive archetype or mirror image of Tennessee's villainous manhood. On those latter occasions, her behavior was as erratic and overbearing as an incensed drill sergeant's.

I was being pulled in opposite directions, and for me, the situation was obviously confusing and scary; it must have been devastating for them. Against terrible odds, they had struggled to maintain their relationship for nearly thirty years since they'd been married in Tunica, Mississippi, in 1922.

Katie Belle Watkins was born in Tunica on March 13, 1905, the daughter of Aggie P. Jones and Harry Chandler. Her father, a young upstart Irish artisan who lived with his family, had stepped across the tracks and the color line to meet and pursue my grandmother despite the era's rigid racial conventions. According to Miss Aggie's sister, Aunt Bert, theirs was a passionate, whirlwind romance, the type that, although seldom reflected in such popular Southern romances as *Gone With the Wind*, had thrived and been whispered about in Dixieland since rumors of Thomas Jefferson's amorous pursuit of his slave mistress surfaced. Given the time and the place, their relationship was unusual in that there was little attempt at concealing the affair. My mother, who was named after Harry Chandler's sister, Kate, was one of the couple's two offspring. Her brother died of edema at age five, but for a time they were both welcome visitors at the Chandler residence. Almost everyone in the small Delta town knew exactly where the skeletons lay, and on one occasion Harry Chandler had threatened to kill a Negro whom he suspected of stalking his young daughter.

Despite Harry Chandler's ardor and honorable intentions, however, it was turn-of-the-century America in Senator Bilbo's Mississippi. Community acknowledgment notwithstanding, while such relationships were sometimes tolerated, they were not publicly sanctioned or accepted. Moreover, even if Harry had been so inclined, interracial marriage was legally prohibited in Mississippi. Miss Aggie took her daughter and moved to a small farm just outside Tunica.

She found employment as a housekeeper and cook with a local family and, within a few years, married Tom Jones, a black handyman from the Arkansas bayous. The relationship was rocky from the start and their marriage would eventually end in divorce. Before they separated, however, Miss Aggie's teenage daughter met Tennessee, who was then a chauffeur for a wealthy plantation owner in the Tunica area. Shortly after Katie turned seventeen, just as the twenties began roaring, she married her eighteen-year-old suitor.

Their union also began on a questionable note since Katie had hastily accepted Tennessee's proposal, in part, to get away from her stepfather, whom she had come to despise. And although my parents grew closer during those early years, problems persisted— many of which were not of their own making. From a distance or in a quick glance, Katie and Tennessee could easily be mistaken for an interracial couple. And if public race mixing was frowned upon when it occurred between a white man and a black woman in the South, as in the case of Miss Aggie and Harry Chandler, it was absolute anathema when it involved a black man and white woman— or, sometimes, even a so-called high yaller woman, who could easily be mistaken for white. In the backwoods country of the Mississippi Delta, my parents stuck out like a Catholic priest at a Klan rally. Their appearance together sometimes elicited taunts and catcalls. Nearly always they attracted a scrutiny that they neither sought nor deserved.

Harassment and the threat of violent encounters with local red-necks was one of many reasons for their leaving Tunica and moving to a larger, more metropolitan city. Although Memphis was nearby—about forty miles north on Route 61, a highway that follows the banks of the Mississippi River as it winds its way along the borders of Tennessee and Mississippi before expiring in New Orleans—the sight of a high-toned woman and a darker man were far less likely to attract attention in that more cosmopolitan setting. The city also offered other advantages not available in the Delta backwater. In fact, when the northern migration of rural blacks escalated during World War I, Memphis became one of the most popular stops on that journey. Most simply passed through on their way to Illinois, Michigan, and Ohio. But many stayed and settled there.

One of the biggest attractions was its work opportunities. There was furious competition and Negroes were not paid as much as white workers, but jobs were available for laborers in factories, the rail industry, and lumber mills. Almost all of them paid far more than the farmwork that was available farther South.

Of course, there was also the excitement and allure of Beale Street. It was not only a mecca for gambling, high life, and entertainment but also a thriving commercial area where Negroes congregated en masse to shop and conduct everyday business. Nat D. Williams—impresario, local radio personality, and columnist for the *Memphis World* and *Pittsburgh Courier*, as well as a teacher at Booker T. Washington High School, where my sister Cherrie attended his class—described it as a "mile-long adventure."

Williams was a key contributor to *Beale Black & Blue*, a book that depicted the street as a "melting pot of black America." As such, it was home to "harlots and mothers of the church; professional men in their black suits and dark ties; country folk in overalls and flour-sack dresses; easy riders in their boxback suits, Stetson hats, and silk shirts . . . wandering minstrels singing their blues, itinerant preachers shouting a hell-fire-and-brimstone blues of their own; conjure men and con men; voodoo and hoodoo women." Beale Street's glitter and glamour were worlds apart from the small-town, deep-South communities from which many of the new arrivals had fled.

The color and variety notwithstanding, there was a downside. Most Negroes were still shunted to the worst neighborhoods in the

least desirable areas. Many lived in squalid surroundings near the
polluted streams of the Mississippi, where the yards of their
crowded houses were dotted with outdoor toilets and refuse piles.
W. C. Handy, who was considered Father of the Blues and would
have a municipal park named after him, once lived in an area
known as Greasy Plank.

By the time my parents were born, Memphis had already earned
a reputation as the murder capital of the world. Rampant black-on-
black violence was generally treated with a slap on the wrist, and
white mayhem directed at blacks was simply ignored. A few years
before my parents arrived, for instance, a white mob had burned a
young black man at the stake when he was accused of raping a
white girl; afterward, his charred remains were strewn about Beale
Street as a warning. Similar incidents had prompted concerned
newspaper editors at the *Memphis Commercial Appeal* to remind
readers that the gratuitous killing of blacks was "being overdone"
and should be stopped since "those white men who kill Negroes as a
pastime . . . usually end up by killing a white man."

It was into this atmosphere that Katie and Tennessee moved
when they left Tunica, in 1923. They were fortunate and found
housing outside both the downtown Tenderloin area through which
Beale Street sliced and the squalid shanty settlements along the
river. They settled on Lucy Street between Wellington and Latham
in an area just beyond the southern tip of the rich south Memphis
district, where many of the city's wealthy whites lived. The house
was modest, but theirs was a safe, stable block in a primarily working-class black neighborhood. Some of their neighbors, in fact,
were part of the city's then expanding black professional class—
schoolteachers, businessmen, and such.

Katie quickly found work as housekeeper and, eventually, secured a job in the household of the Van Fleets, a wealthy Memphis
family by whom she was employed until we moved to Ohio. Initially, Tennessee worked at a series of jobs as a chauffeur, laborer,
and handyman.

Even with the two incomes, they struggled during the twenties.
And when Tennessee was unable to find work after the stock market
crash of 1929, the situation deteriorated. By then, they had four
children. Muriel (Cherrie), the oldest, was born in August of 1924.
Doris followed in October 1927, and in July of the next year, Katie

gave birth to my twin brothers, Herbert and Albert. McKay was born in August 1932, at the height of the Depression.

Times were hard, but they survived—according to my father, even did better than most in their position. The Van Fleets offered some aid, as did agencies that distributed food to thousands of near-destitute families, and by the early thirties, Tennessee found sporadic work with the WPA levee projects. Equally important, throughout the toughest times he always had a hustle. And although he didn't always emerge unscathed, he had a knack for arising unvanquished even from the most adverse confrontations.

No stranger to Beale Street's saloons and gambling dens even before the Depression, he became a more frequent visitor. It was the Prohibition era and, for those bold and determined enough, there was money to be made buying and selling whiskey. Many nights found him at such joints as the Hole in the Wall, where the least affluent went to gamble, or, on occasion, the Monarch Club, one of the better gaming spots. His stake was never big enough to join the high rollers in games frequented by such legendary Beale Street gamblers as Casino Henry or Mac Harris or Red Lawrence, the blond-haired mulatto said to have killed thirteen people between World Wars I and II. Still, he usually managed to come away with enough to help clothe his children and keep food on the table.

There were, no doubt, reasons other than monetary ones that drew Tennessee to Beale Street. It was, after all, an oasis that, for many, provided temporary asylum from the hazards of day-to-day living in the Delta's racist, Jim Crow society. As in Harlem during the same period, Negroes could congregate, socialize, or party without undue interference from whites. Although they owned almost nothing on the street, it had been left to them. Parks, theaters, and restaurants catered to their needs, and whites were content to live and let live if Negroes kept to themselves and didn't stray too far from that one-mile strip. "On Beale you could be a man, your own man," one observer noted. "On Beale you could be free."

Katie, who neither gambled nor drank, was not drawn to Beale's night life. Mostly she worked, came home to Lucy Street, and took care of the expanding family. Like most Memphis Negroes, however, she did spend time on Beale, shopping, taking the children to movie houses like the Daisy or to outings in Church's Park or—later, after Boss Crump was persuaded to name a newly cleared plot of land at

Hernando and Beale after the city's most famous bluesman, in 1931—to W. C. Handy Park. She even accompanied Tennessee on occasion, as when they and the other children went to see Herbert and Al festooned as the Goodyear Twins and perched atop a float in the Negro-sponsored Beale Street Cotton Makers' Fiesta.

By that time, the worst of the Depression woes were fading and Tennessee had found work as a mechanic at a Goodyear service center and auto repair shop, where he remained until he left Memphis. Although his forays into Beale Street's high life had diminished, they had not ceased. A pattern had been established.

> Well, mama don' allow me to fool roun' all night long,
> Now I may look like I'm crazy, poor John,
>     do know right from wrong.
> Now, drop down, babe, and let your daddy be,
> I know just what you're trying to put on me.

The motif was as well worn and destructive as any that ever plagued relationships between black men and women: she the caretaker, guardian of the home; he the free-spirited denizen of the streets. The inevitable clash would hound my parents even as they left Beale Street and Memphis, settled in the North.

In Youngstown, Katie would seek to mend fences, disrupt the pattern. Unable to stop her husband, she seemingly resolved to join him. She learned to play cards, became involved in the house parties that Tennessee hosted in our cellar, and sometimes accompanied him when he went out to gamble. During the early years on Woodland, she seemed to enjoy playing tonk and, sometimes, would even offer advice after my father had decimated and mocked me at the card table. There was a brief period of conciliation, and for a time they appeared to have grown closer, warming to each other's company. But her attempts at rapprochement ultimately failed. Tennessee's resolve was inexorable; the allure of nightlife with its elusive promise of escape from anonymity and the tyranny of white male dominance continued to beckon. Finally, although I had no idea at the time, his need for freedom, liberation, and acknowledgment was the hammer that drove a wedge into the fragile stump of their relationship.

Disheartened and frustrated, Katie turned to religion and the church. It was Reverend Rose's storefront Baptist church that initially comforted and salved her pain. Later she became an avid follower of Katherine Kuhlman, a white evangelist with a large black following; her ministry, although national, was based in the Ohio area. But, even as Katie shifted her burden and trust from secular solutions to the hand and word of the Lord, her faith was sometimes challenged by more mundane beliefs.

It may have been a legacy passed on by the elderly, silver-tongued storytellers who gathered in and around the Delta backwaters and spun out tales of haints and hexes, or the ghostly myths perpetuated by manipulative whites who attempted to frighten and control the Negro underclass. Or perhaps it was the proximity of the hoodoo practitioners who thrived and prospered at the east end of Beale Street. Whatever the cause, both my parents had left the South with an abiding respect for, if not full-blown belief in, the supernatural.

Dream books, an essential tool for determining the day's lucky policy number, and charms or tip sheets secured during occasional visits to psychics or conjure women were ordinary household items. Superstitions were as much a part of the tenor and rhythm of our daily lives as Tennessee's Delta blues tunes. Even if you didn't appreciate them, it was wise to be appraised of their importance; they were accorded a respect that the clergy often reserve for Deuteronomy. At an early age, I had become well versed in the consequences of a raft of trivial occurrences that ranged from generally accepted beliefs about walking under ladders, black cats crossing your path, and breaking glass to more esoteric notions about the dire result of sweeping dirt out the door, combing your hair at night, stepping in another person's tracks, or passing food behind someone's back at the dinner table. Ignorance could be a liability. One of the worst beatings I received, for instance, resulted from accidentally brushing a broom against my father's foot when he was gambling.

In that atmosphere, it wasn't surprising that, even as she embraced the church, Katie sustained some allegiance to supernatural folk beliefs.

Although I was never quite sure she believed it, she often told a story about a Delta man who had come under the spell of a conjure woman. "Name was Hoecake. He beat that woman and walked out on her. Guess he thought was just goin' go on 'bout his business. But she had somethin' waitin' for 'em. Not long after, people started wondering what happened to him. See, ain' nobody seen him for weeks.

"Then, one day, he come downtown to buy some groceries. But he was walkin' backwards. That's right . . . backwards! He tried to act like nothin' was wrong, picked up his bag of food and tipped on out the door, trying not to fall. Then backed on up the road and outta town. Everybody tried not to laugh, 'cause they knowed it was the work of that two-head doctor lived out there in the country. Went on for months. Hoecake kept on walking backwards. And all the while, it seem like he was gettin' thinner and lookin' worst. Then one day he went down to the levee lookin' for somebody. When he tried to leave, he got all tangled up and turned around. I guess he forgot which way he was goin', 'cause he backed right off the levee and fell in that water. Drown to death, right there. Sho' did. And that's the truth. Least that's what they said when I was comin' up."

The mind, they say, can perform miracles: heal the sick, empower the weak. Some even insist it can wake the dead. Now, I'm not so sure about all that. But I do know that faith and true belief can give substance to the most whimsical fantasies. It can rejuvenate or enervate, create its own reality or purge the beliefs of others; can, in fact, compel a man to walk backward just as readily as it can inspire men to build cathedrals on foundations of myth and fear. Since there is ample evidence that some—including many Southern blacks—fervently believed in the power of voodoo, Katie's tale may well have been true. I don't know. What I do know is that for years after she related the story I kept my distance from anyone who seemed to have intimate knowledge of the mysterious workings of goofer dust, mojos, and other hoodoo implements.

Still, for me the story was more amusing than disturbing. There were signs, however, that Katie did not dismiss it out of hand. The visits to conjurers or root doctors continued. Her concern about others working a spell on her remained, and apparently, she had some confidence in charms and incantations such as burying one of my father's shoes near the front porch, its toe pointed toward the house, to assure his return. For a time, those beliefs coincided with her faith in the Bible and the church. Poised between black cat bones and the cross, she balanced them with near-perfect equilibrium as a master magician might simultaneously levitate two disparate bodies.

Even practices that I dismissed as mere recreation or caprice turned out to have much more portentous overtones. Her habit of hanging empty pop bottles on the peach and apple trees in our backyard, as I later discovered, was derived from a traditional African practice. Some West African Kongo tribes believed that such bottle trees could protect their villages by warding off evil spirits; the ritual had been brought to America by slaves and passed on for generations. Its Youngstown revival, I'm sure, was unnoticed by most everyone except those versed in secret rites employing charms, powders, and roots to unleash the fearful spirits that my mother sought to mitigate.

As Katie became more immersed in Katherine Kuhlman's ministry, her concern with conjuration gradually faded. She stopped accompanying Tennessee to gambling parties and, eventually, gave up cards altogether. She also quit smoking after being moved to throw her cigarettes away at one of Miss Kuhlman's revival meetings. Her relationship with Tennessee, however, continued deteriorating.

It was during this time that she most ardently pressed me to accept Jesus Christ and join the church. Often I was required to accompany her to Reverend Rose's sermons or to Miss Kuhlman's crusade. If excused from those Sunday afternoon meetings, I was given a quarter for a donation and sent off to Sunday school at the Third Baptist Church, which was within walking distance of our house. Early on, however, I'd become suspicious of organized religion. Can't explain it, but from as early as I can remember I had an instinctual feeling that most of the churchly folks I'd seen were ducking and dodging, hiding out from the repressive reality of everyday life. Although I'd clapped and swayed to the often overpowering gospel sound of the choir at Mt. Carmel, stomped in time to the rhythm of tambourines and organ that amplified the voices of the bounteous sisters who lead the singing, I could not respond to either the fire-and-brimstone sermons of Reverend Rose or the quiet, joyous entreaties of Miss Kuhlman.

Once, among a crowd of several thousand at spacious Stambaugh Auditorium, I thought I felt the Spirit, the call, when Miss Kuhlman had beseeched the audience, "Come forth. Lay your burdens in the hands of the Lord." My mother had already left her seat and joined the throng that moved toward the stage when, still sitting in my third-balcony seat, I suddenly felt drawn to follow her. Mesmerized, or perhaps hypnotized, I rose and started down the marble stairs. It was as if my mind had been shut down; I was responding solely to the feeling, the wave of passion that had swept me up. The bellowing sound of the choir and thundering drumming of the audience's applause for the faithful who gathered in front of the podium seemed to lift me, pull me along with the others. I was light headed and drenched with sweat when, swept along by the crowd, I made it to the first floor, where the wave of people—young and old, black and white—halted at the narrow entrance to the orchestra floor.

But, there, jammed against those warm, soon-to-be-saved bodies, I froze. If the apparent calling had buoyed and transported my body, the voice that then reared in my head settled and anchored me. The feeling that had drawn me there was real, as powerful and pure as I'd ever felt. But if the hymn was pristine and perfectly pitched, the singer, organized religion, was, for me, irredeemably flawed. I turned, fought my way back through the crowd that surged herdlike toward the stage, and left the auditorium. My heart had been willing but my mind recoiled.

During the revival meeting's remaining hours, I sat outside on the concrete steps, staring across at Wick Park, the luxurious recreational facility that fronted Stambaugh and even then was packed with a crowd of carefree revelers who apparently lived in that then-plush, all-white neighborhood. From within the auditorium, the strains of a subdued sorrow song lilted through the building's massive ionic pillars. "I found Jesus . . . Oh yes, I found the Lord."

I never told anyone about that experience, but it had changed me. My mother had lost me, at least, with regard to that realm of her life. She had entered a place into which, at the time, I could not follow. I had not completely closed the path, however; like those marginal Catholics who depend on a deathbed confession to absolve themselves of a life filled with transgressions, I had postponed my decision, knowing that there was another option.

There would be time to recant, I told myself, time for redemption and safe entry into the flock; after all, according to my mother, suicide and blasphemy were the only unforgivable sins. Still, despite the overwhelming power of the feeling I'd experienced in that auditorium, the church and its biblical lore remained as unbelievable as the tale of the man who walked backward. And unlike Hoecake, I did not intend to stumble backward into anything. If I was to fall, I intended taking Miss Aggie's advice. I'd do it while looking straight ahead; at least I'd see and, perhaps, understand what was tripping me up.

By age ten, I regularly took the quarter allotted for Sunday school and spent Sunday mornings down the hill at Boyd Nabor's poolroom on High Street. I was convinced that the Lord wouldn't object to sacrificing twenty-five cents so that I could learn a skill that might someday prove beneficial. And although Katie had seemingly found herself as she became more absorbed in the church, the breach between her and Tennessee widened. While she found solace in the word, he found rejuvenation in the streets. The bickering and verbal wars continued.

## III

About the same time, the discord in our household intensified. Just before his eighteenth birthday, McKay returned from the army. He had been discharged when they discovered that he had entered illegally. During his brief stint, however, he sustained a foot injury that required a serious operation. Afterward he was treated with morphine; constant use of that medication led to an addiction he tried to kick for the rest of his life. When he returned, as a teenager, however, no one was aware of it.

For me he had been an awesome but shadowy figure from the time I could remember his presence in the house. He was as much sojourner as family member, and because of the time spent in reform school and the army, I hardly knew him. After his discharge, however, he spent nearly two years at home and we grew closer.

More than that, he became a kind of role model for me. Having found that the boisterous, wisecracking front I'd adopted during my first few years at school was only leading to disaster, I'd begun to curb my behavior, if only to stay out of trouble. The piety of the church was not, for me, a reasonable alternative. Confused, increasingly turning inward and becoming more introspective, I was ripe for some positive outside influence. McKay was nothing if not cocksure and persuasive.

Articulate and glib, smooth as the silk suits he wore, and apparently superconfident, his presence was electric, as was his appearance. Tall (about six feet one), slender, and blessed with my mother's

stately features, he could light up a room. In addition, he had acquired a charm and elegance that could disarm the most cynical observer. "Boy could talk a tree out its bark," our cousin Charles
Ernest was fond of saying.

But if he left the impression of a suave lothario, mine was that of
an introspective, mostly inept ugly duckling. I was a skinny, gan-
gling ten-year-old, not only struggling to keep pace with a frame
that was skying at a speed that nearly defied my capacity to adjust
but also desperately trying to come to terms with the seemingly
conflicting priorities of the adult world. Why, for instance, could
Tennessee passionately take me to task for stealing a soda pop in
one instance and, the next, return home drunk after losing his entire paycheck and boldly challenge anyone to criticize him? That
dilemma haunted me until I finally realized that while he accepted
his own limitations and some unsavory aspects of his own life, he
expected much more from me.

When McKay returned home, however, I was still baffled. I hadn't
even perceived or accepted the difference between celluloid fantasy
and the real world. I had just seen the classic western *High Noon*,
and the Gary Cooper role had fascinated me. The hero's quiet resolve was impressive, and because he too seemed lanky and awkward, so was the forceful way he carried himself. Afterward, at
home, I often found myself mimicking Cooper's determined, stiff-
shouldered stride as I tramped about the house mouthing the
movie's theme song, "Do not forsake me, oh my darling," and imagining myself fighting for some high-minded cause. For a time, the
pretense marginally improved my habit of slouching out of embarrassment over my height (I was already near six feet tall), but it accomplished little else. I remained ungainly, hesitant, and without
direction.

My search for an unequivocal ethical cause didn't fare well either.
Celluloid hype about the certitude of Old West moral and ethical
standards notwithstanding, for many working-class black families
the moral arena had a shadowy, slippery playing field. A history of
dealing with a nonblack society for whom ethics and the law were
often bent to achieve its own ends had taught most blacks to adopt
a flexible attitude toward issues of right and wrong. My family was
no exception. Finding a clear-cut cause was not a simple task. Moreover, the stiff-upper-lip approach I'd chosen was greeted with about

the same amount of enthusiasm *Il Trovatore* might have received from an Apollo Theatre audience steeped in the sounds of rhythm and blues. Reserve or seeming hesitancy were seldom rewarded in our house; my fanciful stoicism and attempt to assume a heroic posture was ignored or, at best, greeted with amused tolerance. Unlike the Cooper character, for me no rewards were forthcoming; there was certainly no beautiful heroine waiting in the wings.

My admiration for McKay was evident, but during his first few months at home, he seemed perplexed by my behavior. Moody and often distracted, he seemed to spend most afternoons lying around the house or picking at an old stand-up piano that he'd bought shortly after returning. At night, he disappeared. Like Tennessee, he'd always prided himself on his appearance, and although he wasn't working, he quickly acquired a striking wardrobe. During that time, he walked with a limp, even occasionally using a cane, particularly if he was visiting Dr. Belinky, the city coroner as well as our family physician, for treatment of his foot. The cane, combined with his expensive tailored Nehru suits, jewelry, and cashmere overcoat, made him look like he had just stepped off the cover of *Esquire*. He played the role to the hilt. My fascination increased, even as he ignored or, often, ridiculed me.

It was he, in fact, who put my identification with cinema heroes to rest when, laughing, he stopped me one day and asked: "What the hell's wrong with you, Pepper? This ain't no goddamn Western. Walking around here pretending you a cowboy and singing some jive-ass Tex Ritter song. You crazy, or what? Better figure out a way to get out of this rat hole and make yourself some damn money."

Despite the similarity, at least in my mind, of Tennessee's two-gun-toting image to such Old West heroes as Wild Bill Hickok, Gary Cooper was soon displaced as a role model.

Less than a year after his return, however, McKay collapsed on our back porch. My mother's scream awakened me in the middle of the night when she found him sprawled outside the door. When I dragged myself off the couch, where I'd been sleeping that night, and stumbled into the kitchen, McKay was unconscious. His head was titled back at an awkward angle against the porch's wooden slats, and frothy saliva dripped from the corner of his mouth. Thinking he was dead, I panicked.

My brother Herbert had also awakened, and with my mother, we dragged McKay to the car; then she rushed him to South Side Hospital. I didn't sleep for the rest of the night. The next morning, just before I went to school, she returned and said they thought he'd be all right. She also told us what had happened; it was the first time I heard of an overdose.

McKay survived, but that incident not only changed our relationship but, more importantly for him, upset the scam that he'd been working with our doctor. His foot, apparently, was no longer causing the severe pain that he pretended. Not that his urgent need of morphine wasn't real; if anything, it was probably more intense. But the ailment had shifted from a socially sanctioned physical problem into a murkier domain. Having been busted, in society's view he'd been transformed from ailing patient to addict or, far worse, a mere junkie.

After he was released from the hospital, Dr. Belinky cut back on the generous doses of morphine he'd been supplying, apparently intending to wean my brother from his habit. McKay had other ideas. Soon he was supplementing the doctor's prescriptions with drugs from the street or, when he could, the pharmacy.

There must have been others as well, but shortly after being released from the hospital, McKay enlisted me to assist him in buying paregoric, an over-the-counter drug sold primarily for the treatment of diarrhea in children. It also happened to contain opium.

During the fall of that year, my brother and I methodically visited nearly every pharmacy in the Youngstown area. My task involved a simple bit of deception. It started in the heart of the downtown business district, at a drugstore next to the Strand Theater on Central Square.

I ran into the pharmacy looking distressed and pleading with the owner. "Mister, mister! We need some *par-ru-goric* bad. My sister is sick. She's sweatin' and throwin' up . . . my mamma said you'd sell us some!"

McKay rushed in a minute or so after I did. "Did you get it?" he yelled. "I'm double-parked out here, we got to hurry."

The pudgy, round-faced pharmacist, who was waiting on another customer, looked at us, hesitated for a moment, then told the customer to wait a second. He went back and pulled a small bottle from a locked cabinet at the rear of the pharmacy. McKay tossed $10 on the counter and rushed back outside. I collected the change and the brown paper bag with the medicine inside. "Be careful with that," the pharmacist yelled, as I ran out of the door. "And get your sister to a doctor, quick."

It had worked. In the car, McKay checked the bag, then laughed. "I told you it would be easy, didn't I?" he said. "Let's split."

It was, of course, a one-shot deal. After each charade, we had to move to another pharmacy. For a two- or three-month period, we repeated the scenario, moving in ever-widening circles until we had exhausted drugstores in Youngstown as well as the surrounding suburban communities of Warren, Austintown, and Boardman. It was an exciting game to me; I looked forward to those adventures since, for the first time, I felt some real involvement with my brother. Although McKay had insisted that this was our secret, one that couldn't be shared with anyone, including my parents, I never even considered the consequences if the scam was discovered.

After he had scored, if there was no one at home, I'd sit and watch as he carefully went through the ritual of preparing his fix. He would boil the mixture to isolate its opium base and, spoonful by spoonful, draw it through a piece of cotton into a syringe. Tightening his belt about his upper arm, he'd search for a prominent vein in his forearm and sink the needle into it. Occasionally, when he had difficulty finding a usable vein or fumbled with the syringe, he dropped the end of the belt from his mouth and asked me to pull it tighter so that he could look more closely as he prodded and squeezed to find a suitable spot for the injection. Afterward he would sink back onto the couch, nodding and seemingly relaxed, sometimes nearly unconscious.

I watched all of this with a combination of fascination and curious detachment that, later, seemed bizarre to me. There was no fear or repulsion, not even the rush of excitement one might experience observing some dangerous, forbidden practice. It became, after a while, as routine as watching someone drink a glass of water.

This was, of course, years before drug abuse became a major social problem in America. The practice had not yet spread from the black community to the suburbs; it was not yet a pressing concern for the mainstream.

Since I had never heard of drug addiction and it was a brother whom I admired who was performing the act, I accepted it as an unusual but not extraordinary occurrence. Luckily, the dread of needles that I'd developed during past visits to doctors ensured that McKay's malaise held no attraction for me. Moreover, it was right after we'd completed the drugstore scam that he was most attentive to me. During the car ride and score, he was always tense, nervous, and distracted; but once he shot up and was, as he said, in the zone, his anger and anxiety faded. He mellowed and became a different person.

In that post-fix reverie, after he'd gotten "straight," he was always less guarded, more accessible. The face of the glib and frivolous con artist receded; he became warmer, more musing and meditative. Although he seldom talked about what he did, what scheme was currently supporting his habit and supplying the cash that he nonchalantly flashed, he did express interest in my concerns and activities. We talked about baseball, boxing, and his experiences in the Golden Gloves. We even talked about jazz and women, subjects of which I had absolutely no prior knowledge. I was the baby of the family and McKay, the closest in age of all my siblings, was eight years older. It was at those times that I first felt any real connection to my brother.

I also realized that McKay was not the superconfident player that I'd come to imagine. He was more than just flash and con, panache and deceit. Relaxed and open, he would sometimes talk about his own experiences, alluding to demons that I never imagined existed. "Most people never face bare reality," he once told me. "If they did, it would drive 'em crazy. You know, you're lucky, living in that fantasy world you concocted. I hope it works, my man. Hope you never have to face the real deal—stark reality." I, of course, had no clue as to what he was talking about. Despite my Gary Cooper fantasies, the world I did face often seemed real and scary enough for me.

I began to sense, however, that McKay's life wasn't as carefree and unburdened as I suspected. Soon it became obvious that he was also far more thoughtful and intelligent than I imagined. In fact, although he had little formal education, his IQ surpassed the genius level. Years later, he earned a high school equivalency diploma in prison. And after starting college at Wayne State University in Detroit, he received his degree in engineering while locked up. I never paid attention to his intelligence or the deeper side of his personality until he drew me aside and recited Edgar Allan Poe's "The Raven" in its entirety. From the first moment I heard it, I was entranced with the poem's eerie, otherworldly quality as well as its hypnotic rhythm and cadence, partly because McKay seemed to internalize it, transform it with his own dramatic presentation.

During the fifteen or so minutes he took to move from the opening lines, "Once upon a midnight dreary, while I pondered weak and weary, / Over many a quaint and curious volume of forgotten lore," to its conclusion, "And my soul from out that shadow that lies floating on the floor / Shall be lifted—nevermore!" McKay seemed to be transported, moved to another, darker realm. At those times I was convinced that he had, indeed, come face-to-face with some terrible reality that remained unknown to me, something that in actuality mirrored Poe's "grim, ungainly, ghastly, gaunt, and ominous bird of yore."

There were other poems, many of them also by Poe. But it was "The Raven" that most impressed me. And while he stayed with us, he recited it on several occasions, most often just before he disappeared into the night. Although he always exited with his usual flamboyance, for me the haunting expression of despair rendered in that poem revealed far more than the cavalier mask he wore in the street.

McKay's bond to a specific place or routine shifted as quickly as his moods, however; within two years of his arrival, he had moved away. A few months after leaving Youngstown he was arrested. Tried and convicted of forgery, he was once again imprisoned.

His departure, of course, left a huge gap in my life. I missed the camaraderie and excitement, the piquant sense of danger and brief glimpse of the unknown, mysterious world to which he had exposed me. I was also saddened by his imprisonment. Once, when he was in the Boys Industrial School, my parents took me along to visit him. We were led through a maze of corridors with barred, locked doors before we reached him. Although he seemed perfectly at ease when we sat and ate the food my mother had cooked and brought with us, I couldn't keep my eyes off the armed guards who stared down from the balcony that encircled the large dining hall. I barely touched my food. Nothing, I decided that day, was worth the risk of being locked up there. When I asked my mother if he was going back to the same place this time, she shook her head.

"No," she said. "They done sent him to the penitentiary this time. It's worst . . . much worst than that."

I couldn't imagine how that was possible.

On Woodland, however, very little remained static. The neighborhood was transforming itself as rapidly as our household fluctuated. White flight continued and it seemed that every few months a new black family appeared.

Just over a year before my brother left, the Bright family moved into a house that was only two doors away from us. I quickly got to know them since, besides their four-year-old daughter, Doris, and Richard, a son who was McKay's age, they had a younger son, Alfred, who was only three months older than I. Within a year, we had established a friendship that has lasted over forty years.

For the first time since we left Shehy, I'd met a friend who was my age, someone who shared many of the same urges and faced many of the same adolescent problems I did. McKay and I had grown closer, but he was still eight years older than I. Coming late on the scene, I'd virtually grown up as an only child. Al Bright soon became the brother and companion that I'd been missing.

Sports was the adhesive that initially bonded us. Al's interest in baseball was nearly as fervent as my own. Soon after meeting, we'd devised a variation of the stickball games played in large cities; we played in my backyard, but instead of fireplugs and city blocks determining the value of a hit, my next-door neighbor's garden and grapevines and the fence that separated their property from the next lot became the perimeters of our makeshift field. A drive that scaled that fence and landed in the Mormon family's flower garden was a home run. The problem was retrieving the ball without trampling on Mrs. Mormon's roses or having her spot us when we ventured into her immaculately ordered backyard. Despite annoying the neighbors, after school we spent hours in my backyard honing our batting and pitching skills.

Even more time was spent on the ball fields at Volney Rogers Field and at the Grant school playground. Playing on different teams, we also vied against each other in Little League baseball. And when not competing in sports, we explored the surrounding terrain. Before they were destroyed by pollutants, the woods just below Grant playground were filled with wild fruit trees as well as blueberry and strawberry bushes. On many a summer afternoon we feasted in the huge lot behind the shack where Slobbering Tommy, the apparently retarded son of a family of newly arrived Southerners, lived. Fresh peaches, pears, apples, plums, and berries provided all the nourishment we required until we returned home at dusk. Mill Creek Park, with its picnic grounds, waterfalls, coves, and seemingly unending expanse of natural wonders, was a source of limitless exploration. And there were excursions by bike to Idora Park, where we rifled through refuse baskets to retrieve pop bottles and, though the practice was frowned upon, pedaled three miles back to Woodland and exchanged them for the two cents deposit they garnered at a local store. It was always a lucrative trip, one that financed the cost of refreshments and tickets for many Saturday afternoon jaunts to the Regent Theater—where customers were admitted and seated on a nondiscriminatory basis—or the Strand, where Negroes were permitted to sit in the first four rows.

Although only a few months older, Al was far more socially advanced than I. It was he who awakened my adolescent interest in girls, as first, I watched him flatter and flirt with the newly pubescent daughters of the families who lived near the elementary school playground, then joined him in cajoling and pestering to initiate some physical contact. Thinking ourselves crafty or sly, while actually only pawns in their supple hands, we plotted to create opportunities for copping a feel, momentarily caressing one of those softly rounded areas of the female anatomy that held such mystery. Al, a swain in advance of his years, would often disappear into the woods or behind the school building, he and his companion emerging flushed with hair and clothes disheveled. I was less artful or bold and settled for pushing them on the swings, hands occasionally brushing against summer-light dresses and plump derrieres, playfully wrestling on the baseball diamond's soft outfield grass, or, crotch pressed against budding buttocks, rising and descending in four-person foreplay at one end of a seesaw. The dance of puberty was a magnet for me, endlessly exciting even though it left me confused and frustrated.

Later, nearing age twelve, I would find relief at a party in the cellar of Al's house during a steamy game of post office. Called into a dark, oversized closet by a fourteen-year-old nymphet whose experience and good looks precluded my approaching her, I was led to bunglingly lose, or at least nearly lose, my virginity. Embarrassingly, the deed was quite literally done at her hands and on her thighs. Afterward, furiously brushing her soiled dress, she would ridicule both my aim and ineptitude. Practice, I reassured myself, would surely improve my marksmanship.

During that time, I was a frequent visitor at the Brights' home. It was, in part, to escape the tension between my parents, but more important, it derived from my growing friendship with Al. In fact, we had become more brothers than friends and, until a few years into our teens, were inseparable. He was treated like a son by my parents, as I was by his. It was resources that led us more often to choose his house as a meeting place. Not only did he have more sophisticated games and toys (the electric train that I'd been promised but never received, for example), but his family was also among the first on our block to purchase a TV set. On weekdays, programs were broadcast only about three or four hours each evening, but everyone who either could afford the luxury or had access to someone else's set scrambled to get a view of the grainy, sometimes ghostly images that, for the first time, were magically brought into your own living room.

Several times a week, I would join Al and his family to sit in front of the tiny flickering black-and-white screen to watch television's early sitcoms and variety shows. Many times wrestling matches featuring such stars as Antonio Rocca or Gorgeous George were the only programs shown; Al and I watched those with equal enthusiasm. But nights when *Beulah* or *Amos 'n' Andy* were shown truly became "must see television" nights for those black viewers who had access to a TV set. After a baseball game or an early evening of hanging out at the playground, Al and I would eagerly rush back to his house to view *The Life of Riley*, Milton Berle, or George Burns and Gracie Allen. It was, I believe, after a hilarious evening of watching the then-almost-svelte Jackie Gleason as Riley that I returned home to find my parents once again embroiled in a furious shouting match.

There was no surprise or shock that uncharacteristically hot autumn night. It was a scenario that I'd witnessed countless times before. Outside, unnoticed, I paused and sat on the porch banister, listening to Katie's accusations and loud rebukes, Tennessee's entreaties and duplicitous denials a chorus sounding in rhythmical counterpoint to her furious indictments.

During past clashes, frightened and torn by loyalty to each of them, I had implored, tried to inject reason into chaos—"Daddy, stop it! This is crazy. Somebody's goin' get hurt." Then, pushed or flung away, I would find a spot just beyond the skirmish and hover there, hoping that my presence would forestall the full-scale mayhem I fully expected to break out at any moment, or thinking that, should it get totally out of hand, I might somehow intervene.

But not this time. Instead I stepped silently to the screen door and, for what seemed like an eternity, watched them struggling. Grappling and cursing, they stumbled over kitchen chairs and fell back onto the table. I didn't move, just stood there, absolutely still, hoping I was obscured by the night. Once, Tennessee glanced my way, momentarily pinning me framed in the doorway, then, unfazed, rolled on top of my mother and continued the fray. Outside, as I stood shrouded by darkness, the scene seemed distant and removed, as staged and theatrical as the wrestling matches Al and I viewed on TV, yet still as wrenching, immobilizing, and painful as someone ripping at my guts.

The weight had grown too heavy. I had to put it down, release it. And suddenly, something snapped; an eerie calm settled over me. I could have been a stranger watching a brawl on some nameless street in a foreign land. I stared at them for another two or three minutes, seeming to float backward, outside myself, then turned and stormed down the driveway to the street.

I walked down Woodland to Hillman Street, then, in a daze, started up Hillman, past the Falls Avenue playground, where on many occasions I'd joined kids and adults from that Italian neighborhood in nightly softball games. Kept moving, aimlessly, past Princeton Junior High School, into the all-white, middle-class neighborhood above Indianola Avenue; then farther south to Midlothian Boulevard and the restricted enclave of the well-to-do whites, where a Negro's mere appearance was cause for alarm, and arrest was likely should one be caught loitering on foot after nightfall. Feeling invisible and ghostlike, on that night I moved through their exclusive preserve without interruption. In fact, I barely noticed where I was. Images of my parents, struggling, locked in combat, flashed through my mind like eerie still frames; each time I erased one, another appeared.

Turning west, I lurched toward Market Street and, mind racing, reversed the two-mile trek. Would they be all right? Had I done the right thing? I wondered as I stumbled down that deserted main thoroughfare, blindly passing used car lots, darkened restaurants and department stores. As I neared home, my anxiety grew. Past South High, the school I'd later attend, then back to Hillman, and near midnight now—tense, shaken, and unsure—I stood in front of our now darkened house.

The journey could not have taken much more than two hours, but it seemed like days. Half expecting some terrible calamity, but resigned to whatever awaited, I walked slowly up the driveway to the back porch.

The clamor had ceased, and when I entered, no one stirred. Silence, heavy as fog, had settled over the house. I moved up the stairs toward the room I then shared with Herbert, but before entering, cracked the door to my parents' bedroom and looked inside.

It was as if nothing had happened. They lay in bed together, intact, sleeping soundly. Relieved but, somehow, angry, I stared at them for what must have been ten minutes, then stepped back.

Silently, I closed the door.

Physically and mentally exhausted, I fell into my bed and, staring into the blackness, took a deep breath, at last exhaling. It was over. Nothing more had happened in my absence than if I'd stayed and looked on, torturing and blaming myself.

It was finished.

Alone in the darkness, I lay awake until near dawn. All the while the sound of McKay's voice echoing, rapping in my head like a dirge, *Quoth the Raven "Nevermore" . . . "Nevermore"!*

# 7

## like a
## ball game
## on a
## rainy day

Ostensibly, not much had changed. The next morning I awoke to the
usual breakfast of toast and oatmeal. The eight-block walk to Hillman Junior High School offered no surprises. As always Boatwright,
the burly, six-four school bully, who some insisted should have graduated high school by then, waited outside the entrance, menacing
and intimidating everyone who entered. Inside, teachers droned on,
struggling to invigorate their lectures, which some had delivered
unaltered for decades. Still, I'd gotten up and greeted the day as eagerly as if it had been opening day of the baseball season. Small as
it had been, a transformation had occurred. In walking away, removing myself from my parents' skirmish, I'd moved a step closer
toward independence. I didn't know what the next step would be or
where it would lead, but at least I was not standing still.

Despite the ideal home life suggested by grade school teachers
such as Mrs. Smith or the breezy accord between married couples
that radio projected on *Father Knows Best* and *Ozzie and Harriet,* I
knew that my parents' domestic conflict was not just an aberration
of our household. No, not even as menacing and uncontrolled as the
battles that spilled from the house of our young hillbilly neighbors
and more than once sent the scrawny wife fleeing—half undressed,

her tangled dirty-blond hair stuck to the tears that soaked her face and bruised lips—into their backyard in a vain attempt to escape her husband's drunken wrath. But whether it was unique or not, my complicity had become unbearable.

Sooner or later, connections have to be dissolved, cords cut—as when surgically severed at birth before we're slapped awake by an anonymous physician's cold hands and take our first gasping, solo breaths. Later, we initiate the split-ups. Whether we silently walk away or aggressively rend the connection, time comes when we're forced to back off—disclaim our ties to painful, debilitating roles. Sometimes, as James Baldwin wrote in another context, we're obliged, to "decide between amputation and gangrene."

The cut, of course, was not clean. I'd moved away from the fray, but the distance was qualified. Obviously my dependency hadn't vanished; fortunately, food, shelter, and the encouragement and support I needed to grope my way through adolescence were nearly always available. Despite their personal battles, they rarely gave me reason to question their affection for me. It sometimes took strange forms, but I was blessed in knowing that however the deal might go down, they'd be there in my corner.

There were also occasions when I'd regress, slip back into the swamp of confusion and anxiety that led me to believe I might still somehow influence the two adults who had brought me into the world, head off what I perceived as the crash course they had chosen. Mostly, however, I maintained my distance. I became an observer, looking on as a stranger might watch through a knothole from the safety of another room.

While the shift hardly influenced my relationship to my mother, it totally revamped the bond between me and Tennessee. Perhaps because he had seen me, knew that I had silently watched and walked away, both his estimate and treatment of me were permanently altered. It was as if some primal accord had been reached, some covert agreement that, for him, signaled my passage into manhood. It wasn't my intent, of course; I had not taken sides, but my father seemed to assume that we'd entered into some conspiratorial alliance.

Most dramatically, Tennessee never attempted laying a hand on me again. I was reprimanded, but loss of privileges replaced those dreaded basement encounters with his belt. A reflection of his newfound respect, I assumed. More frequently, it surfaced in simple gestures: the way he reached up to touch my shoulder (I was several inches taller than he by this time) when we entered a room filled with his running buddies; the smile that lit up his face when he introduced me; the collusive tone he adopted when he whispered, "Now, don't say nothin' 'bout this to yo' mamma, boy," as he slipped me a few dollars after I'd hit a home run in a Little League game or when he made an unscheduled stop at a house in which, I surmised, the female occupant was turning over more than her policy numbers. It also surfaced with his confidence, the new responsibilities he allotted me—as when he insisted that I scrutinize a warranty before he bought new automobile parts or examine the terms of an extended-payment contract when he bought a new appliance or contracted for repairs on the house.

I'd been trying to get away, to avoid being sucked into their battle, but surprisingly, stepping back from my parents' conflict had created a new stability, a sense of father-son equilibrium that I had not even imagined.

Katie, no doubt, noticed the change, but to her credit, she seldom objected. Yes, she sometimes issued ominous warnings: "You watch yo'self when you out there with that devil," she'd say. "Don't be gittin' in no trouble." But, perhaps because she knew I would always be closer to her than to him, she never insisted that I reject his attention. And although their arguments continued, I never witnessed another physical fight between them. Once, about a year later, they came close when my mother picked up a skillet and hurled it at Tennessee as he stood by the back door. He ducked and, looking at me as if to say, "See, I told you," turned and walked out. We didn't see him for three days.

Once I came to terms with, or at least walled myself off from, their conflict, sports became an obsession. Beginning with Tony, the hard-nosed Italian playground director who first urged me to join his softball team, at age eight, several coaches had encouraged me to develop my athletic ability. And by age twelve I'd become one of the better baseball players in the area. In truth, somewhat embarrassingly so, since I had grown to six feet by then and, as the mothers of many of my opponents pointed out in no uncertain terms, towered over most of the preteens with whom I competed. Although a skinny 130 pounds, I was still a behemoth among dwarfs. The disparity was so great that I batted over .600 in my final year of Little League play. I had, some assured me, potential, and might well become an excellent prospect.

But unlike today's professional sports world, where African-American athletes dominate, during the forties and fifties the exploits of Negro athletes were seldom advertised except in boxing and track. Southern Negro colleges offered scholarships, but press coverage of Negro college games was limited and the schools could not accommodate the vast numbers of excellent high school athletes who were emerging. Even the 1936 Olympic hero Jesse Owens had been ignored by Negro college recruiters when he left high school. At major nonblack colleges, athletic scholarships for Negroes were rare; and when they were awarded, the athletes found themselves isolated and, often, ostracized on campus. Despite the success and fame of All-Americans such as Paul Robeson, their achievements were frequently ignored or minimized by coaches and sports writers. Athletic excellence might earn some local recognition, but it did not guarantee access to education and social advance as it does today.

Nor did it offer an escape from poverty or second-class citizenship. Television, which was in its infancy, had not yet generated the hype or created the frenzied national interest that would elevate college and professional sports to the level of multibillion-dollar industries. So the allure of megabuck contracts and instant celebrity did not exist. The near-perverted worship of attitude that marks today's sports world was also nonexistent. The egoism and self-puffery that now permeates team sports would have been dismissed as mindless belligerence or simple lack of upbringing, and "bad boys" such as Dennis Rodman (and Howard Stern and Imus, for that matter) would have been greeted with disdain, barred from sports arenas and the airways, and probably dragged off to mental institutions.

In the early 1950s Negroes were as scarce in baseball and other (admittedly floundering) pro athletics leagues as they were in the medical, legal, and political arenas.

A few Negroes had competed in the American Professional Football Association and the National Football League when they were organized in the early 1920s, but a "gentleman's agreement" between franchise owners in Boston, Chicago, and Pittsburgh excluded them in 1933. The ban lasted until 1946, when the Los

Angeles Rams signed end Woody Strode and halfback Kenny Washington. During that same year, the Cleveland Browns signed Marion Motley, a fullback. Despite these breakthroughs, resistance to black players continued. George Marshall, the Washington Redskins owner, held out until 1962, when he finally signed future all-star Bobby Mitchell after a trade that gave the Cleveland Browns draft rights to Ernie Davis, a Syracuse University All-American against whom I competed in basketball at college.

Independent black basketball teams such as the Renaissance Big Five and the Harlem Globetrotters had competed successfully against white pro teams since the 1920s, but the National Basketball Association did not sign an African-American player until the Boston Celtics drafted Chuck Cooper in 1950. During that same season Earl Lloyd joined the Washington Capitals and Nat "Sweetwater" Clifton signed with the New York Knicks. A trickle of blacks slowly enlarged the ranks of NBA players until the late 1950s, when such superstars as Oscar Robinson, Bill Russell, Elgin Baylor, and Wilt Chamberlain opened the gates for the huge reservoir of black talent that had gone untouched. Even then, they were recruited sparingly.

In professional baseball, the color line was, of course, broken in 1946 when Jackie Robinson signed with a Brooklyn Dodger farm team. Next year, despite rabid opposition from fans and opponents, he started at second base for the Dodgers. With the National League leading the way, others followed. Larry Doby became the first black player in the American League when he signed with the Cleveland Indians in 1947. Although the Indians' manager, Bill Veeck, also signed first baseman Luke Easter and Negro League pitching legend Satchel Paige during the next two years, few American League managers followed Veeck's lead.

During the years I played Little League baseball, the number of black major-league baseball players could be counted on your fingers. The same could be said of the NBA and NFL.

Even so, Cleveland was only a one-and-one-half-hour drive from Youngstown, so I accompanied either my father or my brother-in-law Leroy to watch the Indians at Municipal Stadium on at least a dozen occasions during the late forties and early fifties. It was a thrill to sit in the bleachers and watch the pros perform, particularly when they played the New York Yankees, their chief rival. Despite the two or three black players in the Indians' starting lineup, however, I seldom dreamed of becoming a major-league ballplayer. As the Yankee's all-white roster demonstrated, most teams still barred Negroes. Moreover, there were no journeymen black players on pro teams; the few black professionals who emerged in the forties and fifties were usually franchise players, clearly a cut above almost everyone else in their sport. Unless one imagined playing at the level of such superstars as Robinson, Doby, and Willie Mays, professional baseball did not loom as a promising career choice.

Still, as indicated by the Browns' and Indians' pioneer efforts in recruiting black players, sports was one of the few areas where blacks could compete on a more or less equal basis in Ohio during the fifties. It was, perhaps, with an unconscious sense of that increased opportunity that I turned to athletics. Looking back, I'm not altogether certain; hindsight brings continuity to the most haphazard events. What is certain is that sports offered a chance to excel with little interference from the confines of race. And since those restrictions were becoming increasingly more apparent to me on a social level, I devoted my energies almost exclusively to athletics during my early teens.

Although I saw it as simply recreational, I loved baseball and it remained my favorite game until my middle teens. In fact, the game seemed to be revered by nearly everyone in Youngstown. The city prided itself on having more ballparks than any community its size in the country, and although conditions and upkeep varied, parks with baseball diamonds could be found in nearly every neighborhood.

In addition, the Parks Department maintained a dozen or so perfectly tended ball fields that not only were used for organized leagues that catered to local players of all ages but also attracted events such as the National Amateur Baseball Federation tournament. And although they stopped before I was old enough to attend, professional Negro League games drew large crowds of black and white spectators until the mid-forties, when the league disbanded. I heard my brother-in-law Leroy and my father talk about games between the Pittsburgh Crawfords (whose roster at one time included future Hall of Fame legends Satchel Paige, Cool Papa Bell, and Josh Gibson) and the Cleveland Red Sox that they'd seen at Oakland

Field. Youngstown, like many Midwestern cities, had a long-standing tradition of reverence for the national pastime. In fact, despite the concentration of major-league teams in large cities and the publicity accorded such marquee franchises as the New York Yankees and the Brooklyn Dodgers, most baseball players came from the South and Midwest. The slow, measured flow of the game, the absence of a clock or time as a governing factor, and its original idyllic, pastoral setting, are starkly contrasted to the fast-paced frenzy of big-city life. Wild cards such as Ty Cobb and teams such as the old Gas House Gang brought a dose of spirited aggression, color, and eccentricity to the sport, but it was color with a decidedly rural cast.

Prior to the disclosure of the big-bucks obsessions of owners and players and the emergence of glitzy, artificially turfed pleasure domes, baseball and its pastoral field of dreams seemed the perfect symbol for an American ethos that thrived in the Midwest. The game was so revered that even intimate encounters were regularly assessed in baseball terms: still, the path from first base (kissing) to home plate (intercourse), at least for most teenagers, was usually interrupted by some errant play and ended with a cold shower.

The isolated face-off between the pitcher and batter, as many sports pundits have suggested, was a perfect symbol of America's romanticized self-image: fair play, self-determination, and the solitary frontiersman's heroic confrontations with nature, Native Americans, and outlaws. Indeed, I often stepped into the batter's box with the same resolve and sense of stoic determination I imagined Gary Cooper felt during his showdown with the villains in *High Noon*. Alone, face-to-face with a treacherous foe, it didn't matter that instead of a wicked gun-toting adversary there was a hurler armed with a sharp curve and seventy-mile-an-hour fastball.

That one-on-one duel, along with the game's pace and orderliness, its emphasis of tradition and precise rules, reflected concerns that were revered in America's heartland. "Whoever wants to know the heart and mind of America," Jacques Barzun wrote, "had better learn baseball."

No accident, then, that for myself and most other teenage boys, summer meant baseball. In addition to playing organized ball in Little League, Pony League (when thirteen and fourteen), and Class

B (when fifteen and sixteen), I played softball in playground leagues and spent afternoons and free evenings in pickup games at Volney Rogers Field or one of many other local fields.

Since I had reached my full height, of just over six foot three inches, by the time I was thirteen, however, many of my friends began suggesting that I try my hand at basketball. Although initially not only extremely awkward but also hesitant about straying from a sport in which I had gained some local recognition, I began hanging out at basketball courts on local playgrounds. At first, my ineptitude was matched only by my frustration. And since I'd begun to take my athletic prowess for granted, it was a lesson in humility.

By the time I'd worked up enough courage to attempt competing at the basketball court in Volney Rogers Field, where the Youngstown version of the city game was played at its highest and most ferocious level, I was only an adequate player. Since those games attracted the best current and former high school players as well as members of the Youngstown University basketball team, I initially observed more than I played. It was rough, cutthroat basketball with little of the superficial civility and order I'd become accustomed to on the baseball diamond.

Elbows and forearms flailed. Players four inches shorter than I skied above my outstretched arms for easy layups or snuffed jump shots that I thought were untouchable when I released them. Moreover, trash talking and signifying seemed as crucial to the game as defense.

"This ain't the Little League, chump," someone would yell as he rammed what I thought was a pretty reverse layup back into my chest and the crowd of onlookers whooped and broke up with laughter. "Don't bring that shit in here. Take it to the toilet!"

The dialogue was not new or particularly innovative. Since I had begun Hillman Junior High, the daily trek to school had involved a continuing war of words with classmates that both entertained us and honed our verbal skills.

Al Bright, Carmel Brawley, and Frank Owens were among the group that I joined each day. Snaps and gibes flew like missiles. Most were impromptu retorts that escalated in intensity when, inevitably, the sessions got more personal. Mere signifying, or individual disparagement, shifted to the dozens—a venue where, at least among friends, nothing was sacrosanct—sisters, mothers, whatever.

We drew on everything we'd heard. Redd Foxx's old Confucius gags: "Panties not best thing in world, but next to it," or, "Better to sleep with old hen than *pull-et.*" Off-color street rhymes: "Fucked your mamma on a red hot heater / Missed her cock and burned my peter." Or

> Take off them old silk panties
> That used to be your aunties'
>     That we found layin' in the hay.
> With the hole in the middle,
> Where your uncle use to diddle. . . .

Frank was by far the most glib, artful, and outrageous of our group. He could effortlessly isolate any one of us and turn the entire crowd against that person whenever he chose. And since he was also the darkest, therefore most susceptible to jibes focused on color ("Boy, you so black you cast a shadow on coal"), he had armed himself with an arsenal of raps that most often silenced anyone who chose to go in that direction. He could, without hesitation, recite such folk rhymes as "The Signifying Monkey" or "The Sinking of the Titanic," turning them into personal put-downs without a hitch. In fact, with his boldness and aggressiveness, Frank came closer to the so-called Bad Nigger stereotype than any one of our friends. Fiery and undaunted, at times he seemed to personify Shine, the hero of the "Titanic" folktale that he recounted with such vigor.

> All the millionaires looked around at Shine, say,
> "Now, Shine, oh Shine, save poor me."
> Say, "We'll make you wealthier than one shine can be."
> Shine say, "You hate my color and you hate my race."
> Say, "Jump overboard and give these sharks a chase."
> And everybody on board realized they *had* to die.
> But Shine could swim and Shine could *float.*
> Shine could throw his ass like a motorboat.
> Say Shine hit the water with a hell of a splash,
> And everybody wondered if that black sonovabitch could last.
> Say the devil looked up from hell and grinned.
> Say, "He's a black swimmin' muhfucker.
> I think he's gon' come on in."

Yes, I had heard most of the raps, but never in the context of sports. There was no trash talked in the organized baseball leagues in which I'd played. Basketball at Volney Rogers Field was a new experience.

In that heated competitive atmosphere skirmishes flared like lightning during a flash storm. They seldom proceeded beyond pushin' and wolfin' or one punch before someone intervened, but if not halted, the spectacle could approach the bizarre.

On one occasion during my initiation to the game, an overly emphatic foul and cavalier remark about the victim's mamma led to an extended fray that almost convinced me to confine myself to baseball. The slightly smaller victim, who had been flung to the ground when he was fouled, obviously felt that the combination of physical and verbal abuse crossed the lines of propriety. In order to rectify the situation, he ripped a large branch from a tree near court's edge and, as the unsuspecting assailant dribbled toward the basket, blindsided him. The game stopped immediately, but the branch-wielding victim didn't pause. He continued beating his slightly dazed assailant about the head as he explained why it was inappropriate to have brought his mother into the discussion.

Now, normally, someone would have stepped in and stopped the clash. But as I later discovered, the original assailant was not very popular. A mediocre ballplayer as well as a bully, he had no friends at courtside. It was time, everyone seemed to feel, that he got his comeuppance. And that he did.

Shielding his face, he had rolled over near the foul line of the adjacent baseball field in an attempt to escape the onslaught. Finally he struggled to his feet and took off across the infield, the former victim in hot pursuit. But scrambling to get away, he stumbled and tripped over second base. He fell again and, in the process, unhinged one of the heavy straps from the metal spikes that held the bag in place. The former victim didn't miss a beat. He quickly tore the half-unleashed bag from the ground and began pummeling the bully, who was now rolling around in the infield dirt, about his back and legs. By this time everyone had given up the attempt to stifle their laughter and, howling, had gathered in a circle to watch the mayhem.

I don't know, but the former victim must have beaten the bully for about four, maybe five minutes. I lost track since, each time two or three blows were landed, the bully rolled into the fetal position and tried to shield his head and eyes with his hands and arms. When he did, the former victim would pause, circling his fallen prey like a vulture, waiting for him to move his hands, look up, or try to escape. Then he'd renew the assault. Finally the bully successfully dragged himself to his feet and, holding his back, sprinted across the outfield grass. "And don't bring your ass back here," the former victim shouted. "Next time I'll whup yo' ass with home plate."

The basketball game didn't resume until at least fifteen minutes after the bully raced across two baseball fields and stumbled up the hill to Glenwood Avenue. Every one of the dozen or so remaining players was either bent with laughter or sprawled on the grass and benches surrounding the court. I was laughing as heartily as anyone even as I thought to myself, Damn, this stuff can get serious.

It took more than a year for me to become anything more than a liability in those pickup games. Gradually I adjusted to the fact that, unlike baseball, basketball is a game of continuous motion, snap judgments, rapid adjustments, and endless improvisation. Where baseball was cool, requiring occasional heated responses, basketball was sizzling, requiring grace and composure under fire. During the next two years basketball would consume most of my time.

In a sense, sports had become my religion, sportsmanship my ethical code. The drive for perfection in basketball and baseball took precedence over nearly everything I did. But while I continued advancing in those areas and was satisfied with my progress, life beyond the baseball diamond and basketball court was becoming more and more frustrating. I had neutralized the tension within my own household, but more and more found myself confounded by outside impediments.

Ironically, it was indirectly through sports that those outside, social problems made their first serious impression on me. The incident that triggered my awareness did not directly involve me, however; it centered around Al Bright, my best friend.

Al was the only Negro on his team, Donnell Fords, which had won the city Little League championship in 1951; to celebrate they scheduled a team picnic at the end of the season. Players and parents were invited to the event, which was held at South Side Park, a recreational facility with picnic grounds, a ball field, and a swimming pool. Al's parents could not attend, so he was picked up by one of the coaches. When they arrived at the park, the festivities had already begun. Coaches, parents, and players had gathered and set up the picnic inside the wire fence surrounding the swimming pool.

When Al tried to enter, he was stopped by one of the lifeguards. In Youngstown, despite demonstrations since the mid-1940s and Mayor Harold Smith's attempt to establish a nonsegregation policy at city pools in 1949, Negroes were welcome on a daily basis only at the Chase Park pool, which had separate pools for blacks and whites; a few others allowed entry on one designated day each week.

Someone on Al's Little League team had overlooked a crucial element in the city's social arrangements. The embarrassed coaches and some parents argued with park officials for a short time, but the lifeguards would not budge. The unwritten rules, they insisted, were clear. Negroes were not permitted in the pool area.

The best they could do was to set up a blanket and allow Al to sit just outside the fence. No one would object to that. Food could be brought out for him, and teammates could gather just on the other side; it would, they argued, be just as if he were actually there.

Reluctantly, Al agreed. From time to time, one or another of the players or adults came out and sat with him for a few minutes before returning to join the others. An hour passed before a team official convinced the lifeguards that the situation just wasn't right. They should at least allow the child into the pool for a few minutes. Finally, the park supervisor relented. But there were several important stipulations. First, everyone else would have to get out of the water.

When the area was cleared, Al was led to the pool and placed in a small rubber raft. One lifeguard waded in and, swimming along side the raft, took Al for one turn around the pool. "Just don't touch the water," he warned. "Whatever you do, don't touch the water."

For an agonizing few minutes, Al was guided around the pool, a hundred or so white revelers looking on in astonishment at this obviously dangerous encroachment on traditional social values. Having completed his circular journey around the perimeter of the pool, Al was escorted outside to his assigned spot without the fence. The celebratory picnic, having lost some of its festive spirit by this time, came to a premature end shortly afterward. An apologetic member of the coaching staff offered Al a ride home as the team

packed up and prepared to leave. Al declined and, with championship trophy in hand, walked the mile or so back to Woodland Avenue alone.

I'm not sure what Al was thinking during that long trip back
home. He didn't say anything about it for months. Not to me or anyone else. He held it in, as if refusal to disclose would somehow di-
minish the impact—postpone the loss of faith in a vision we shared.
Inevitably, however, the incident had a devastating effect on him,
undermining and, for a time, eroding his belief (or at least trust)
that achievement, correct behavior, and adherence to the rules
might be fairly rewarded, judged solely on the basis of individual
merit.

I had no such sudden revelation during adolescence. Even after Al
shared his experience with me, I was reluctant to completely abandon my belief that no adult could be dull witted enough to judge
people solely on the basis of appearance or a heredity, over which
neither they nor those making the judgment had any control.

Al had experienced a sudden jolt, a form of shock treatment, but
for me the grim revelation eased up, like a slick pickpocket in a
crowd of unsuspecting revelers. It surfaced piecemeal, in incre-
ments: at first, no more than insignificant ripples—teachers who ignored my raised hand when a question was asked or assumed that I
initiated any disturbance that arose in their classrooms. The Shirley
Temple look-alike who was convinced I was the bogeyman. The parents of white playmates with sisters who stopped inviting me to play
in their homes once I reached the age of puberty. Those slight annoyances soon intensified, however; the ripples quietly gathered
strength and, within a few years, came crashing over me with the
force and momentum of a tidal wave.

Afterward, I realized I'd somehow missed a cue, wrongly assumed
that the near absence of tangible signs of racially based restrictions
on my behavior and the surface cordiality with which I'd generally
been greeted meant that I could expect unbiased treatment from the
outside world. That in society's estimate I was equal to everyone
else, black or white. Naive, perhaps, but there had been little in my
experience to suggest otherwise. Moreover, since after the second
grade I'd glided through school at or near the top of my classes and
had been assured that I was an exceptional athlete, I actually felt superior to most of my peers. I, of course, had no idea that before

reaching my teens, to most of the outside world I was an anomoly—
a Negro who, not knowing what he was expected to be, had impetu-
ously gone off in search of his identity.

Mind you, it wasn't entirely my fault. This hazardous self-
deception derived, in part, from the curiously apolitical atmosphere
at our home and the restricted range of public school education in
Youngstown at the time.

As I mentioned earlier, casual references to honkies and niggers
notwithstanding, race was a minor issue in our household. Compared to my parents' experience in Mississippi and Tennessee,
racism in Youngstown must have seemed comparatively benign.
The see-no-internal-evil, hear-no-internal-evil philosophy that generally dominated the media during the fifties was accepted without
question; blame for most domestic discord was assigned to communist sympathizers and outside agitators. And since neither of my
parents were high school graduates and were not aware of the substantial writings of Negro intellectuals or early freedom fighters,
there were few references to black historical figures.

Beulah, Kingfish, Rochester, and mild-mannered heavyweight
champion Joe Louis were the most notable black cultural and historical figures discussed at home. No one talked about Nat Turner
or Sojourner Truth or mentioned Negroes such as W. E. B. Du Bois
or Frederick Douglass, authors whose writings might have suggested a distinct, separate black heritage or pointed toward a tradition of struggle and achievement with which young Negroes might
have identified.

Nor was there any significant mention of Negroes in our textbooks or classrooms. Although the first black teacher was hired by
the Youngstown public school system in 1940, during my twelve
years in the city's integrated schools I had no black instructors. Except for George Washington Carver and Booker T. Washington, who
were briefly noted, black historical figures were also consistently ignored. Class and racial antagonisms were glossed over in our classrooms. The Horatio Alger myth persisted, and despite contrary
personal beliefs that sometimes surfaced, to their credit most teachers outlined a colorless American history and struggled to give the
impression that race was a negligible factor in one's future success
or failure. It was a meritorious goal but (in addition to that historical interpretation being out of synch with the real world) it masked

a collusive silence. Slavery and other historical episodes that might have cast America in a negative light were seldom or only briefly discussed. We learned that Lincoln freed the slaves, for example, but were never instructed as to how those Africans arrived in America, what conditions they lived under, or how they survived after emancipation. In the Youngstown school system curriculum, Negro history was a phantom presence, an embarrassment that was, seemingly, better ignored or swept under the carpet than explained.

Through avoidance and silence, and seemingly with the best of intentions, my grade school teachers perpetuated a myth of equality that many white Midwesterners publicly embraced and, perhaps, even imagined was real.

No wonder, then, that without the kind of traumatic incident that Al had confronted, I'd sailed through school with only the slightest hint of racial discord. In effect, raised in a vacuum and, until age twelve, lulled into accepting the heartland's affirmation of Cold War sloganizing that touted the harmony and fairness of America's democratic values while deemphasizing or covering up the country's internal racial strife, past and present.

Later I discovered that the *Buckeye Review,* a local black newspaper founded in 1937 by the attorney J. Maynard Dickerson, offered alternative views of the local political and social scene. Throughout World War II and the fifties' and sixties' civil rights movement, its editors provided a voice of dissent that aired grievances and pointed out inequities in segregated public facilities, housing, and employment. The newspaper's editors also emerged as prominent elected officials and political appointees: attorney Dickerson became the city's first black city prosecutor and was appointed to both the state Industrial and state Liquor commissions; attorney Nathaniel Jones, who took over the paper in the sixties, was selected as a judge for Sixth Circuit Court of Appeals by President Carter in 1979; and McCullough Williams Jr., who became *Buckeye Review* editor in 1982, had not only been a city councilman and a member of the Youngstown Board of Education but had also served on several city commissions.

While growing up in Youngstown, I, of course, didn't know any of these men. The town's middle-class, black-bourgeois set was as far removed from my Woodland Avenue household as the Hollywood Hills are from Watts. The paper occasionally turned up in our house but no one, with the exception of our former boarder, Robert, had paid much attention to it.

And apparently, despite its dissenting political voice and a few loyal black supporters, most other Negroes snubbed the review and ignored its call for aggressive protests. During the forties and the fifties, the area's prevailing racial attitudes were most clearly reflected by the city's lone mainstream newspaper, the *Youngstown Vindicator.* Its editorials, for example, urged Youngstown's "naturally patient Negroes" to resist "exploitation" by "disloyal radicals," "communists," and "undesirables" who were prompting them to exercise their undisputed legal rights and integrate the city's public swimming pools. At the same time, the paper continued confining its news coverage of Negroes—except for arrests and criminal activity—to a column called "Interesting News Notes for Local Colored Folks." Written by the paper's lone Negro editorial contributor, it was a mixed-bag listing of births, deaths, parties, and social functions that sometimes read as if they were part of an *Amos 'n' Andy* script: "At Miss Alice Jones' party last week, collard greens and ham hocks were served to twenty hungry guests."

Quaint now, if nothing else, but representative of the era.

It was, of course, the pre-civil-rights-movement fifties in America's heartland. And despite efforts to control them, according to media and government caretakers "Red agitators" were popping up like dandelions all over our well-groomed, free-market, democratic landscape. Stalin and the "Red menace" were real enough threats, but too often, necessary vigilance escalated to paranoia or, worse, the sly imposition of an ideological scapegoat to discredit anyone who challenged the status quo, defied the established hierarchy, or as in the incident mentioned, threatened to tarnish the city's chlorine-purified waters. Within a decade the Red finger would be pointed indiscriminately at Hollywood filmmakers, Martin Luther King Jr. and the civil rights movement, labor unions, even Alan Freed and that upstart cultural threat, rock 'n' roll music.

Meanwhile, across the country, Negroes were assured that they never had it so good. And given my adolescent tendency to accept the adult world at face value, I generally acquiesced in that assessment.

There were telltale signs of the contrary, but I paid very little attention to them during my preteens. Negroes were restricted to the balcony in most downtown theaters, for instance, but like most children that was exactly where I wanted to sit. What better place to watch a Saturday matinee than a darkened balcony where teenage white ushers were hesitant to enter and young black boys had free reign to unleash their rowdiest behavior, grope unsuspecting adolescent girls, and occasionally "accidentally" spill popcorn or soda pop down onto the white orchestra audience, who, we were convinced, would rather have been sitting in the balcony.

I, for one, had no idea that in the South and, presumably, among many Youngstowners, the balcony was known as the "buzzard's nest" or "nigger heaven." At the time, it didn't matter. Nor was it important that most downtown restaurants did not serve Negroes or that blacks were not welcome at the city's hotels and motels or that the ballroom at Idora Park, unless leased by some Negro organization for a specific occasion, was roped off in two sections with the Negro policeman Sam Holmes posted in the middle to assure that no blacks wandered into the white section near the bandstand, although whites regularly strayed into or hovered near the fringes of the black section to watch, loosen up, and learn how to shake their booties. It didn't even matter that we were forced to buy hot dogs—to this day, the best I've ever eaten—from a takeout service window at Jay's Restaurant. What was important at that age was that a ball driven over the fence was a home run regardless of one's color, that the Wildcat and other rides at Idora Park were not segregated, and that local Isalys Dairy stores, the originators of the now famous Klondike bar, even though they had been restricted a few years earlier, were then open to everybody.

Except for the discord at home, it had been, for me, an unburdened, free-and-easy time. My most intimate contact with the blues had come when a baseball game was postponed—*feel so bad / feel like a ball game on a rainy day.*

When all was well at home, like most Midwestern teenagers, I could happily spend an evening chasing and catching fireflies or sitting on the front porch with a six-pack of Popsicles trying to guess the make, model, and year of passing automobiles before they reached our house or—when my sister-in-law Julia or her boarders were about and had the time to spend with me and my next-door neighbor Huck—laughing and learning the intricacies of the rules and attendant verbal feints that accompanied rousing games of bid whist. Then there was always the allure of listening or, sometimes, eavesdropping as adults swapped tales about World War I, the high life of Paris (where they "treated Negroes like kings"), or the idio-syncrasies and curious achievements of various and sundry "col-ored folks." This was particularly so if one of the storytellers was my next-door neighbor George Hicks, who held the coveted title as the town's biggest liar.

On many summer evenings, Big Six, as adults used to call him, drew a sizable audience to his front porch, where he held court as he and others spun out one tall tale after another. Wild and wooly stories that were mostly outrageous and nearly always hilarious—like the tale of the Negro League player who, during an afternoon game, hit a pop fly so high that, by the time it descended, the ball-park lights had to be turned on so the infielder could see enough to catch it.

Some even had a thread of truth to them, just enough so the teller could insist, "Yall don't believe me. Go 'head and check the facts—if I'm lyin', I'm dyin'."

Like the story Mr. Hicks told after he interrupted another tale with, "Ah fool, that weren't nothin'! You ever heard tell of Boneset-ter Reese? Nah, well he live right here in Youngstown—over there on the west side, near them Polish people. Wasn't no ordinary nig-ger, neither, elsewise they wouldn't let him stay there. Fact is, he stayed out dere so long, he got to thinkin' he was Polish. Say, he wanted to light a cross in front his own house. *Hah, hah.* Yaasss-sir, boy had a international reputation though. Couldn't read nor write. Fact, wasn't nothin' but a gard'ner when he started out. Use to fix up people's trees, you know, put splints on the branches. Keep 'em from fallin' off. Say he could take a tiny saplin' branch and turn that sucker into a fruit-bearin' tree twenty feet tall in just 'bout two or three days. Come to find out, he could do the same thing to folks' bones. Fix up folks doctors wouldn't even touch. This was back there in the twenties, you know, and even though he ain't had no medical degrees or licenses, people come from all over the world to have him tend to 'em.

"Yeah, that's right! King of England come over here to have his shoulder relocated. Drove right down Federal Street. Picture-show actors and ballplayers came too. I heard tell Babe Ruth come down here after he tripped and fell down the stairs in one of them after-hour, juke joints in Cleveland. Bonesetter fixed him up, and next day, boy went back to Cleveland and hit two home runs. You *do* know that he was colored, don't'cha? Sure nuf was.

"Anyway, Bonesetter got so famous that the governor give him a special license to practice. Mayor give 'em the key to the city. Only colored boy ever had the key to this city. Trouble was, the nigger lost it the next day. . . ."

It didn't matter that although, surprisingly, there was a Bonesetter Reese, he was a Welshman, nor that although many celebrities did visit Youngstown for his services, none of those that Big Six had mentioned were among them. On those evenings, the whoops and hollers, groans and laughter of the assembled audience were enough. It was a simpler time. One could easily suspend belief, take things at face value, and accept the unlikely as readily as everybody else did.

Much of that changed for me when Al Bright told me what happened to him at the South Side Park pool.

# 8

## lawn jockeys
## and other
## grotesques

Al's disclosure, of course, had not come as a complete surprise. At least unconsciously, I had long been aware of the swimming pool controversy. Despite the earlier protests and an occasional uneventful use of some pools by young Negro girls, attempts by black males—whether children or adults—were most often met by threats and intimidation. Not only were Negroes allowed free access to select city pools only one day a week but, adding insult to injury, at the close of that day those pools were drained and cleaned before being opened to white swimmers the next day. Tired of struggling to actualize the mayor's integration order, most Negroes had accepted that compromised, unspoken agreement. The situation, however, had so disturbed me that despite the allure of splashing and frolicking in cool, refreshing water on many a hot summer day, I'd abstained, vowed never to set foot in a city pool. Afterward, I buried the matter in my unconscious. The implicit insult and contempt shown for blacks was more than I could rationally handle. The downside was that I never learned to swim.

My friend's experience, of course, forced me to again confront those feelings. It was the peculiar circumstances of the event, however, that most shocked and surprised me. Despite thinking that equal opportunity in the professional arena was unlikely, I had come to expect fairness in sports, particularly baseball, at the local level. Al Bright's poolside episode severely tarnished that expectation. But while it brought a note of gloom into what had been a cheerful, unassuming period for me, it also led both of us to look more closely at racial bias and, eventually, reevaluate our decidedly little-league fantasies.

Most immediately, it prompted us to confront the situation, talk candidly about race and the consequences of growing up as a Negro in Youngstown. It is one of those grim but necessary labors that most black Americans have to perform at one time or another if they are to clear the air, learn to cope and survive. We wrestled uneasily with what, for us, was the central question: how could anyone be driven to such hate, cruelty, and complete disregard for others' feelings and well-being on the basis of color and race? And coming to the discussion without any real sense of history, (not even of the role that a similar bias had recently played in Hitler's rise and World War II), we found no answers.

Still, the sessions themselves vented some of our anger and outrage, led us to an uneasy laughter over other ironies. We began, for instance, to examine how negative symbolism regarding nearly everything associated with Negroes permeated the English language and helped perpetuate racism and a contemptuous view of black Americans.

We explored everything our young minds could conjure up, starting with the obviously invidious associations suggested by the most common designations for the races: "black" and "dark" with their connotations of evil, despair, mystery, and the forbidden; "white" or "light" and their insinuations of purity, optimism, clarity, and the alluring. Then, later, as we pushed further, we laughed and marveled at more subtle expressions of the same theme: how even the descriptions of the Negro's hair, when compared to that of Europeans, could assume sinister, derogatory overtones—kinky versus straight; curled, circuitous, and perverted versus upright, candid, and right minded. The exercise, of course, solved nothing. It simply corroborated what had been a suspicion—that, somehow, an intricate web had been woven, a matrix of superficial perceptions, illusions, and exaggerations that, when threaded together and united with that crazy-glue concoction called race identity, conspired to obliterate individuality and cast Negroes in a seemingly inescapable trap.

Somehow, despite that determination, neither Al nor I immediately succumbed to the anger or gloom that easily might have led us to react with the hostility or debilitating despair that already had begun to affect some of our friends. Although we had no answers, we sensed that defiant outbursts or sullen withdrawal would only worsen matters, confirm the stereotype. Not that we always checked our anger; we simply vented it covertly.

As one might expect of children, we reacted primarily to incidental transgressions, annoying visible reminders of the predicament. High on our list were those ebony jockey figurines depicting grinning Negroes with white caps and red waistcoats that were prominently placed on the lawns of hundreds of white suburban homes. They were, we felt, the most obvious symbols of the fate white folks had in store for us, as if the occupants of those homes were announcing, *Niggers, beware. Unless you can conform to this image, don't bother setting foot on the property or in the neighborhood.* They were vulnerable targets, however; so we went on a rampage, executing nighttime raids during which we stealthily rode our Schwinn bikes into those quiet neighborhoods, lassoed one or more of those bug-eyed, big-lipped, minstrel-faced caricatures and dragged them off into the night. We might have worn white sheets and hoods, since those excursions amounted to a series of symbolic lynchings.

The ritual continued until the night when the clamor of our efforts to remove a resistant jockey in the secluded Mill Creek Park area awakened and brought an infuriated resident screaming onto his lawn. The statue had been uprooted and dragged about twenty yards from the lawn before it slipped our noose. We left it laying battered and dented in the middle of the street and quickly ducked into the woods about fifty yards away when the enraged homeowner ran from his house. A few minutes later, several patrol cars arrived. Apparently, they were intent on solving the mystery of the missing lawn niggers.

I had to stifle my laughter, couldn't believe what was happening. The cops paid more attention to that cast-iron jockey than they had to real Negroes that I'd seen sprawled, bloodied and beaten, on East Federal Street sidewalks after a brawl. I thought they were about to call an ambulance. I started rolling in the weeds as I imagined their conversation. Al had to restrain me. *Don't worry, Mr. Jones, he's gonna be just fine. Nothing but a few dents and bruises. Here, we'll help you get him back to the house. He'll be all right, good as new.*

They carried it back as if it were a child who'd been felled by a hit-and-run driver. A few minutes later, after the policemen had calmed the owner, they drove up and down the winding street for a few more minutes, shining spotlights into the woods. But we were securely hidden in the brush. We stayed there until the uproar subsided. Afterward, discretion led us to search for other targets. Although it was hardly revolutionary, even in retrospect there was a certain satisfaction in destroying those stereotypical cast-iron icons.

Fortunately, our discussions also led us into more fruitful pursuits. Curiosity about the language drove us to go beyond the racial implications of words. We began systematically studying the dictionary. Starting with "aardvark," we moved through the alphabet memorizing and testing each other on the most arcane entries. A few other teenagers joined us from time to time, but Al and I were the core of the group, which he fancifully dubbed the Abecedarian Club. We never made it through the entire dictionary—stumbled at "habanera" and quit shortly after "histaminase." But the exercise itself had opened new vistas for me, unveiled an avenue of interest and expression that would soon assume as much importance as sports.

In fact, I'd become obsessed with finding answers to why Negroes and whites were treated so differently, with discovering what, I assumed, must be a rational justification for the suspension of our democratic beliefs, not to mention a sense of fairness and good sense, when blacks were concerned. That determination led me to attempt convincing my mother that we needed an encyclopedia. Reluctantly she agreed and began a time-purchase plan that brought a volume of Funk & Wagnall's to our house every two weeks. As with the dictionary, however, the project never reached completion. Purchases stopped when more necessary items, like food, interfered with the expenditure. We at least got to *N* and the entry for "Negro" before Funk & Wagnall's realized they were not likely to receive any further payment. Still, during the next few years, that half encyclopedia set was put to good use.

The vocabulary games and probing of the encyclopedia, combined with the ongoing talks that Al and I had about our own experience with subtle racial bias, drew me into a different realm. It was becoming apparent that as a jock with an obsession for *E.C.* comic books, my future was not too bright. I began trying to more seriously examine the world around me. Sports, of course, were still important, and during my early junior high school days I not only continued playing baseball but also developed into a fair basketball player. Between the ages of twelve and fourteen, however, sports took a backseat to a more pressing problem—the seemingly disproportionate focus on race that gripped the community and the struggle to come to terms with my own identity.

Raised in an integrated setting, I'd assumed that I belonged to an extended nonracial community. And initially, my assumptions weren't seriously challenged. I'd grown up unencumbered by any rigid social conventions or specious assumptions about race and prejudice and, like most children, sought connections, not separations. I thought of myself in terms of nationality, not race. Assumed that I was a part of the larger *us* and celebrated our victories over the villains, *them*—Nazi Germany, imperialist Japan, the ongoing communist threat, and even, according to a raft of Hollywood Westerns, the American Indian. It was a shock for me, as well as Al Bright, to discover and, finally, accept that despite our allegiance, in the minds of a considerable number of white Americans, *we* were *them*!

Suddenly McKay's warnings about the devastating nature of stark reality began to take on an eerie resonance. Miss Aggie's cryptic allusions to the disparity between fact and truth, her suggestions that things ain't always what they appear to be, assumed more meaning. If I'd been more perceptive and aware, I might have seen it earlier, looked beyond the surface serenity and realized that the harmony and equal opportunity espoused by teachers and the media were, in fact, reserved for a specific group. It was a dead-out scam, a hoax.

The problem, however, was that despite the well-publicized gangland flare-ups, a pervading sense of tranquillity cloaked Youngstown's quietly restrictive social arrangements. Conformity reigned among both blacks and whites. It was as if everyone had determined to grasp and tenaciously hold on to a brief moment of calm and apparent order. Peace, security, prosperity, and a superficial equanimity held sway. Somehow, at least unconsciously, everyone seemed to understand that the illusion or fabrication, like an inexpensive knit sweater, would completely unravel if even one loose strand were pulled too forcefully or examined with any real intensity.

Growing up in that small eastern Ohio industrial town was to experience a subtle, seemingly inexplicable sense of outwardly imposed restraint and negation of self-worth. It was like being trapped in one of Franz Kafka's nightmarish fictional allegories—I might just as well have been the frustrated land surveyor who vainly searches for the ruling lord in *The Castle,* or Joseph K., who despite not knowing and never being told the nature of his crime, is accused, tried, and convicted in *The Trial.* Madness and traditional social custom masqueraded as sanity. And since nearly everyone with whom I came in contact accepted the situation as not only ordinary and expected but also unalterable, defiance seemed imprudent unless one were himself willing to be labeled a troublemaker, deviant, or psychotic.

Negroes had first taken up residence in the area in the early 1830s. But except for mild verbal protests against police intimidation by a few church and civic leaders in the twenties; overt, if short-lived and futile, demonstrations against segregated eating facilities in the thirties; and the swimming pool protests of the late 1940s, Youngstown Negroes had mainly acquiesced to their restricted acceptance and second-class status. A paper titled "The Negro in Youngstown," issued by a Kent State University seminar headed by sociologist August Meier, claimed that "nowhere is there any indication of real indigenous Negro leadership or any sign of real unity among the Negro community" and concluded that the Youngstown Negro "was as much an apostle of gradualism as Booker T. Washington could want."

By the mid-1950s, even as Martin Luther King Jr. began the bus boycott in Montgomery, Alabama, little progress had been made. Some Negro leaders apparently worked behind the scenes, quietly making small gains; but without active community support, little was accomplished. The most visible resistance came from the upstart Black Muslims or from black preachers, who while deploring the Negro's condition, usually urged a go-slow policy. Meanwhile, most downtown restaurants remained segregated, as did the central YMCA and YWCA and nearly all hotels; segregated seating was the rule in downtown theaters; Negroes were still allowed only restricted use of public pools; and discrimination in housing and employment was rife.

Given the Negro population's long-standing passivity, there was little need of an intimidating Ku Klux Klan presence or formal racial covenants in Youngstown during the fifties. Unlike the South, there were no signs indicating COLORED ONLY or WHITE ONLY. It wasn't necessary. As if by some silent edict, everyone knew his place, knew also that he was expected to stay in it. It was the key to survival and social acceptance. Most quietly complied.

Therefore a sizable proportion of the town's Negro population lived either in the segregated Westlake Housing Project or a confined area in an adjacent ward. The latter became known as the Monkey's Nest shortly after it was abandoned by European immigrants and Negroes began moving in, at the turn of the century. During the forties and fifties, there was no estimable drug problem. Cocaine and, most certainly, crack were unheard of. The only noticeable substance abuse, in fact, derived from the nearby steel mill's *coke plant,* whose towering chimneys regularly spewed out a sulfurous stench and fine spray of orange dust that drifted across the railroad tracks and chemically polluted river to settle on the area like a scarlet cloak of inferiority. Not even Nathaniel Hawthorne's Hester Prynne was more dramatically stigmatized.

But despite the impoverished surroundings, upstanding Negroes struggled to build a community in their neighborhood. Amidst a score of gambling dens, dives, and night clubs such as the Black and Tan and the Cotton Club, traditional family institutions thrived. There were churches, small businesses, recreational activities at the Caldwell Settlement, and as in most black areas at the time, a communal sense of responsibility for neighborhood children. Still, it was a tough section, and much of its reputation was derived from the face its residents presented to outsiders. It paid to carry a chip on your shoulder if you were from the Nest, if only to deflect the mockery that arose from time to time. "Yeah, I'm from the Nest," a former resident used to boast. "Don't take no mess. And if you grab my chest, you get your rest."

There were, some insisted, reasons other than its racial makeup for the derogatory name attached to the area. I'm not sure. I do know that, when I was a teenager, the mere mention of the name set off gales of laughter among blacks—at least, when there were no whites or residents from the area among the crowd—and polite, knowing smiles among whites. It was our place, those smiles seemed to suggest, even if we didn't live there.

For their part, most white Youngstowners, reassured, perhaps, by local newspaper headlines that advised, "Negro's Progress Is Surprising Even to Himself," basked in this generally unquestioned harmony and accord. Casual interactions between blacks and whites were generally marked by a polite, if sometimes disingenuous, affability. Local whites even winked and looked the other way when, on weekends, celebrations by Negro revelers escalated into rowdy, sometimes violent, disturbances. That's just the way they are, prevailing theory seemed to suggest. It's okay as long as they keep it among themselves—as it were, stay in their place.

Youngstown was generally characterized by its surface politeness and amicability. While not quite as slow paced and seemingly guileless as television's Mayberry, North Carolina, where Andy, Opie, and Aunt Bee set the tone, neither was it as fast paced, cold, and indifferent as large urban centers such as Chicago and New York City. It was, according to the 1950 census, the fifty-eighth-largest city in America. But as in many small heartland cities, a kind of homespun Midwestern hospitality reigned. Youngstowners were given to such euphemistic expressions as "Gosh darn it" and "Holy cow" and regularly expressed excitement with quaint outbursts such as "Yes siree, Bob!" (I, for one, never figured out who Bob was.) People customarily smiled and greeted one another on the streets, asked directions without fear of being insulted or snubbed. Gave them without seeming hurried or taxed. Although perfunctory, that openness and courtesy was part of the region's protocol, a civility that in most instances was extended without regard to race.

A good deal of the time, as Al Bright had discovered, it was fraudulent and misleading. As with Sherwood Anderson's so-called grotesques, the fictional characters that inhabited *Winesburg, Ohio,* for many whites in Youngstown polite civility was apparently simply a mask concealing less-virtuous passions, more intensely felt aversions. Once inside their own homes, no doubt, many dropped the facade, began passing ethnic slurs around the dinner table as easily as they passed the bread and butter. How the transformation occurred was and yet remains a mystery to me.

Was it simply legerdemain, a kind of mental sleight of hand that insured the outcome of every coin toss—heads I win, tails you lose—or did they really believe it? And if so, how intense must their fear and self-loathing have been. What possible trauma justified lumping an entire religion or race of people into one indistinguishable unholy lot, effectively eliminating them from consideration as individuals? What? Some recurring, wishfully thought, neominstrel fantasy in which blacks inevitably meld into a mass of homesick field niggers pining for de massa and dem cotton fields way back home? A berserk black man or latter-day Catholic inquisitor terrorizing their family? Some time-warped vision in which an ebony Jeffrey Dahmer takes up residence in the suburbs and, during Sunday afternoon barbecues, gorges himself on marinated white folks? Surely not those mirror images of rice- and pancake-box caricatures that filed docilely into Reverend Rose's church on Sundays; not even the overly cheerful and somewhat pretentious proprietor of Shylockson's Tailors. What synaptic dysfunction triggered the illusion, even among the most simpleminded, that they were inherently superior to an entire race or group of people? For the life of me, I could come up with no answers.

And that was the problem—the elusive nature of the racism.

Where was the potentate who authorized this madness? Who was in charge of the asylum? Not the inmates, either black or white, since most seemed consumed by some soporific daze.

Unlike Al, I never faced direct or overt segregation in Youngstown. In part it was luck, of course, but primarily it was because as a child, I had usually followed the lead of others without question—complied with the unwritten rules, and without even knowing it, effectively stayed in my place. Later, when I became aware of the restrictions, I simply refused to put myself in a position of asking or insisting on being accepted anyplace where I was clearly unwanted. My own arrogance prohibited it. It was over a year after leaving Youngstown, when the Colgate University basketball team traveled to Annapolis, Maryland, for a game against Navy, that I was caught by surprise and refused service at a local Jim Crow restaurant.

Again, unlike in the South, where whites expressed their contempt openly and without restraint, in Youngstown white attitudes were for the most part evasive and muddled, reflecting a moral ambiguity that may have stemmed back to the nineteenth century. After all, the Youngstown-Warren area had been a major stop on the Underground Railroad. Some whites had enough belief in Negro equality to risk their lives and help runaway slaves escape to Canada. And, of course, Ohio fought against the South in the Civil War; Youngstown's Soldier's Monument, which still stands in Federal Plaza, lists hundreds who died in that war. Not their primary goal, perhaps, but they died helping to free black slaves.

Whatever the cause of the area's peculiar brand of racial bias, the effect was eerie and unsettling. It may even have been easier in the South—although, with my attitude, I don't think I would have survived. Still, the adversary was clear-cut. No games of hide-and-seek. No one felt any urge to disguise contempt for Negroes. Southerners knew where they stood. There was no ambiguity and, therefore, much less chance of Southern Negroes internalizing racist indictments and assuming even partial culpability for the stifling sense of repression.

In Youngstown, aside from the often irritating patronage of some, and a few outspoken racists whose voices were heard rarely enough to be considered oddities, in direct confrontations whites were generally apologetic about their biases and the imposition of rules regarding segregation. Few even acknowledged the existence of an ebony ceiling that limited Negroes' access to all but the most humdrum, grueling pursuits. It was as if those rules were heavenly inspired, had been handed down by some nameless higher authority. Often the individual enforcing them appeared to be doing so only under duress or coercion.

Once, at age twelve, after rushing into the Palace Theater and finding that the movie had already started, I forgot where I was supposed to sit and took a seat in the orchestra section. The usher calmly walked over, smiled, and said, "I'm sorry, sir. I'm going to have to ask you to sit upstairs. It's theater policy, you know."

It was all done so courteously that, as I stood to leave, I felt a sudden obligation to *thank him*. Nearly asked if there was anything I could do for him. After all, it was my place—where I had intended to sit all along.

The peculiar character of the area's racial attitudes was further revealed to me several years later, again at a downtown movie house. While sitting in the State Theater after its segregated seating policies were relaxed, I overheard a conversation between a frail, aging white couple who sat in the row ahead of me. In the middle of a tense scene between Sidney Poitier and John Cassavetes, the woman turned to her companion and asked, "How does he wake up every morning and look in the mirror at that black face, dear?"

"Well, Martha," her companion answered thoughtfully, "I suppose he's gotten used to it by now."

For a moment, I flashed on sitting upstairs in the balcony again—tossing shit over the rail on folks just like them. But somehow, this was more ludicrous than insulting. Two wizened near-octogenarians expressing apparently heartfelt pity at Sidney Poitier's appearance! Beyond inexplicable, it was truly weird. I bit my tongue to keep from laughing when it happened, but later realized that their comments revealed more about the nature of racial bias in Youngstown than most of the books I'd read by that time. It was quite often a bizarre mixture of irrationality, self-delusion, and ethnic arrogance, tempered by what might even have been sincere concern. Despite the latter, by that time I'd concluded that arrogance and stupidity, even when humorous, are nearly always a toxic mixture.

Ultimately, however, the most intense bias against Negroes centered on employment, housing, and fraternization or miscegenation. The first was an economic matter. The others, although artfully wedded to the first by the seemingly innocuous good-old-boy network, constituted the most inflammatory aspect of bigotry in the heartland and elsewhere. When I was an adolescent, the employment issue was a minor one for me personally. In my early teens, I'd easily found a job setting pins at a local bowling alley. Later, largely because of changes effected by McCullough Williams Jr., I was hired as a caretaker at a south side playground. After becoming the first Negro appointee to the city's Park and Recreation Commission in 1955, Williams disrupted the long-standing practice of visually eliminating Negro applicants when he began removing the photographs that, in the past, had been required with every application. It was the way things had to be done in those days. Along with several other black students, I benefited.

Neither did discrimination in housing affect me, except in an indirect manner. When we moved to the south side, our block had been an integrated area that roughly paralleled the city's racial demographics. About 20 percent of our neighbors were black. Twelve years later, when I left for college, only two white families remained. But curiously, I thought, while Negroes continued moving into homes north of Woodland, almost none bought property east, west, or south of our block. It was as if a line had been drawn in a war zone—someone had decided that there would be little or no further penetration.

Later, I'd discover, lines had been drawn. In the area of housing, at least, racial agreements had been established in Youngstown. Until the mid-1950s, for example, Negroes were restricted from buying property east of Hillman Avenue, the street that established one end of the block on which I lived. Realtors, even loan associations and banks, apparently conspired to maintain that border, directing Negroes to other, mostly less desirable housing, usually in near-downtown sections such as the Monkey's Nest, which had been abandoned by European immigrants, or those areas at the city's extreme northeastern border that, since the early twentieth century, had been predominantly black.

We had moved into a neighborhood that allowed entry to the newly built Hillman Junior High as well as South High, at the time one of the city's best schools, so the housing agreement didn't negatively affect me. In fact, since I could walk one block in any direction, as I often did, and find myself surrounded by an entirely different culture, it probably expanded my horizons. For my sisters and brother Al, however, it presented a serious problem. When starting their families, they were steered to neighborhoods that reflected neither their aspirations nor their incomes.

Still, the housing issue was largely a smoke screen for the more emotionally heated issue of fraternization. Except for those occasions when whites attacked Negroes brought in by the steel mills as strikebreakers, the most bitter white reactions to Negroes' presence had revolved around attempts to integrate previously all-white neighborhoods or, as with the swimming pool disturbances, to demand access to facilities where intimate contact between the sexes was likely. Revealingly, the pool riots occurred when Negro males attempted using the facilities; few objected and no one fumed when young Negro girls arrived with their white girlfriends.

Southern racism, more often than not, did not flinch from intimate interracial contact. Black mammies suckled white babies.
House servants worked and lived among their masters and, later,
employers, who figuratively and often literally slept with "their" Negroes. It was not a problem when (as with the case of my grandmother and Harry Chandler) a white man and Negro woman were
involved, or those Negroes permitted inside the household assumed
the proper obsequious posture and accepted a class hierarchy that
placed them at the absolute bottom of the social structure.

Most Southern whites, from what my parents had told me and
what I'd seen on television or experienced during my brief visits to
the South, carried their biases like a badge or club. Stepped right up
and got in your face. Defied you to deny their supremacy, your nigra-
hood. It was a *personal* matter. From state and local officials down
to the poorest dirt farmer, there was no question that in their eyes
you were and always would be nothing but a nigger.

Northern whites, on the other hand, were detached. Segregation
was an impersonal phenomenon and most were perfectly willing to
accept the *appearance* of equality as long as Negroes kept their distance—stayed in their place. They eagerly embraced the idea of
equality but were reluctant to embrace actual Negroes. Whites folks
in the South, to paraphrase Dick Gregory, didn't care how close you
got as long as you didn't get too big. Northern whites didn't care
how big you got as long as you didn't get too close. In many instances, even those local whites who had helped runaway slaves, according to published reports, were disinclined to invite their
beleaguered refugees into hiding places within their homes. They
were usually hidden away in barns and outdoor tunnels until they
were safely dispatched toward Canada. I got some hint at age thirteen of how fervently some white men embraced those beliefs, during an encounter with Joey, a swarthy, macho, thirty-year-old Italian
shoemaker with whom I'd previously had a friendly relationship.

His shop was at the corner of my block, and apparently he had
seen me walking past it with a young white girl who was in one of
my classes while we were returning from school. When I entered
the shop to pick up a pair of my father's shoes a few days later, he
took time to share a bit of his Sicilian folk wisdom. I wanted to get
to the basketball courts before dark, but I listened impatiently as he
wound through a seemingly friendly harangue, which ended with,

"You know, Pepper, I love you people. Give you the shirt off my back. You can have my clothes, my liquor, my money—but don't ever mess with *my* women!"

At first I was honestly confused, didn't know precisely what he was talking about. I wondered, frankly, how far the boundaries of his clan extended. So, as he walked over and placed the newly repaired shoes on the counter, I asked, "Ahhh, *your women*? Do you mean your sisters, your wife . . . your mother?"

Of course, the minute I said it, I realized how the remark might be taken. I was aware of the dozens and I'm sure he was also. But despite its sarcastic overtones, my response wasn't intended that way; I'd simply blurted out the question that his comment immediately brought to mind. It was naive, no doubt, and in retrospect I'm surprised that he didn't pick up his hammer and leap across the counter. Instead, Joey's normally cheerful expression turned to ice. He stared at me coldly for a moment, then took the money my father had given me to pay for the shoes and walked away. Never said a word, just busied himself hammering on the spiked heel of a woman's pump until I walked out the door. He never spoke to me again, and I always found excuses when my folks tried to send me back to his shop.

Perhaps it was my age, the fact that my childhood innocence had run its course and, imagining what life would be like as an adult, I'd been shocked into awareness, or maybe it was the times. I'm not sure, but it was only a year or so after the incident with Joey that those annoying ripples that I'd previously disregarded began to loom as serious problems. Something was in the air. Rosa Parks had just made the fateful decision to defy a Montgomery driver and refuse to assume her place at the back of the bus, precipitating the boycott that launched the civil rights movement. The little white lies were no longer flying. In the South, black folks were turning up the heater, and as Stevie Wonder would later write, it was "gettin' ready to shock . . . gettin' ready to pop." Even in Youngstown, where accommodation of second-class treatment was entrenched, one could sense it. At least, by the mid-fifties, I could.

Although none was singly decisive, the accrual of small slights and the prospect of their continued interference suddenly seemed overwhelming. Sometimes, without warning, they'd flash into my mind, clicking into place as if called up by one of those automatic carousel projection devices: the knee-jerk embarrassment I'd felt as muffled laughter broke out whenever one of those *National Geographic* films about Africa was shown in class; the realization that, while I'd stood outside in the rain or snow to buy a hot dog at Jay's, the restaurant was not only warm and dry inside, but often nearly empty; my teachers' slick avoidance of nearly all references to Negroes in history or sociology classes, or the benevolent smiles that had settled on some of their faces as they glanced at me while the class gleefully harmonized Stephen Foster's "Old Black Joe" ("gentle voices"?—my ass!).

Increasingly I became more attentive to subtle everyday occurrences such as the patronizing aloofness of clerks who deferred to white customers as I stood in line to purchase some bauble or the condescending treatment my father received from white salespeople, even as he agreed to pay inflated interest on a household necessity. The stark contrast between East Federal Street (the rowdy, unkempt section of town where Negroes were encouraged to shop, eat, and find recreation) and West Federal (where they were greeted suspiciously, segregated, or excluded from its clean restaurants and hotels, plush theaters and shops) suddenly seemed to leap out at me. Even customs that I'd previously ignored began rankling. I preferred sitting in the balcony of movie theaters, but the notion that I *had* to sit there began to infuriate me.

The more Al Bright and I discussed the matter, vented our repressed anger, the more frustrated I became. Astounded by the indifference that seemed to have settled over almost everyone—family, friends, teachers—and unable to devise any solution, at first I withdrew.

Part of the problem, I realized, was my own. I had come to resent any unfair restrictions on my development. And growing up within Youngstown's quietly enforced separatist society was increasingly becoming intolerable. I wanted complete access—the whole cookie—thought I deserved it and knew that I would never accept sitting idly by and being denied the opportunity to express myself fully, intellectually, socially, or in the workforce. Exasperated, I finally went to my mother and directly asked, "How do they put up with it? How can so many black people just sit around like nothing's wrong? Not even complain?"

"I don't know, son. We just do. Colored folks been doin' it for years 'cause seem like ain' nothin' we can do about it. No cause to fret, though, you'll get used to it, same as I did. Just trust in the Lord. He'll show you the way."

Neither her explanation nor her solution were acceptable.

I did not have the patience of Job, nor did I aspire to it. If the Lord had anything to do with it, I concluded, then he too was suspect, capable, perhaps, of the same duplicity that marked Sherwood Anderson's Winesburg, Ohio, grotesques.

No, I had to do something—make some changes. And if I couldn't change the attitudes of the people around me, then I'd have to change my attitude, my approach. It may have started with them, but the second-class status and sense of powerlessness had become as much a figment of my stunted vision as it was a consequence of their restrictions. I had to transform myself.

The next evening, I went to the room I shared with my brother Herbert and spent most of the night silently cursing God and the church. Although frightened and halfway expecting a thunderbolt to rip through the ceiling and destroy me, I directed every profanity I'd ever heard toward an unseen heavenly father that I felt either did not exist or, worse, had deserted me. If my mother had been right about unforgivable sins, I thought, then there was no way back. I was beyond acquittal.

Near morning, I lay there tired, sweating, and still apprehensive about that thunderbolt. I did, however, feel a sense of giddy relief. If nothing else, I was now on my own. What had the barbershop philosopher Pines said? "Sink or swim, that's what they told you— knowed you niggers couldn't swim a lick." Well, regardless, as *they* apparently intended, I was on my own. If Katie was right, there was certainly no chance of heavenly intervention. Although I hadn't even learned how to float, as Shine might have said, *it was time to hit the water*. I was determined to swim on my own.

*9*

# school daze

South High School was little more than a mile walk from my home. An imposing Gothic and Italian Provincial structure with an ornate portico sheathed in ivy, the building was set back far enough from the noise and hubbub of Market Street to give it a calm, almost secluded air. A semicircular cement walk cut through the neatly landscaped lawn, leading from the street to the arched tripartite doorways at the entrance. Similar facades, I'd later discover, might be sighted from a gondola while gliding along a Venice canal. Or, given a shift in setting, another century and a more rural locale, one might have easily imagined horse-drawn buggies pulling up to the entrance to dispatch visiting country squires as genteel Southern belles and self-fashioned aristocrats sipped mint juleps on the balcony above the portico.

Opened in 1911, it was the second high school built in Youngstown. By the 1930s, its grounds had been enhanced by construction of a football stadium seating thirty-five thousand and a field house that held over three thousand spectators; it had become the city's premiere public school. The student body reflected the area's residential pattern, so until the mid-forties, Negro attendance was minimal. But things had changed. When I first made the half-hour trek from Woodland Avenue and began my sophomore year, nearly 18 percent of the student body was black. The graduation class of 1958 would count forty-three Negroes among the 254 who received diplomas.

Besides its racial makeup mirroring the city's demographics, South was a microcosm of Youngstown life in other ways. Nearly every segment of the city's diverse ethnic and religious mix was represented: Irish, Scotch, English, Germans, Italians, Hungarians, African Americans, Asians, Greeks, Catholics, Jews, and Protestants, as well as, I'm sure, some fundamentalists and holy rollers all intermingled. Generally, whites and minorities received equal treatment. It was the 1950s, of course, so there was a general understanding that, according to social prescript, whites were destined to assume positions of authority in the community after graduation. Still, we played, studied, and rubbed shoulders with our fairer-skinned classmates, competed against them in everything from debate and chess to basketball and football. And for the most part, schoolmasters judged us on individual merit.

There were, of course, some exceptions. At the time social custom was nearly as restrictive of women's roles as they were of Negroes', so female participation in the school's varsity athletic programs was limited to sideline roles as boosters and supporters. And although there were many vivacious, attractive Negro girls who might have represented the school as majorettes or cheerleaders, none were chosen. Still, most school activities were governed by an impartiality that was starkly contrasted to the world outside. It was as if we were a part of some surreal social experiment in which, for six or seven hours a day, society's racial strictures were relaxed, democratic principles observed. At day's end, released from our *casa grande,* we were sent back into rigidly separated and distinctly unequal black and white worlds where we once again donned our racial masks and assumed our designated societal roles.

In the mid-fifties, however, even this compromised arrangement was encouraging. The civil rights movement was just beginning and most Negroes faithfully clung to the belief that America would respond to the call for equal opportunity. Optimism abounded and most blacks and whites seemed to agree with the views expressed by the black novelist and essayist George Schuyler, who a few years earlier had written in a *Reader's Digest* article, "the progressive improvement of race relations and the economic rise of the Negro in the United States is a flattering example of democracy in action." So long as moderation was observed and no one demanded much more than cosmetic change, racial harmony reigned. Deliberate speed, you know.

Why not? Although there was little happening in their own backyards, Northern Negroes could look to the South and see signs of progress. In Alabama, Montgomery whites were still resisting demands for an end to segregated seating on buses; they had, in fact, adopted some extreme measures to keep Negroes riding in the back of the bus. Attempts to break the boycott included intimidating carpoolers and harassing Negroes who had the energy and temerity to attempt walking to work. Bus or be busted, no less. Still, the boycott continued and word was the authorities would soon capitulate. In December of 1956, they did. Moderation and a deliberate response to "reasonable" demands seemed to be affecting progress, even in the heart of Dixie.

But then, Gov. Orval Faubus had not, as yet, taken center stage. He would soon signal the extent of the hard-core resistance that lay ahead by calling in the Arkansas National Guard to block the court-ordered admission of Negro students to Little Rock's Central High School. His actions would force President Eisenhower to dispatch federal troops. For the remainder of the year, the school hosted a ritualistic procession in which federal paratroopers escorted nine Negro children through a hateful mob of taunting, egg-and-rock-flinging white rabble-rousers. Inside, although still monitored by troops, the sons and daughters of that mob would continue the harassment, turning each day—as a few of those black students later admitted—into a journey through a cracker-ruled Dante's inferno.

And of course, no one talked about the lynching of Emmett Till, a vacationing Chicago teenager who, during the summer before I entered high school, had made the fatally grievous error of winking at a white woman in a backwoods Mississippi town. It was whispered about or avoided altogether by both whites and Negroes, the latter primarily for political reasons since, at that time, almost no one wanted to publicly confront the racial juggernaut's real bugbear: the explosive, emotionally heated issue of race mixing that actually fueled the insistence on separation of the races in housing, at social gatherings, and at public functions. As if equality could be meted out in small doses and contained—recognized here, forbidden there. We hoped, perhaps, that human nature would not vault our fabricated racial hurdles; that, despite resistance from both sides, it would not run its course and demonstrate that true equality meant exercising freedom of choice in mates as well as in jobs, housing, and traveling, in eating or sleeping accommodations.

Still, despite our sidestepping the race-mixing issue and blindly ignoring signs that furious clashes lay ahead, South High offered a relaxed learning environment where equanimity and cordiality ruled. It was, in comparison to today's schools, a virtual Eden. Drugs were rare enough to be considered nonexistent. Weapons or organized youth gangs had not spread from big cities to small-town America. Altercations did arise. But at a time when the TV violence was mostly confined to Hopalong Cassidy shoot-'em-ups, Ralph Kramden threatening to belt his wife (*"Pow*—to the moon, Alice, right to the moon"), the mock mayhem of wrestling matches, or a few legitimate boxing matches, arguments seldom escalated to anything more than fistfights. Black and white students interacted with little tension and, generally, at the end of the day, went their separate ways. Knew their places and stayed there. In a sense, we grew up in the calm before the stormy sixties, a brief interval during which Negroes' rapidly eroding patience and acceptance of accommodation could comfortably mesh or, at least, harmoniously coexist with the heartland's amiability and apparent good intentions.

In fact, when most Americans talk about the fifties and good old days, if they are not cynically referring to a time when Negroes were securely locked into second-class status, they are usually alluding to the era's youthful optimism and apparent wholesomeness, its uncontested belief in an American dream that promised tranquillity, suburban prosperity, and unlimited leisure. They fondly recall its dress, music, sanguine outlook, and innocent, if sometimes weird, recreations. That guileless faith was insistently passed along to fifties' teenagers, the oldest of the so-called baby boomers. Not since the twenties had American teens been given license, in fact urged, to adopt a carefree, irresponsible attitude. *Father Knows Best* was more than just the era's most popular TV sitcom; it expressed an attitude that, while not always actualized, reflected assumptions shared by much of the nation's heartland. Religion and family were icons, hallowed institutions. Parental control was unchallenged. Youth was, by dictate, on holiday—an arrangement that most college and high school students eagerly embraced.

On college campuses panty raids or frivolous attempts to squeeze scores of students into a telephone booth or Volkswagen Bug grabbed headlines. College deans and psychiatrists dismissed the antics, compared them to the harmless revelry of the Roman Feast of Saturn, excused the shenanigans as healthy expressions of youthful ardor. And while innocuous pranks and diversions such as swallowing goldfish and demolishing pianos or automobiles were tolerated as examples of young adult recreation, almost any behavior threatening to disturb the complacence of the real, adult world was discouraged or repressed. Discussions of current social or political issues were rare, despite the Cold War, threat of the bomb, and the ominous rippling of black protests in the South. Little wonder that historians would call ours the silent generation or that, in 1954, a survey of Oklahoma A&T students revealed that their greatest worry was finding a parking space.

The harebrained hijinks that erupted on many college campuses rarely surfaced at South High, but in most ways it was typical of the era's small-town Midwestern secondary schools. Despite, or perhaps because of, its insistent gaiety and enthusiasm, I began my first year there with a good deal of suspicion and apprehension— not because of the academic challenge, which, as I anticipated, wasn't overly demanding, but because of the social arrangements, which I feared would only intensify my own discontent.

Studies were, of course, the main focus. But unlike in junior high, where classes and outside activities did not generally overlap, at South the school day was closely connected to a swirl of weekend and after-school social events.

The South High social scene, as I quickly discovered, was a lively, somewhat exclusive world of pageantry, pep rallies, formal dances, hayrides, sock hops, and picnics that most often revolved around sports events or were sponsored by a variety of social and recreational clubs or organizations, admission to which at least partially determined one's status. Before classes each morning students gathered in groups to chat or dance or simply listen to the pop music piped into the auditorium, mostly the bubble-gum sounds of such

artists as Patti Page, Eddie Fisher, and Kay Starr or cover recordings of rhythm-and-blues hits by the Crew Cuts, Georgia Gibbs, or
Pat Boone. When I started school in the fall, that derivative assortment was being enlivened by a few new, exciting pop voices as well
as a few selections from the R&B charts. Elvis Presley had arrived
with his "Blue Suede Shoes," and occasionally a ballad by the Plat-
ters or Orioles could be heard.

There was an aura of childlike playfulness about it for most of us,
a reflection of a more innocent age, no doubt. Still, high school was
home to our fledgling teenage courtship rituals. In that sexist, pre-
sexual-revolution era, the rites generally proceeded no further than
swollen lips, hickeys, dry humps, and afterward, cold showers. The
overriding mainstream consensus was that "good girls" never went
all the way—saving themselves for marriage, you know. Most often
it was, as Richard Pryor, the Peoria-born comedian who cut his
teeth in the Cleveland-Youngstown area, would later quip, the
"great pussy drought of the fifties." Only the most persuasive studs
got past second base (bare skin), and if his partner was disclosed,
she was quickly labeled a tramp. Loose lips, whether boasting of actual encounters or airing macho fantasies, could and sometimes did
sully or ruin reputations. Even those of girls who had righteously
and successfully blocked access to home plate.

But while the scent of raging testosterone hovered over most activities at South High, it was—as in Rosemary Clooney's hit song
"Come On-a My House," which euphemistically promised, "I'm
gonna give you candy"—most often insistently cloaked by a veneer
of wholesomeness and naiveté, or even more effectively, stifled by
snickering innuendo, coarse jokes, and bungling come-ons that mirrored the tittering advances of Bob Cummings's hapless nephew in
*Love That Bob*, the popular fifties precursor of the voyeuristic butts-
and-bosoms format that shapes such 1990s TV hits as *Baywatch*.

Following contemporary fashion, most girls arrived in penny
loafers, bobby socks, sweaters or blouses whose Peter Pan collars
were ringed with ribbons, and midcalf-length skirts or dresses. Rosy
cheeked, with hair pulled back in ponytails or coiffed nonchalantly
in the short, pixie style June Allyson had popularized, they aspired
to the girlishly plump (buxom, if resources allowed) girl-next-door
look Hollywood had established in the person of such young stars
as Doris Day and Debbie Reynolds. And while the image may no

longer appeal, it exuded a healthy, squeaky-clean allure that confounded even as it enticed. So pristine and firmly enshrined on a
pedestal that mortal excretory functions were unimaginable.

Only a few were bold enough to affect the era's contrasting image,
the glamour and sensuality of a Rita Hayworth, Ava Gardner, or
Dorothy Dandridge with long, flowing hair, dark sultry makeup, and
hip-hugging dresses. The risk was too great for most. It was too easy
to be labeled a slut on appearance alone. And in the fifties, appearance was paramount.

During that first year of high school, I mostly stood back and observed the festivities—as it were, treaded water. I had gotten off to a
bad start even before school began. Word of my athletic promise
had preceded me, and during the summer, both Merle Rosselle, the
basketball coach, and John McAfee, the football and baseball coach,
had called. But while I looked forward to trying out for basketball, I
had no intention of playing football. Having twice sustained a broken arm, one while playing football in a Peewee League game, I'd
decided to avoid the risk of further injury. Moreover, since I intended playing basketball and baseball, participation in football
would have meant involvement in sports throughout the school
year as well as a good deal of the summer. I knew that I needed time
to myself.

The problem was that McAfee, who had been my Little League
coach, had already set up a locker, assigned a uniform, and penciled
me in as a wide-receiver prospect. Despite his urging, I declined the
invitation to attend summer football practice. When school started,
he informed me that I not only was not welcome on South's baseball
team but also would be required to attend all those physical education classes from which varsity athletes were routinely exempted.
Although he changed his mind and allowed me to join the baseball
team the following year, we rarely spoke to each other during that
first year at South.

In addition to being blackballed by McAfee, I took some razzing
from the football players during that first year. "What's wrong, Pep?
Football too rough for you? Why don't you try a man's game?" Despite the pressure, I held to my decision, waited for the basketball
season, even though I soon realized that football players had a
unique status at South High.

In the fall, football fever swept through the school like a cyclone.

It was a passion that engulfed not only the school and city but the entire region. The blue-collar, lunch-bucket communities that surrounded Ohio and eastern Pennsylvania's industrial towns produced some of the nation's finest football players, linemen in particular; they were a traditional recruiting ground for Midwestern colleges such as Notre Dame, Michigan, and Ohio State. South High's schedule included teams such as Massillon High, which had risen to national prominence when coached by Paul Brown, who by this time was on his way to becoming an NFL legend as coach of the Cleveland Browns. Although South was mostly routed by that elite rival, they often challenged and occasionally upset them. Those games as well as contests against less prestigious opponents were approached with something akin to religious fervor which started before the games and extended beyond them.

During pregame pep rallies in the auditorium and at the games, perky cheerleaders dressed in lettered sweaters and short flared skirts which, in that modest era, would have been condemned as risqué in most other circumstances drove the student body to near frenzy with their zealous exhortations and acrobatics. In many ways, it was like a revival meeting, with the hype, pomp and ceremony, and delirium intensifying until the night of the game and the dance and parties that followed the contest. Caught up in the hysteria and excitement, I began to realize how much athletes, particularly football players, were revered. It was at those times that I most regretted—in fact, almost reconsidered—my decision not to play football.

My frustration didn't subside until the coming of winter and the beginning of the basketball season, when I surprised some by making the starting five. During the course of the season, largely due to my own tentativeness and lack of confidence, I was later relegated to sixth man. Despite vying for the city championship, the team fell short, lost a decisive game to our crosstown rival and the eventual champs, Rayen High, by four points in the season finale. That year's basketball team didn't create the excitement that the football team had inspired, but it did expose me to a kind of limited celebrity within the school and whetted my appetite for more. Still, it was a disappointing season, as was most of my life off the court that year.

I groped my way through the year without any real goals, dodging minefields and trying to stay out of harm's way as I searched for answers to questions that, curiously, did not seem to bother anyone except me. I didn't sink, but there were some serious dips and plunges, extremely close calls.

One of the most unsettling occurred in the spring as my mother drove me to school one day. On the way, I asked her to stop at a small, family-owned grocery store so I could buy some chewing gum. When I entered, the proprietor, who was in his sixties and, judging from his broken English, a recent European immigrant, immediately stepped away from the counter and mumbled what sounded like, "No, No. Go away . . . go away." Late for school and having no idea what was bothering him, I impatiently placed a nickel on the counter and asked for a pack of Juicy Fruit gum.

The old man took another step backward, waving his arms as if frantically signaling an unwary motorist to halt before they plummeted over some unseen precipice. His voice, quaking now, again mumbled, "Go away. No more, no more."

Mystified but undeterred, I pushed the coin toward him and, more insistently, demanded, "Look, man. Here's the money. I just want a pack of gum."

Finally, he reached toward the candy rack and, shaking as if he'd seen a ghost, picked up a pack of gum and tossed it onto the counter. Infuriated now, I almost walked out without taking it. Instead, I snatched it from the counter and yelled, "What's wrong with you, man? You crazy motherfucker." When I stormed out of the door, the old man remained pressed against the shelves behind the counter, still shaking his head and mumbling to himself.

Later that afternoon, Mr. Kennedy, the boys' advisor and school truant officer, stepped into my English class. After briefly whispering to my teacher, he asked me to step out into the hallway with him. Two police officers were waiting. I'd been identified as one of two thieves who had stuck up a nearby grocery store the past weekend, they told me. Although not cuffed, I was escorted out of the building, put into a patrol car, and taken directly downtown to the station.

Apparently, the distraught grocery store proprietor had taken the license plate number of my parents' car and called the police after I'd left his store. A few hours later, several officers had arrived on Woodland. My parents' house and car were searched for stolen property. I never could imagine what they were looking for—hot

Wonder Bread or soda pop? Contraband cold cuts, cigarettes, chewing gum?

Even though they found nothing, I was hauled in under suspicion.

As it turned out, I had a perfect alibi for the Saturday afternoon on which the armed heist had taken place. Along with other members of South High's Rotary Club, I'd volunteered to assist the local American Red Cross in stuffing envelopes to be sent out for contributions. I had been assiduously stuffing and stamping that morning and well into the afternoon. At least a dozen witnesses could have confirmed my whereabouts. It didn't matter. I was questioned by an officer whose wry smile made his feelings about my guilt apparent. "Yeah, right," he finally mumbled when I told him where I'd been when the robbery took place. "Sure you wasn't at church or visiting your rabbi? That's all fine, but we still want you to get in there with the rest of them boys."

I was herded into a lineup with five or six other black students. Fortunately, even though he had positively fingered me no more than seven hours earlier, the store's proprietor was unable to identify me or anyone else when faced with a group of black teenagers. The gist was that a Negro—short, tall, fat, skinny, light, or dark, who knows?—had robbed his store. And since we all looked alike, every Negro was suspect.

Although I was let go at the end of the day, there were no apologies. I was just released and told, "Well, it looks like you're okay." I was surprised when they didn't add, "this time," since despite Mr. Kennedy's support, the general consensus was that I was guilty—if not of that crime, then surely of something else. Even my parents questioned my innocence at first, grilling me until they were satisfied that, unlike McKay, I had not decided to step completely outside the legal system.

Years later, while working at the *New York Times*, I'd laughingly consider that I'd missed a rare opportunity. If I'd again been mistakenly identified and convicted—but had somehow managed to get through college and become a journalist—I would have had material for a best-selling confessional that validated mainstream notions of the system's sanctity and confirmed our suspicions about Negroes' innate malfeasance. I could have perfectly fit a profile that, by the eighties, had assumed immense popular appeal: the black profligate who, after discovering the error of his ways, remorsefully confesses, returns to the fold, and repudiates his errant past.

At the time, however, the incident rattled me, further eroded my faith in the system and its treatment of Negroes. It also helped solidify my determination to get out of Youngstown and resist the lure of the steel mills. Still, I had no idea of what direction to take unless, by some miracle, I was recruited by a major-league baseball team. There was definitely no money for college, as I'd found out when I asked Tennessee about it in junior high school. At first he'd laughed, apparently thinking I was kidding. Then, seeing the look on my face, he said, "Well, if you set on it, you better start savin' money now. You know we cain' help you much."

University life didn't look very promising.

Even my brother Herbert jumped in on the conversation. "And what you need wit' college anyhow? Nigger out dere at my job say he got a college degree and he unloadin' trucks right 'longside me."

Instead, I entertained the vague, romantic notion of becoming an artist or hustling pool for a living. I imagined myself a successful comic book illustrator living in New York City or a vagabond pool shark, moving from city to city, custom pool cue in hand, fleecing unsuspecting locals as I toured the country. Not that either my artwork or pool game justified those aspirations. My friend Al Bright was a far superior artist and went on to become a well-known abstract expressionist painter in the Ohio area as well as a professor of art at Youngstown State University. In pool, I was good but inconsistent, certainly nowhere near the level of my sister Cherrie's husband, Billy, or his brother Ray Wallace, whom most considered the best players in town. Not even as good as Vernon Martin, a classmate and baseball teammate with whom Al Bright and I often played. Still, I haunted the pool halls—my search for a satisfactory groove or consistent stroke a reflection of the struggle to come to terms with more serious problems. The most pressing was that I wasn't sure of my own identity, really had no idea who I was.

I'd learned the operative social game by this time and, in most circumstances, was able to affect a cheerfulness and civility that usually camouflaged my real stress, confusion, and inner turmoil: subterfuge, of course, but the public face I maintained was not as deliberately deceitful as that suggested by the unnamed hero's grandfather in Ralph Ellison's *Invisible Man*, "overcome 'em with yeses, undermine 'em with grins, agree 'em to death and destruction." I could not have even feigned that minstrellike guise. Still, in dealing with everyone except my family and closest friends—white or black, students or teachers—I assumed a nonassertive, polite yet formal demeanor that, while affable, did not invite easy familiarity. An attempt to appear collected and impassive even while wracked with self-doubt, it was a kind of cerebral cool that was only tenuously connected to the guile of the truly accomplished yesmen. Many of them had perfected that gamut and attained prime jobs as waiters at exclusive white clubs and restaurants; some were among the elite of Youngstown's "colored" middle class. Nor did it resemble the calculated, coolly objective manipulations of the predators and hustlers who frequented the Brass Rail, Sportoree, Forty Club, or other late night hangouts.

In truth, it involved little pretense. For while ferociously competitive in sports, games of all sorts, I was tentative and painfully self-conscious in many social situations. On the baseball diamond or basketball court I was oblivious to everything but the immediate goal, winning. There was no concern over appearance or the opponent's subjective estimate of my ability or worth. The game determined supremacy. Talent and ability won out. There were no postmortem justifications or excuses—no reexaminations or recountings based on social privilege or predetermined rank. Without those clear-cut, competitive situations, however, I was often lost—floundering hopelessly.

Suspicious of *what* people said, I shifted my focus to *how* they said it. I honed in on askance glances, listened for false tones, watched for pauses and hesitations, and weighed those nuances as methodically as a jazz buff might assay the meaning of the pregnant pauses and silences in a Miles Davis or Ahmad Jamal jazz solo. Bound by some elusive sense of group culpability, I'd cringe with embarrassment and guilt at the raucous buffoonery or drunken impropriety of some black stranger as if his or her behavior were, as the smug expressions of most white observers suggested, truly a personal indictment. Sometimes, inexplicably consumed by an anxiety attack that could thrust me into a cold sweat, I'd panic. I'd sit stone still, frozen by the blank stares of surrounding passengers whose unblinking eyes—like a parliament of owls or one of those eerie paintings where the subject's gaze follows wherever you go—

seemed to shadow my every move. Anticipating their examination
and indictment, I would sit petrified rather than stand and attract
attention. I'd sometimes ride several stops beyond my destination
before mustering enough nerve to rise and submit myself to their
scrutiny. Then, enraged with myself, I'd stomp back to my true destination, like Joseph K. wondering why I was being charged. What
was the crime? Who among those around me was pointing the ac-
cusing finger this time?

It was only after the school year that I began clearing the air and
finding some direction. By the summer of 1956, despite a middling
year at South, I had become one of the area's best basketball players. The reputation was earned in park pickup games more than in
organized play. In those unsupervised, freelance, one-on-one contests I felt liberated. I'd found my niche and, by summer's end, had
built a reputation imposing enough to be invited to the most competitive games with the area's best players. We gathered regularly at
two or three select parks on the south side to challenge one another
and test our games.

It was through contacts made on the basketball court that I met
Aubrey and Steve, two New Yorkers who were enrolled at
Youngstown State University. Neither played on the varsity team
during the time I knew them, but they were tough, streetwise players who had grown up playing at New York City parks. The fact is,
they introduced me to some of the trickery and mind jukes that had
been developed in the city game, where such street legends as Con-
nie Hawkins and Earl Manigault made their reputations. I was immediately impressed by their hip New York attitudes.

The cosmopolitan flair that marked their assertiveness and brim-
ming self-confidence set them apart from any Youngstowners I'd
met, even McKay. Brazenly flouting many of our provincial customs, they mocked our acceptance of the town's narrow behavioral
confines and slyly lampooned the authorities charged with enforcing them.

The comely, mostly naive teenagers who stepped up to serve us at
frozen custard stands or soda pop fountains after a ball game, for
example, were always challenged. The alabaster smiles they flashed
with the initial "And what can I do for you all today?" nearly always
turned crimson after a leering grin and husky "Well, dig it,
baby . . . question is what can we do for you," or even a flirtatious

"Not sure, baby. What did you have in mind?" Aside from testing local girls' innocent, knee-jerk affability with presumptions of intimate invitation, they'd playfully twit store owners and salesclerks who greeted them with superficial largesse.

"Hi, there. Come on in," an overly cheerful clerk would offer. "Best buys in town—we're practically giving things away today."

"Oh yeah," one of them would shout before they walked around the store piling expensive items in their arms, then started for the door.

They'd crack up when the clerk rushed over to intervene. "Wait! Wait a minute. Not so fast, boys. Just kidding, you know," he'd stammer as he retrieved his goods. "Now what can I really do for you?"

They enjoyed pushing buttons that most Youngstowners I knew left untouched. And I marveled as they mischievously pricked the thin surface of Midwestern hospitality and, frequently, revealed its less convivial underside.

It was rare in Youngstown, and some resented their cocky, cavalier manner. For me, however, it signaled the existence of other possibilities; if New York City had shaped their attitudes, I concluded, it was a spot that I'd have to check out. Their disdain for local custom, however, sometimes collided head-on with the town's backwater conventions. Aubrey, for instance, was forcefully removed from the Palace Theater and arrested after refusing to move to the balcony when an usher's cordial invitation was greeted with, "No thanks, I'm perfectly comfortable here."

By the fall, they had become friends, and, perhaps most important, they introduced me to some exciting books by so-called Beat Generation writers as well as a few European authors—existentialist, they called them. They swore those writers would open up an entirely different way of looking at the world. "They'll blow your mind," Steve insisted, "open your eyes to some shit you can't even imagine." As it turned out, they didn't exaggerate the outcome by much.

# 10

## and shine
## swam on

Al Bright and I revived our friendship during the summer between my sophomore and junior years. Not that there had been a rift. It was simply that, since he was a grade behind me, we had seen less of each other during the previous school year. I was caught up in the excitement of the basketball season and the struggle to adjust to a high school social scene that he had yet to confront. Contact was limited to shooting pool after school and a few occasions when we double-dated. But by summer I had passed my driver's test and convinced Tennessee to occasionally trust me with his 1953 Pontiac Chieftain. With a ride and more free time, we began hanging out together again.

Al and I had been fastidious dressers since we reached our teens. The inspiration for me had come from Tennessee and my brother McKay, who was about my size. And since whenever McKay mysteriously disappeared, he left most of his belongings behind, I had access to a wardrobe that most high school students couldn't match. Al's brother, Richard, was also known as a sharp dresser and had influenced him. Attention to the details of dress and hairstyle was something we came upon without even thinking about it.

While we leaned toward a more conservative look in clothes, we had adapted the dapper, marcelled look we'd seen McKay and

Richard wear, not to mention the slickest of the local hustlers and such famous black entertainers and athletes as Jackie Wilson, Sugar Ray Robinson, and Nat King Cole. Al and Richard not only sported waved and straightened "mops," as we called them, but had also started a bootleg hair-processing enterprise in the cellar of their home. I began as a customer in their basement barbershop and, eventually, began helping them cut and straighten hair on weekends—a hazardous undertaking, since Konkolene, a lye relaxer whose ads promised that it could straighten anything, including barbed wire, could inflict serious burns or cause eye damage if not handled properly. A few customers nearly drowned themselves dousing their heads in the cellar's huge washbasin when the concoction got through the protective Vaseline shield and scorched their scalps. The risk was worth it for those of us who aspired to the smooth look that *Ebony* magazine promoted and Negro celebrities from nearly every field flaunted.

The previous summer, both Al and I had worked at a bowling alley and saved enough money to enable us to dress moderately well during the school year. But there was no prospect of work for either of us before we returned to school for my junior year. And as I pointed out to Al, attention to attire was heightened in high school. Even the rebels and roughnecks had their own style. A small group (the so-called greasers), probably influenced by movies such as *The Wild Ones*, with Marlon Brando, or *Rebel Without a Cause*, with James Dean, had donned jeans, black leather jackets, T-shirts with cigarette packs rolled into the sleeves, and had taken to wearing their hair with pompadours in front and ducktails in back. Almost everyone else, however, adapted a relaxed Ivy League look, which we called the Princeton; sweaters, khakis or casual slacks, and white or tan bucks were staples for them. The latter was the style Al and I had affected for a few years, heightening it with sports jackets, Mr. B or tab-collar shirts, ties, and other accessories that gave it a more hip, personal flair. At South, we felt, even more would be required to distinguish ourselves.

What we needed, both agreed, was a hustle, a way of picking up some extra cash to augment our wardrobes.

For us it was an ad hoc social club called the El Doradoes and a raffle that promised to give away a $100 gift certificate. The notion was triggered when we passed a print shop's display window. The array of signs, cards, and tickets caught our attention, and a brief talk with the stout but oddly whispery-voiced owner revealed that raffle tickets were available at a mere $20 per thousand. He never questioned or asked for verification of our club's supposed charitable purpose. We had seen our parents sell tickets for raffles benefiting the church or other causes, so the idea wasn't new to us. Why not form a club, give away a prize, and raise money for ourselves?

Al and I walked back outside to confer. After taking another quick glance at the tickets, we turned, looked at each other, then slapped hands and broke out laughing. It was on. What the hell? No one would be hurt, and some lucky person would get a great gift.

Back at home, we told our parents about our new club, never mentioning that we were the only two members. Shortly afterward, we began leaving home one evening each week under the guise of attending a club meeting. Of course, the "meetings" were usually held at a poolroom where no one from either of our families were likely to appear. By the beginning of the school year, we had purchased tickets that assured the buyer, NEED NOT BE PRESENT TO WIN, and began a hustle that continued into my senior year.

Before starting my second year at South, however, I'd begun reading short stories, poems, and essays by some of the authors Steve and Aubrey had recommended. It started as simply recreation, a way of passing the time when I'd returned exhausted from the basketball courts. Despite my friends' insistence, I never once assumed that any critical revelations would surface. In fact, I initially approached those writers with the same wariness with which I regarded assigned readings of works by Jane Austen and George Eliot (which I had only cursorily perused) or the inexorable wisdom of organized religion.

And although I immediately identified with the disaffection and alienation evoked by J. D. Salinger's *Catcher in the Rye*, Jack Kerouac's *On the Road*, and Allen Ginsberg's long poem *Howl*, for me they didn't provide the insights my friends had guaranteed. Salinger's Holden Caulfield, for instance, must have appealed to nearly every youth who, like myself, was wallowing in his own estrangement and social awkwardness while blaming his predicament on the outside world. For him it was the vulgar and insensitive middle-class world in which he was trapped; for me it was the narrow strictures of race and the hypocrisy of those who ignored or tolerated them. But while those books confirmed that Negroes were not the only ones alienated by the fifties' insistently homogenous culture, they did not offer any solutions. In fact, they seemed unaware of or uninterested in the race issue that bedeviled me.

When I turned to the existentialist writers, however, I was startled by their insights. It took only a few months to realize that they were exploring areas that were crucial to me. They had seemingly penetrated the superficial level of discourse that typified the literature I'd read as well as the views espoused in institutional rhetoric or expressed in most social interactions. Not a difficult task, of course, since sex and racial issues were subjects that rarely surfaced in traditional literature or in polite conversation in Youngstown—particularly if the discussion involved members of different races. Not only did the existentialists acknowledge and address problems similar to those with which I'd been wrestling, but they also hinted at some solutions.

For that reason, the works of Henri Barbusse, Luigi Pirandello, Albert Camus, Franz Kafka, Dostoyevsky, and Jean-Paul Sartre, meager as was my initial exposure, swept over me with a rush that was comparable to that exquisite moment when I'd realized I could regularly drop a twenty-five-foot jump shot touching nothing but net. As if stepping into that magical athletic *zone,* I was suddenly immersed in ideas that seemed to support my own nagging suspicions about the absurdity of the social arrangement. Nearly all of my perceptions suddenly seemed perfectly synchronized, as attuned and on target as if those writers had been reading my mind. I'd discovered a source of external confirmation for my own beliefs. Those writers, particularly Sartre, provided a rationale and context for dealing with an estrangement that I'd previously considered a personal idiosyncrasy.

As important, they led me to expand my own inquiries—move from a narrow personal and racial view to another level. I'd already begun to suspect that in mainstream America segregation and race camouflaged other, deep-seated human concerns, more primordial fears. Sartre and the others seemed focused on that complicated underlying terrain. They engaged issues of freedom, choice, self-determination, identity, and the burden of counterfeit, externally imposed social roles, all of which were related to racial identity and social equality but not limited by them. Their ideas spun and shifted in my head like the colorful bits and pieces of glass and plastic in a kaleidoscope, rearranging themselves, taking new shapes, creating new designs and constructs. In those works I discovered a link to a reality that increasingly loomed as more revealing and valid than the fabricated, polarized racial roles that defined life in Youngstown.

About that time I began jotting down my own thoughts. I never intended for anyone else to read what I'd written and didn't think of it as keeping a journal. I was simply trying to record ideas triggered by my reading or express some of the pent-up emotion that had been unleashed by it. I also tried my hand at poetry and wrote short vignettes about either real or imagined characters who seemed alienated and ostracized. The Shehy madman and Robert, our mysterious socialist boarder, became models for fictional sketches. I tried to combine the surprise endings of the hundreds of *Crypt of Terror* and *Vault of Horror* comic book stories I'd read with the elusive profundity I sensed in Camus's "Myth of Sisyphus" and Sartre's *Being and Nothingness*. Usually, late at night, I'd scratch out the poems or stories in a loose-leaf notebook, then tear out the pages and hide them. I wrote slyly, furtively, hiding the scribblings from everyone. They seemed too revealing of a shadowy personality I wanted to conceal.

I was moving uneasily from the grisly if frivolous intrigues of *E. C.* comic books to the more real if no less disturbing insights of writers who questioned or openly challenged society's complacent assumptions about the nature of social reality. The shift got off to an unsteady start that summer.

Still, I couldn't help feeling that the raffle was a faltering, beginning step in the process, a bit of surreptitious chicanery that, if nothing else, signaled my awareness of the society's duplicity and confirmed my determination to undermine it, exact some justifiable retribution.

That resolve, however, was tested from the outset. On the first day of school, as Al, Carmel, and I began the trek up Hillman Street to South High, we heard that Frank Owens had been killed. He had gone to visit relatives in the South during summer vacation and never returned. He had been felled by a shotgun wound in his back. It shocked us all. And since the circumstances of his death were veiled by mystery and rumor, the entire affair took on sinister overtones. Some said he'd been involved in a fight with a group of teenagers (black or white, depending on who told the story) and had been shot when he tried to walk away. Others insisted he'd been shot by a white farmer while stealing a chicken, a story that, although evocative of Stepin Fetchit and Hollywood's silent-film image of the Negro, held no credence for those who knew Frank. A few contended that the chicken story was a cover-up, that he had been taken to the fields and shot after whistling at a white woman. Emmett Till revisited. It was never confirmed, but considering Frank's brashness, we did not dismiss the latter speculation.

Although we never discovered what had actually happened, during the first few weeks of school we all had to deal with the grim reality of Frank's departure. A mixture of anger and despair throttled the excitement and expectations of the beginning of my junior year. We missed Frank's laughter and vitality, at the same time knew that his aggressiveness and free-spirited approach was a liability for any of us if we made a misstep or forgot where we were. A bit of the South's growing tumult had snaked its way to Ohio.

## III

Autumn arrived under a shroud for me and Al Bright. It was hard to submit to the glee and enthusiasm of teenage revelry when death had brushed that closely. So, even as South's football team began the year with consecutive wins, blanking three opponents and scoring 145 points, and our schoolmates wildly celebrated its success, we languished. Frank's absence hovered like a cloud over the school's merrymaking and jubilance until near winter.

Still, despite my excitement being mostly contained, there was a growing sense of elation and anticipation over the prospects for the coming school year. It was barely recognizable to anyone else, I'm sure, but a seed of confidence had sprouted and was gradually building. However vague, the notion that there was a possibility of eluding the restrictive social role that shadowed me had reared itself. Nothing tangible, you understand; it was still little more than a premonition.

Sports, I concluded, was the most promising pathway for me. It was the area where I'd had most success, and although I'd treated it as mere recreation and taken my prowess for granted, I began to sense that being good was not enough. I had to take it to another level—had to be better than most. Athletes and entertainers, it appeared, were the only Negroes whose individual achievements were recognized by the society. The Brown Bomber, Sammy Davis Jr., Nat King Cole, Sugar Ray, Jackie Wilson, and, a year later, Elgin Baylor would become my role models. And since I couldn't sing a lick and had at least temporarily boycotted sock hops and dances, the basketball court became my stage.

That fall, basketball became an obsession. After school and on most weekends, I spent nearly every available hour working on my game. I dreamed of levitating that extra second and, like Elgin Baylor, hanging just long enough for my opponents to descend as I kissed a bank shot off the glass. I played in the rain, the dark, in December even shoveled snow from the local court on frigid evenings and played wearing gloves. Not because the game was important in and of itself, mind you—at the time, I didn't even consider its long-range value as a possible ticket to college, let alone anything after that. It was, for me, a means to a more short-term goal, a vehicle, I imagined, that might ease me out of the shadows and confer a scrap of the status and the accompanying freedom that I assumed Negro entertainers and sports celebrities enjoyed.

During the fall, I began carrying on an internal dialogue. Lying in bed, practicing, or walking to school alone, I would silently coax, prompt, and exhort myself. Voicing a private self-declaration that, although muted and hushed, was as emphatic and hyperbolic as the frenzied public boasts and assertions that Muhammad Ali would later use to fuel his ego, purge himself of self-doubt, and elevate his performance. You will be the best player in the area, I'd tell myself. Nobody can touch you. You're bad, man. Bad! The greatest. You will score twenty points a game. Every game!

The words, repeatedly intoned, became a personal mantra that caromed about my mind as if chanted by a chorus of giddy cheerleaders.

Now, I'm sure that if overheard, the dialogue would have elicited amused ridicule. I could have easily been mistaken for one of those crazed Negroes who, mistaken for someone else since birth, accede to the fantasy and become unalterably disoriented. We've all seen them aimlessly wandering the streets, eyes glazed, pointing and gesticulating as if engaged in heated discussions with an invisible double—that ubiquitous doppelgänger that society had appended like a deformed Siamese twin. Bizarre and generally laughable, they are the fruit of a quintessential American phenomenon. We regard them with amusement or pity until, as with the Long Island Railroad slayer Colin Ferguson, that enigmatic double materializes, rebels, and, like a real-life Bigger Thomas, monstrously asserts itself.

> DEFENSE ATTORNEY FERGUSON: Are you saying my client, Mr. Ferguson, shot you? (Points to an empty chair behind him.)
> WITNESS: No! I'm saying it was you who shot me.
> DEFENSE ATTORNEY FERGUSON: What? You're saying two people shot you!

Circumstances, of course, had not driven me to such freakishly deadly extremes. But without outside support, the trancelike focus and near self-hypnosis I'd adopted was crucial. I had to exit the dead-in course that I'd been following. If I'd been more attuned to current fads and pop psychology, I would have realized that my self-encouragement technique was not unique. It was, in fact, merely a personal, makeshift version of a motivational approach popularized by Norman Vincent Peale in *The Power of Positive Thinking;* still on the *New York Times* best-seller list after three years, the book had sold over 2 million copies.

In addition to my heady ruminations about success during the coming basketball season, more tangible signs of progress surfaced. The El Doradoes' raffle got off to a better start than either Al or I imagined; truthfully, almost veered out of hand. We had planned on selling tickets ourselves, confining sales to a select circle of friends and family. For a quarter each or $1 for a book of five, we anticipated a modest return. A month after beginning, however, the project had mushroomed.

Not only had our parents enlisted in selling tickets, but some South students and teachers had also volunteered to help our cause. Tickets were being sold at the hospital at which Al's mother worked, at my father's job in the steel mill, and, presumably, to mobsters at Sandy Naples's sandwich shop—even at get-togethers in middle-class white suburbia. By the end of November, we were usually greeted by a dozen or so students who not only returned stubs and cash but also asked for more tickets. At home, our parents were no less diligent. The club and raffle had taken on a life of its own. Unnerved and nearly overwhelmed by its popularity, Al and I nevertheless took up the challenge, continued the deception, and gleefully accepted the windfall. That first year, we didn't even bother giving away a prize. Instead, we lied, telling our parents that a teacher was the winner and convincing South High ticket holders that a steelworker had won. No one questioned us. The next year, we did give away a $50 gift certificate (we'd changed the amount when we ordered a second batch of tickets) to an employee at Republic Steel.

While the charade taxed our ability to create plausible explanations for the club's activities, it provided the monetary source we needed to gild our images. We became frequent customers at several of the best men's shops downtown; draped ourselves in Hickey Freeman and Botany suits and sports coats, Stacy Adams and Florsheim shoes, Van Heusen shirts, silk ties, and cashmere sweaters; added custom-made Eisenhower suits with militarylike waist-length jackets, shirt-suits with French cuffs, covered buttons, and pleated backs, and trousers with dropped belt loops, half-inch seams, and sixteen-inch pegged bottoms from Shylockson's Tailors. We were, at least in our minds, bad as we wanted to be. It was, perhaps, unfair, given the source of our funds, but both Al and I were designated the best dressed in our respective graduating classes.

Increasingly that fall, I began stretching out, often abandoning the pool halls at night to date or, along with Al and other friends, cruise the streets for girls in Tennessee's car, looking for a rap, now, with nearly as much intensity as, on the basketball court, I'd drilled myself in feints and jukes in pursuit of an easy score. Different moves for different grooves. *Searching . . . every whichaway* but, like the Coasters, most often ending with comic defeat. No Boston Blackie or Bulldog Drummond, I brought nothing in. In fact, at that time, a steady girl was not the goal. I was too disoriented—fucked up—for that responsibility. The search was for more immediate, fleeting satisfaction. *"Don't want it all,"* as another song intoned, *"Just want a little bit . . . Just a tiny weenie bit of your love."*

It didn't matter who, black or white, middle or working class, freak or prude. Whether alone on a date, double-dating with Al, or—on those rare occasions when cruising produced something more than snappy repartee with clamorous flirts who laughingly declined our invitations—with some duo bold enough to take up the challenge of a carload of horny athletes, the scenario was most often the same. First, a search for some isolated spot, usually in Mill Creek Park, where, at night, darkened roadside stops and picnic parking areas provided excellent cover. There, the cajoling and imploring began. "Just a kiss, baby. Yeah, that's all. Uummm. Yeah, that's it." Then exploring and pleading. "Just a little bit, baby—don't leave me like this."

Backseat Don Juans locked in a tug of war with not only the immediate object of our desire but also with a host of cultural assumptions and prescriptions that quickened or slackened our ardor as surely as the hands that fought us off or invited further exploration. Good girls don't do it. Some black girls, freer and less inhibited by mainstream mores, might. White girls probably wouldn't, although, unlike most sisters, they would often give lip service to the idea. (I didn't meet a black woman who even admitted knowing the meaning of the word "fellatio" until I reached college, and even then it remained an abstract concept.) And all the while James Brown's entreaty echoed in our minds if not on our lips: *Please, please, please.*

They were hit-or-miss encounters—exciting, sometimes dangerous, as when what we thought was a patrol car pulled up beside my car and directed a spotlight inside as Al sprawled in the backseat with a date and I tried to convince a new acquaintance that if it felt that good it couldn't be all bad. Hastily rearranging our clothes, we sped away. With headlights off, we roared through a stoplight at a busy intersection while exiting the park and grazed one car while barely missing several others. Scared nearly to death that time, we survived.

In December, basketball practice began and my interests shifted. This was to be my year, I'd promised myself. I approached it with an almost religious zeal, blotting out nearly everything else. With several seniors returning, we were expected to have a great year. Anticipation increased when, after its incredible start, the football team faltered, winning only three of its last six games.

After an opening loss to Farrell High, the eventual winners of the Pennsylvania state championship, the basketball team exceeded everyone's expectations except, perhaps, my own. We established the school's longest single-season winning streak with twenty-one straight victories before finally losing in the state regional tournament at Kent State University.

In a game played before more than five thousand fans, including Youngstown's mayor and city council president, our late rally fell short and we were defeated by Akron South. I'd had a miserable first half, scoring only three points. Then, after the intermission, I'd found the groove and hit ten of twelve shots. I was in a bubble, couldn't miss. So was my teammate Bob McMasters, but it was too late. It was a devastating loss for us; left us one win away from the state finals in Columbus and a possible meeting with future pro legend Jerry Lucus and Middletown, the eventual Ohio state champs. Although the team didn't advance as far as I thought we could, I did reach my personal goals. An all-city selection as Youngstown's leading scorer, I'd averaged twenty points a game during the regular season and over twenty-five during the postseason tournament.

The success of our team that year, combined with my own personal accomplishments, thrust me into a spotlight that had its own demands and expectations. Many of the binds that secured my marginal place in the school were loosened. The narrow options were slowly expanding.

Not that the year brought unlimited fulfillment. During the winter I'd developed crushes on two classmates, Jill and Barbara. Jill was a freckled-faced, strawberry blonde whose personality and smile brightened any gathering she attended. One of the most popular girls in school, for me she was the personification of the era's image of the squeaky-clean, carefree-but-innocent, ideal woman. Barbara, while just as ebullient and outgoing, was one of the most beautiful girls in the class. And like most stunning young black women whose appearance attracts a steady stream of admirers, she carried herself with a sophistication that belied her years. Although I became friends with both, the romances that I alternately imagined did not evolve in either instance. With Jill's popularity and visibility, racial taboos would have precluded dating even had she been interested. And while I did date Barbara on a few occasions, I never even got to first base. I was much too unworldly and blundering for someone that socially advanced, someone "far too hip for your dumb ass," as one of my acquaintances bluntly offered.

The social scene, however, was not a total loss. It didn't hurt that local sports writers had warmed to the sobriquet "Marvelous Mel." It had its advantages and rewards. Backseat one-night rendezvous increased, and although they were inspired more by others' initiatives than any artful maneuvering on my part, my self-assurance grew. Toward the end of the school year, events overtook me and the attention forced me out of my social shell, as on my seventeenth birthday, when, after our second tournament victory at South Field House, some fifty classmates, including cheerleaders, showed up at a surprise party at my sister's house. It was an unusual occurrence under most circumstances but, given the era's conventions, probably unique, considering that the mostly white celebrators had ventured into a nearly all-black neighborhood.

By the end of the basketball season, I'd started occasionally dating a sophomore from East High School. A lively brunette of Slavic descent, she had boldly introduced herself before a game at her school earlier in the year. During the spring, without her parents' consent, we arranged to see each other, began a furtive intrigue requiring machinations rivaling those that kept the El Doradoes' raffle afloat. Fired by the thrill of the deception as much as our own ardor, that clandestine, off-and-on affair continued for more than a year. Disclosure was forbidden, so the park and the town's drive-in movies became our meeting places. We spent my prom night in the back row of the West Side Drive-In necking and occasionally laughing at two atrocious B movies. Up at the crack of dawn the following day, I spent most of the morning removing the crumbs, popcorn, and stains of spilled beer and misspent bodily fluids from Tennessee's front seat.

More important than the immediate social benefits, the basketball success had radically shifted my future plans, forced me to reevaluate my fanciful visions of life as an itinerant pool hustler and explore other avenues.

In the spring, South administered aptitude tests for juniors to determine their qualifications for college entry. Future educational plans notwithstanding, it was required, which is the only reason I took it. Even then, I entered the exam room with little preparation and, if possible, less concern. Several weeks later, I was amazed to find that I ranked in the upper first percentile of our class. No doubt Mrs. Smith, my second-grade teacher, would have been shocked. Certainly South High's school administrators were as stunned as I was. They promptly had me repeat the exam.

"Mel, we're really proud of your test scores," Mr. Fleming, the principal, said when he asked me to step into his office a day after the test results were announced. "But there seems to have been some confusion in the scoring. The board asked us to have a select few students retake the examination. Now, I know it's a lot to ask, but would you cooperate with us on this?"

The smile, which always seemed somehow etched over his drooping jowls, was as phony as the reassuring pat on the back that he gave me when I left. The following week, I took the test again. There were only eleven other students present, and the two I talked with afterward had not taken the exam before. It was a very select group.

The results, however, were the same. And having discovered that I was academically suited for college, several schools approached me with scholarship offers before the school year ended. When summer vacation began, I'd been contacted by over a half-dozen colleges. That number doubled during my senior year as insistent alumni recruited me for both baseball and basketball. Most offers came from schools in the immediate Ohio area, but queries came from schools as distant as the University of Kansas, in Lawrence, and Dartmouth College, in Hanover, New Hampshire. The blind alley I'd faced was starting to look like a cross-country superhighway.

At first, my parents reacted to the news with reservation and disbelief. For one thing, they had never really understood basketball. Tennessee loved baseball and had been a big fan of the old Negro League, so he and my mother were often spectators when I played organized baseball. But until South attracted citywide notice by advancing to the regional finals, they seldom attended a basketball game. They couldn't for the life of them figure out why someone would pay anyone's college tuition because they ran up and down the floor throwing a ball through a hoop. By the following year, when they were convinced that the offers were real, not just some white folks' trickery, Katie became my most avid supporter. Whenever my enthusiasm waned or some other option reared itself, she would speak out. "Don't even be thinkin' 'bout nothin' else, boy. You get that education and everything else fall right into place."

The college offers also caught me off guard. A few years earlier, basketball scholarships for Negroes at mainstream schools had been rare. One problem was that many Northern schools that might have offered tuition to Negro athletes had schedules that included games with Southern colleges that still refused to compete against integrated teams. That Dixie tradition could be seen in communities just beyond the Ohio border. About forty miles south of Youngstown, one could still find West Virginia high school districts where interracial sports competition was banned. By the late fifties, however, civil rights protest, integration of more Southern colleges, and the visibility and achievements of such basketball greats as Oscar Robinson, Wilt Chamberlain, and Bill Russell had radically altered the collegiate basketball ranks. Scholarships for Negroes were on the rise. Totally unaware of that trend, I had never even contemplated the option. I was, in fact, completely unprepared for moving on to advanced studies.

Although I'd maintained a high B+ average at South and was a member of the National Honor Society, I had taken few college preparatory courses. I danced through my first two years with only the minimal requirements, spending most of my time in art or shop classes. Advanced science and foreign languages, I'd figured, wouldn't carry much weight in a pool hall. I quickly discovered, however, that attending any college would require filling my senior year schedule with prerequisite academic classes. A full load of history, English, chemistry, physics, geometry, and biology was needed to meet college admission standards. So, while elated at the prospect of college as I ended my junior year, I didn't leave school with the relaxed, unassuming sense of security that some others possessed. My last year at South would not be the carefree finale that most seniors anticipate. Instead, academically, it would be the most demanding year I'd faced in high school.

That summer, I played Class B baseball, practiced basketball, and worked as an assistant recreational director at Volney Rogers Field. Essentially, the job required that I tend the five baseball and softball diamonds, clean the tennis courts, and hand out equipment, while the senior director, a South High teacher, supervised. For a summer job, however, it paid well; I didn't complain. Also, trying to prepare for the full slate of college preparatory courses for which I'd signed up, I read as much as I could. It was during that time that I stumbled across Ralph Ellison's *Invisible Man* and George Schuyler's *Black No More*. I rushed through them that summer, missing much of the underlying meaning, I'm sure. But I thoroughly enjoyed those books, and during the next few years, I'd return to them again and again.

It was a hectic few months, which were made more interesting, if not any easier, by McKay's return home from prison.

# 11

## slippin' and slidin'

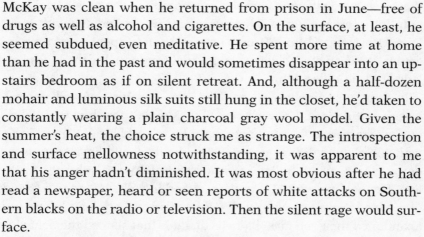

McKay was clean when he returned from prison in June—free of drugs as well as alcohol and cigarettes. On the surface, at least, he seemed subdued, even meditative. He spent more time at home than he had in the past and would sometimes disappear into an upstairs bedroom as if on silent retreat. And, although a half-dozen mohair and luminous silk suits still hung in the closet, he'd taken to constantly wearing a plain charcoal gray wool model. Given the summer's heat, the choice struck me as strange. The introspection and surface mellowness notwithstanding, it was apparent to me that his anger hadn't diminished. It was most obvious after he had read a newspaper, heard or seen reports of white attacks on Southern blacks on the radio or television. Then the silent rage would surface.

"Look at this crap, man," he'd rant, as if talking to himself. "Whitey is stone crazy. Jive crackers throwing bottles and eggs at black children. Why do they take it? Why?"

Initially, his barely contained anger didn't affect our relationship. A wink or approving nod would sometimes offer a hint of reluctant recognition of my success in sports and prospects for college. He didn't say much, however, and I could feel his loathing for the white world into which I was being drawn. For a month or so we avoided the inevitable clash. Instead, when I wasn't playing basketball or baseball, reading, or otherwise occupied at a drive-in theater, we sparred over a checkerboard in the summer heat, capturing each other's men with flourish, brandishing them as if we had snatched pieces of an opponent's armor and exposed vulnerable flesh. Two siblings on disparate courses, we juked and jockeyed for position even as we struggled to remain on the neutral ground that separated our paths. As if by a silent mutual agreement, we confined our conversations to safe topics such as sports and jazz, and listened to the avant-garde bebop albums he had brought home.

He'd tried to introduce me to the sounds of Dizzy Gillespie, Charlie Parker, and other bebop pioneers before he left. But in my early teens, I'd recoil. Reared as I was on rhythm and blues and bombarded with the bubble-gum sounds of Youngstown radio, it was impregnable to me, hard as Chinese trigonometry. Since then—although much more attuned to the cooler sound of the Modern Jazz Quartet, Miles Davis, even the West Coast sound of Jerry Mulligan—I'd come to terms with bebop. I was beginning to pick up on the accelerated riffs and complex harmonies, so the music became a point of reference for us. That summer, I was inundated with Prez, Dizzy, Bird, and Clifford Brown as McKay and I spent more time together. We even stumbled onto a mutual fondness for the blues ballads of Little Willie John.

In July, he somehow discovered that despite frequent dates I wasn't getting laid. I never knew how. Maybe I just had that delirious sex-starved look. I do know that I hadn't told him I was seeing a white chick who didn't put out. The ridicule would have been thunderous. Anyway, he pulled me aside and offered to solve the problem. He took me with him to Warren and introduced me to a friend of a friend. Seven or eight years older than me, she had long since abandoned the good girl / bad girl dictates that shaped the behavior of most teenagers I knew. I can't remember a word that we said to each other, only that we laughed and howled, and that an hour or so after we met she quickly laid my sexual anxiety to rest.

I saw her only twice before McKay took off on another of his periodic journeys. In his absence, I returned to my covert drive-in rendezvous; but despite impassioned entreaties and the fact that we often rounded third base and streaked toward home, we never quite made it all the way. I was still drawn to what had become a kind of frivolous pastime—an erotic game in which we pushed ourselves to the limit of endurance, then breathlessly backed off at the culminating moment. It was frustrating, but the stealth added an irresistible excitement. Small wonder that a Little Richard hit became our song: *Slippin' and a slidin', peepin' and a hidin' . . . Ain't gon be no fool no mo'.*

More important in the long run, during that time Charles Petrovich, a *Youngstown Vindicator* sportswriter, informed me that I was one of two local players selected by Detroit Tiger scouts to participate with players from Ohio and Michigan in an intersquad game at Tiger Stadium. Andy Kosco, or Pudgy, as he was called then, was the other Youngstown player selected. A week or so later we drove to Detroit, spent the night in a downtown hotel, and, the next morning, reported to the stadium. It was the first time I played in a major-league ballpark and I was, of course, awed.

I spent the first few hours on the field dreaming about the fact that many of my sports idols had run those same base paths, stood in the same batter's box. Despite my overenthusiasm, I was fairly impressive in the intersquad game. After making a shoestring catch on a low drive to left field, I threw a runner out at third. I also walked and hit a line-drive single to center field in three at bats. Andy had an even better day. He hit a towering fly ball to the track in center field and tripled, barely missing a home run, on a drive that hit the top of the fence near the 370-foot marker in right center field.

Shortly afterward, we were informed that the Tigers were interested in signing us. Andy, whose power display had definitely impressed the scouts, was offered a bonus and the opportunity to begin at a higher level than I. Later he joined the Tigers' farm system and went on to play in the majors for Detroit, Oakland, and the New York Yankees. I decided to wait until the next year before making a commitment.

I had some doubts about the situation. Foremost was the tumult in the South. Assuming you made the cut, playing minor-league baseball in the late fifties meant earning about $200 a month and traveling on a team bus through backwater Southern towns with segregated accommodations. Since Detroit had yet to bring a black player to the majors, the prospects for quick advancement were not great either. My faith in the organization was further damaged after we'd dressed and prepared to leave the stadium. Charles Petrovich was talking with one of the team scouts when an All-Star player whom I'd always admired walked up. He spoke to the scout briefly before turning to leave. When I asked for an autograph, he looked at me, frowned, then hurriedly walked away. I tried to shrug it off, but I never forgot that incident.

Despite the snub and my reservations, I was floating on air when we returned to Youngstown. It didn't matter that I wasn't sure about trying my hand at baseball or that I had no idea which college I might attend. The options were there. It was my call. Opportunities had increased so quickly that it would have been easy to forget the questions that had nagged me during the past few years. And I might have done so if I hadn't stumbled onto Ilse Aichinger's short story "The Bound Man" a few weeks after returning from Detroit.

The tale mesmerized me. It was as if I had been fumbling in a dark room, fingering objects whose shapes, while nearly discernible, remained elusive and disconnected. Then, as if suddenly illuminated, they assumed recognizable definition.

The story opens when a man awakes to find himself mysteriously bound from head to toes: apparently he has been mugged and robbed. Since he has limited mobility, he accepts his condition, rises, and stumbles off toward town. A carnival owner who passes by spies him and, intrigued by his lurching movements, recruits him as a performer. The bound man becomes an immediate hit. Audiences flock to the carnival and he becomes its most revered act. Even though he is aware that he could remove the ropes, his success and the approval of the crowds lead him to remain bound. He even sleeps in the ropes. Eventually, however, the crowds begin to doubt that anyone could move with such dexterity and ease while confined. Gradually they turn on him, and in order to protect himself, he finally slips out of the ropes. Frightened and infuriated, the carnival's owner, its performers, and the bound man's former fans form a mob and run him out of town.

Although open to all manner of interpretation, for some reason that tale sparked my initial understanding of racism as well as my own identity crisis. It suddenly occurred to me that, as with Aichinger's hero's binds, racial stereotypes were dictating my behavior. They were confining me as surely as the ropes that restricted him, and would, unless I could somehow discard them and risk alienating almost everyone, continue shaping my identity.

The dilemma was that whether you resisted and struggled against racial boundaries or accepted them (as the bound man had) and worked within them, their legitimacy was confirmed. And in Youngstown during the fifties, few other options were offered. Generally Negroes were restricted to one of two choices: defying the racial stereotypes either by actively protesting or by boldly flaunting them—in essence, abandoning mainstream society by becoming a troublemaker or so-called bad nigger; or quietly accepting the social arrangement, becoming a silent accomplice, or quasi-Tom, and reaping whatever leftover rewards the situation might offer. Both reactions were generally applauded and greeted with gracious smiles by nonblack spectators in that carnival atmosphere. If defiance or protests moved too far outside the black community and threatened mainstream spectators or the status quo, however, swift reprisals could be expected. Either way, the binds remained intact.

A select few, of course, fostered the illusion of respecting the restraints but managed to loosen them, learned to work within them and stealthily infiltrated the mainstream professional world or opened their own businesses. If they were too proficient, however, although they might attain some grudging respect, their achievements, like those of Aichinger's hero, elicited jealousy, fear, and anger from whites as well as blacks. The mainstream world's uppity Negroes, those who established alliances in the white world and even commanded a bit of reluctant esteem in that quarter, were the same folks the black community ridiculed as snobbish or "dicty" niggers since, by securing an economic foothold and partially escaping the vise of segregation, they had allegedly abandoned the race.

Reading Aichinger's story that summer led me to begin earnestly scrutinizing my own behavior. It wasn't long before I realized that under the guise of conforming to acceptable standards, I'd allowed racial stereotypes to shape my conduct. Confining my assertiveness to the basketball court and baseball diamond, I'd subdued a temperament that was, without outside influence, reserved—softened my voice, contained my laughter, affected a humility that neared self-effacement. I'd even eschewed dancing and, in public, wouldn't touch a watermelon or a piece of fried chicken. Consciously countering stereotypes at every turn, in effect, I'd been ducking and dodging someone else's fantasy. As a result, I'd turned myself into a no-dancing, non-watermelon-or-chicken-eating beige replica of the bland, dispassionate caricatures that peopled mid-fifties TV sit-coms. In attempting to avoid the stereotype, I'd actually allowed it to shape and mold my actions as surely as if, like Tennessee's grand-parents, I'd been raised in bondage.

Coming to terms with that insight, of course, embarrassed and angered me. But it also accelerated a transformation that would continue at least until I'd completed college. Most immediately, however, it very nearly led me to accept the views of my brother McKay, who, when he returned late that summer, announced that while in prison he'd become a Black Muslim.

I was only vaguely aware of the Muslims. They had opened a mosque in Youngstown in the early fifties and their members could occasionally be seen selling *Muhammad Speaks* on street corners. At the time, however, I regarded them as ironic, even comical fig-ures—something like stumbling upon a group of arrogant peddlers decked out in secondhand tuxedos. Still, it wasn't easy to ignore their defiance and challenging accusations, their rodlike posture and austere appearance—white shirts, black bow ties, and impos-ing, if often threadbare, dark suits. Even their closely cropped hair, a rarity at a time when marcelled mops or slicked-back hair coated with Murray Pomade were the fad, added a more serious if menac-ing note. For reasons as superficial as my distaste for bean pies and unwillingness to give up pork, however, I'd never inquired about their beliefs. Like most other Youngstown Negroes, I'd dismissed them as a radical separatist group that worshiped a black God and advocated violence.

I'm not sure why McKay broke his silence that summer. But I've always suspected that he saw a change in me, realized that despite the favorable prospects, I'd been shaken by something. I'm not even exactly sure of what led up to our talk. I do know that it was a scorching August afternoon and that we had been drinking lemon-ade and listening to Charlie Parker, Walter Bishop, and Roy Haynes jamming on "I Get a Kick out of You," and that my forearm stuck to the dining room table's moist red-and-white oilcloth covering each time I picked up my glass.

"Look, my man," he said, "you got a chance to do a whole lotta things. In fact, it seems like you can do whatever you want. So, tell me, why do you bother hanging out with all these honkies? Don't you know you dealing with the devil? You get involved with their lies and trickonology, they'll turn you around—take you down with them. And I guarantee you, they goin' down. We been hoodwinked, my man, listening to a bunch of Uncle Toms who want us to integrate, join the white man on his sinking ship. You can't trust them or those redneck devils, no matter how much they smile in your face. You need to cut 'em loose, bro, get down with your own people. It's brothers like you who can make a difference, you dig."

Before I could even interrupt, lodge an objection, he continued. "Let me tell you something about the Honorable Elijah Muhammad . . . ."

For the next hour or so, McKay glibly laid out the Muslim philosophy and cosmology. Pacing the floor and, as if warding off some unseen adversary, accentuating every point with abrupt jabs into the noonday air, he rattled off the Muslim doctrine as deftly as he'd reenacted Poe's poetry. The edgy con man's glint in his eyes nearly obscured by a fervor that rivaled Reverend Rose's vehement hellfire sermons, he passionately explained Mr. Muhammad's interpretation of the Negroes' journey into ignorance and bondage. And since I'd heard little of it before, he had my complete attention. Drawn in by a graphic recitation of the history of America's repression of blacks and the repeated declaration "You don't even know who you are! They brainwashed you, my man," I was initially hooked. He had either read my mind or, at the very least, somehow figured out what was on it. No matter. I was as attentive as the fawning parishioners at Mt. Carmel Church. Had I been more demonstrative, I might well have begun shouting, "Amen! Tell it like it is!"

Dazzled by the initial rap, I nodded in agreement and listened intently as he switched to the particulars of the Black Muslim faith. Their insistence on a puritanically strict moral code seemed extreme, even for the 1950s, but the emphasis on the value of self-reliance and independence and outspoken advocacy of self-defense when under attack (a welcomed alternative, as far as I was concerned, to Martin Luther King Jr.'s nonviolent stance) seemed sensible enough to me. So did my brother's presentation of their view of the inequities blacks had suffered during slavery and the injustices they still endured in America. I was ripe for the message and, at times, hung on his every word.

Never having heard of Malcolm X, I didn't realize that McKay was echoing much of his colorful, evocative speech. And when my brother voiced the now famous quip "We didn't land on Plymouth Rock; Plymouth Rock landed on us," I was astounded. For me, the metaphor immediately struck a cord, connected with the bound-man allegory. The idea of black Americans having been mugged and bound by America's racial policies was still ricocheting through my mind like a laser beam; Malcolm's metaphor seemed to illuminate and confirm the insight. My eyes lit up as I stood and slapped McKay's outstretched hand, smiling at our shared recognition and appreciation.

As he continued, however, the spiel began losing its impact. When he shifted from the reality of Negroes' condition and began outlining the religious and racial dogma that undergirded the Muslim's outlook, my nods of approval halted and the smile that had greeted his every word faded into a blank stare. For me, the credibility gap began with his discourse on the Freemasons, a secret international organization whose membership, he argued, included the most powerful politicians and financial power brokers in the world.

"Remember when I told you about stark reality," he asserted. "Well, let me pull your coat. Most people don't know it . . . I didn't know myself until recently. But the reality is, the Masons rule the world. Not just this country . . . the entire world. You dig it! That's about to end though. You see, the Masons are ruled by the devil. But as powerful as they are, they still only have thirty-three degrees of knowledge. You can check it out. Ask 'em if you want." He paused then, smiling at the confused look that settled on my face.

"You do know that sum total of a circle is three hundred and sixty degrees, right? In fact, the total sum of anything you look at is three hundred and sixty degrees, and that includes knowledge. What you probably don't know is that only Allah, the God of Islam, possesses that full, three-hundred-and-sixty-degree range of knowledge. That knowledge was passed onto us, you dig. God, a black man, came to America and passed the word to the Honorable Elijah Muhammad. The devil's time is over, my man. You see the devil, the white man, uses Masonry to control the world . . ."

He continued. But I don't remember exactly what he said after that. I was still reeling at the idea of knowledge having three hundred and sixty degrees.

The gist of it, however, was that among the original humans, who were black and founded the holy city of Mecca, arose a group of twenty-four scientists or wise men. One of those scientists created the tribe of Shabaaz, the ancestors of the American Negro. Among that tribe, about sixty-six hundred years ago, Yacub, a precocious, troublemaking youth with an unusually large head, was born. He had graduated from all of the nation's universities by age eighteen, establishing a reputation for both his discontent and his ability to scientifically breed races. When he began preaching in the streets, convincing followers to abandon the religion of Islam, he and his converts were exiled. The vengeful big-head scientist decided to create a race of bleached devils who would torment his former tribe. Although Yacub died at age 152, he had trained assistants and left instructions for his followers to continue his work, and after eight hundred years of selective breeding, a race of blond, blue-eyed devils had been created. Six hundred years later, these white devils returned to the mainland. The havoc they created turned what had been a peaceful paradise into a living hell. The black race rounded them up and marched them off to Europe, where they lived in caves as savages.

After two thousand years, Allah sent Moses to civilize them and bring them out of the caves. They were to rule the world for six thousand years, and during that time, some of the original black race would be enslaved in North America to allow them to understand the true nature of the white devils. But the original black race was to birth a wise and knowledgeable man with infinite power, in the twentieth century. This mighty God, according to the Honorable Elijah Muhammad, was W. D. Fard. Half black and half white so that he could move among both races, Fard journeyed to Detroit, where in 1931 he gave Allah's message to Mr. Muhammad. With Allah's divine guidance, Mr. Muhammad was instructed to save North America's lost nation of Islam from Yacub's race of white devils.

"Time is here, my man. Right now," McKay declared. "This definitely is not the time to be romancing the devil. Yeah, I know they been courting you, offering you this and that, promising you nearly everything you can think of, right? Hey, take advantage of it if you can, don't be no fool. But you better be careful. They're lying, my brother. It's a stone trick! Don't let 'em dupe you."

By that time, I sat staring wide eyed at McKay, so stunned by Yacub's outrageous tale that I merely nodded weakly.

"Hey, man, be cool. It's hard to digest. I know. You're as suspicious of this religious thing as I was. I'm just trying to hip you to something real before it's too late. A year ago it didn't make sense to me either. Nobody could've told me I'd be in this bag, joining the Nation of Islam. But think about it. It's genuine, my man. One way or another you're going to have to deal with these white devils."

His face lit up with that familiar, cocky hustler's grin, McKay turned off the phonograph midway through one of Bird's explosive riffs and turned to leave. "I got to split," he said, "but give it some thought."

I must have sat there for fifteen minutes, not moving a muscle, sweat dripping from my chin onto my T-shirt. I was thinking, all right, but not about the validity of the Muslims' bizarre theology, or demonology, as Malcolm X would call it in the autobiography that I read years later. In truth, I'd shut down just after the "big-headed scientist" was introduced. I avoided the urge to disrupt McKay's recitation with a cynical rebuttal by focusing on a more somber childhood memory that had been buried in my subconscious.

When I first began playing softball, there was a house across the street from Grant school yard in which an attractive black woman— a single mother, I believe—lived with her son. Each morning, if it was warm enough, she wheeled him out onto the porch and left him there. His emaciated body was dwarfed by a head that was more than twice the normal size, and being kids, we all laughed and joked about him, called him the "big watermelon-head boy." (I would later discover that he had encephalitis.) It was only after I'd had to retrieve a ball from under his porch and was forced to take a closer look at him that I parted ways with the hecklers. One look into his pained, distended eyes rid me of any impulse to make fun of him. Embarrassed and contrite, I smiled weakly and slunk back to the ball field. For the next few years, until he succumbed to the disease, I went out of my way to smile and wave at him whenever he appeared. Still, I could never erase the guilt.

That reverie was probably what kept me from laughing aloud at the Yacub tale. At first I wasn't sure if McKay had been serious. The tale reminded me of an imaginative mix of comic book fantasy and one of my mother's hoodoo stories or, perhaps more pointedly, a blend of Buck Rogers science fiction and Charlton Heston's improbable Cinemascope parting of the Red Sea, which I'd witnessed the previous year at a downtown theater. What shocked me, kept me sitting there after McKay left, was his seemingly unconditional acceptance of the mythology. Still, during the last few weeks before my senior year at South, the hodgepodge of ideas and assertions he introduced remained on my mind.

If nothing else, the Muslims' appraisal of the Negroes' plight affirmed my own assessment and heightened my sense of frustration and outrage at American bigotry. I had, for instance, not even considered how thoroughly the curse of blackness had been accepted by Negroes themselves, how we had internalized mainstream America's color hierarchy—pridefully basking at the happenstance occurrence of a light complexion or, belligerent and resentful, railing against our own darkness. McKay's exposition of the Muslims' dismissal of the civil rights movement's turn-the-other-cheek attitude also rang true for me.

It reinforced my instinctual sense that, despite any immediate gains, passive protests finally only confirmed blacks' subordinate status and lack of empowerment in the eyes of most mainstream Americans. This was, after all, a country that lavished respect on those who carved out their own destinies. Our heroes, whether outlaws or philanthropists, robber barons or benevolent shapers of the New Deal, nearly always assertively *took* what they needed. With that traditional esteem for rugged individualism, although we might sympathize with those who scrape and bow, beg for handouts, we rarely respect them. Gandhi's tactics had a chance for lasting effect in a country where protesters vastly outnumbered colonizers, could even bring the country to its knees. But in America, with blacks outnumbered ten to one, I was convinced it would only produce marginal concessions, the "table crumbs" that the Muslims disdainfully rejected.

As civil rights protests mounted in the South, although I admired the participants' courage and dedication, the thought of joining a sit-in or freedom ride never occurred to me. Even the thought of asking someone for permission to join them when it was obvious that you were unwanted was untenable for me. I couldn't imagine subjecting myself to abuse at the hands of Southern racists without some attempt at retaliation or, at the very least, making immediate plans to exact revenge.

Despite those points of agreement, the Muslims' program simply did not work for me or, apparently, for McKay either. (Several months later he had slipped back into former habits, discarding the sect's spartan apparel and resuming his old ways.) Since I had already severed all ties to organized religion, the Muslims' theological doctrine held no appeal for me. The allure of a black God was not enough of an inducement. Moreover, I came to see the Muslim view as a thinly veiled adaptation of the same racist fabrications that fueled mainstream bigotry. It had been reversed, turned inside out, but it was the same sham that had been used to repress and dehumanize Negroes for centuries.

Still, it was as odd, then, seeing the American media condemning the Muslims as racists as it was ironic, some forty years later, seeing white Americans react with astonishment and bitter, self-righteous accusations after a black attorney supposedly played the race card. Race was, after all, nothing more than a game whites had instituted, a kind of three-card-monte hustle in which, with a charlatan's sleight of hand, they invariably chose the white king or queen while Negroes always selected the black knave.

Now, one might assume that with all these miraculous insights, I'd have found some solution to the problem. The fact is, I was right back where I'd begun, faced with the same dilemma. Starting school in September, I decided to stop thinking about it and simply wing it, follow those instincts that, despite not unearthing any solutions, had served me fairly well in the past.

My status as a jock, a popularity derived, in part, from an insistently conciliatory personality, along with the influences of the blues, the heartland's Pollyanna pop culture, cool jazz and bebop, hoodoo, existentialism, the Black Muslims, America's pioneer spirit, and blacks' larcenously distrustful regard for mainstream society, had produced a rather bizarre admixture. And despite any external resemblance to an all-American black boy with a bright future, I was struggling to unite all those disparate influences. When I entered my senior year at South my mind was swirling with unanswered racial inquiries and ontological platitudes, one foot planted in the heartland's supersanguine reality, the other entrenched in the dark suspicions and intrigues of the fifties black world. Despite a heavy academic load and the need for some fancy high-stepping, I would dance through the year with much more freedom than I expected.

That course was made easier when I discovered that by virtue of athletics or the interest of college recruiters or the sudden recognition of my academic potential, I'd been granted preferential treatment. It was sometimes embarrassing. Caught in the men's room while smoking a cigarette with several other students, for instance, I was told to go to my next class, while the others were reprimanded. And later, busted at lunchtime in the off-limits poolroom adjacent to the school, I was ignored while my three companions were marched back to be punished. Such incidents didn't increase my popularity among those friends who didn't share my newly discovered immunity. But like it or not, in the eyes of most teachers and school administrators I'd become a kind of golden boy.

At other times, the favoritism was confusing, as when, Mr. Moore, an assistant faculty advisor to the student council, seemed to take me under his wing and lose track of who I was. I'd been elected president of the council, and early in the year, during a discussion about an upcoming sock hop, I argued that anyone in the class should be able to buy tickets, whether with a date or alone. Mr. Moore was adamantly opposed and, when pressed, pulled me aside. In a conspiratorial tone, he explained that *we* had to assure that not too many of *them* came to the dance by *themselves*. Trouble, you know. *They* might want to dance with the wrong people. Although he wasn't explicit, never actually identified "we" and "them," the meaning was clear enough. I was, of course, not opposed to being included in this elite "we" category. But something was awry. (Who did he think I was, some turncoat house Negro?) Since I had no other recourse, I submitted. But whenever I was on the door collecting tickets at a dance, a required duty for council members, and a single black guy appeared, I'd advise, "It's couples only, you know. But if you step up with one of the other guys out there, that would be a couple. I'd have to let you in." Moreover, I went out of my way to dance with every one of *them* when the possibility arose.

Despite that and a few other similar encounters, I soon realized that I'd unwittingly stumbled into a strange new twilight zone where the racial lines of demarcation faded and the rigid partition that separated black and white life had been partially lowered. I was, of course, not the only one. I didn't know the others, however, since most were part of Youngstown's insistently insular black bourgeois class. Most belonged to a small group of professionals, municipal appointees, teachers, and small business owners; the majority kept as far away from the city's Negro working class (where my family was firmly entrenched) as real estate agents and the city's boundaries would allow. Among the more visible were the city's half-dozen or so policemen. A few of them could regularly be seen sipping coffee or eating in one of the downtown restaurants that was off limits to ordinary Negroes. Some insisted, however, that they paid a heavy debt for the privilege.

Assigned primarily to black sections of town, their work didn't bring them in contact with many white citizens, so they rarely arrested them. Charged mostly with keeping Youngstown's rowdiest Negroes in tow, some had quickly established reputations for the vigor they brought to their jobs. One or two, known for the excessive force they exhibited when corralling malingerers on East Federal Street and in the Nest, were despised by most Negroes. While their enthusiastic deployment of street justice ingratiated them to the powers that be, when off duty they were seldom welcomed in the black community. Nor were they thrilled to see members of their families associating with Negro underclass upstarts who were too low on the social scale or, for that matter, too dark on the color spectrum. Youngstowners still talk about one of the city's Negro finest who, discovering that his daughter was dating a working-class boy whose dark-chocolate skin didn't pass the paper-bag color test, handcuffed him to a pole and whipped some sense into his head.

Fortunately my entry into the racial twilight zone was not dependent on any conspiratorial alliances with whites and didn't require my exacting any penance from blacks. Apparently my only obligation was to continue playing basketball and play it well. To that end, gratuities were readily extended. Since my full academic load required taking a course during what should have been the study hall period that athletes regularly used for team practice, for example, my physics teacher, Mr. Wiggins, allowed me to skip his class during the basketball season if I appeared for ten minutes of special tutoring during lunch period each day. His assistance and the cooperation of other teachers assured that I received all A's in my senior year.

While our football team raced to a perfect record of eight wins and no losses (the first since 1929 and the stock market crash), I began exploring my newly discovered latitude. There were student council sock hops and parties with council members, Honor Society dinners and parties, as well as invitations to small get-togethers with white students whom I'd met in our yearbook staff or Rotary Club meetings. I usually declined the latter invitations since, most often as the only Negro presence, I still sensed some awkwardness about the situation. After the basketball season, the activities continued with picnics and year-end dinners to celebrate the year's accomplishments. These social interactions with white students proved illuminating.

Confined to a nearly all-black environment, I'd found it easy to lump all whites into a negative, monolithic whole, even consider my brother's assessment and condemn the entire race as evil oppressors or, as he'd put it, "blue-eyed devils." The urge to wrap up all of my personal and social problems like a bundle of soiled clothes and quickly launder them with a dose of racial accusation was tempting. But although I never deluded myself into thinking that I'd been totally accepted, that year's foray across the tracks altered my view. I soon discovered that the students I cavorted with were not the malevolent racists I'd sometimes imagined.

Naturally, there were some—most often, those with the least ability, intelligence, or self-esteem—who eagerly embraced the idea of Negro inferiority and made their feelings evident. Most, however, were simply guileless teenagers, as much confounded by the era's conservative, conformist views as I.

It was most clearly evidenced through my friendship with Kathy, a senior classmate who served on the yearbook staff with me. Except for Al Bright, she was one of only a few South High students with whom I shared any personal feelings. Bright, serious, and extremely sensitive, she seemed as leery of the insistent hoopla as I was. I never saw her outside of class or yearbook meetings, but, perhaps drawn by some shared sense of alienation from the overzealous optimism that prevailed, we grabbed every moment we could to talk to each other. The friendship evolved enough for me to ask her to read and discuss a few of the stories I'd written—a major step, since no one had seen any of my writing until that point. Her encouragement and our continued discussions helped fire my interest in writing. That friendship lasted well into our freshman year at college as we continued corresponding after she entered Kent State University.

What separated me from Kathy and other white students was the privileges they had enjoyed since birth; by that time they'd accepted them as part of the natural order. They were rarely questioned. But the silent collusion no longer shocked me. After all, despite feeling some guilt, I hadn't insisted on being punished when the truant officer busted my buddies in the poolroom. I'd learned from firsthand experience that it wasn't difficult to abide a rigged deck when the cards were stacked in your favor.

That insight didn't solve anything. Despite the preferential treatment, there were numerous reminders. My friend and I, for instance, were still ducking and hiding, our dates confined to drive-in trysts and backseat moonlit conversations in Mill Creek Park. And even the attempt to affect some slight cultural change by switching the records played each morning in the auditorium (a student council responsibility) was stonewalled. Besides substituting Little Willie John's version of "Fever" for Peggy Lee's, I'd carefully "misplaced" all of Pat Boone's recordings, substituting the original releases by Fats Domino and Little Richard, and even slipped some current rhythm-and-blues tunes by the Moonglows and Spaniels into the morning mix before some teachers realized that things were getting a bit too funky. The raucous finger popping was soon stilled when Pat Boone's white-bucked mimicry was returned. The attraction of imitation black life was irresistible as well as safe.

Outside of school, Al Bright and I still hung out, regularly shooting pool and occasionally double-dating and cruising for girls. Determined to end my exile from black nightlife, I joined him once or twice for a night at the New Elms Ballroom, which was leased to Negroes for an evening every month or so; those dances featured such headline acts as Ray Charles and Sam Cooke. It was there that I first saw and became a lifelong fan of James Brown.

The basketball season was, of course, the key time of the year for me. Although I hadn't eliminated the thought of trying minor-league baseball, I was leaning toward college and knew that the offers that had been dangled were largely dependent on my performance during my senior year. Pressure was increased since, despite losing our center and best rebounder, Buddy Smallwood, and our second-best scorer, Bob McMasters, we were expected to have a great season. We did well, finishing with eighteen wins and five losses and going nearly as far in the state tournament as we had the previous year. During the regular season, I averaged nearly twenty-four points a game, but my average dropped in the tournament when opponents smothered me with zone defenses. On a team level, it was a disappointing year.

College recruiters, however, were not disappointed. I was again the city's scoring leader. And, in addition to making the all-city team, I was an all-state selection. After the season, several more scholarships were offered. With my mother's prompting, I decided that baseball could wait, and during the spring, I visited a half-dozen schools. By mid-April I had narrowed my options down to University of Pittsburgh, Colgate University, and Dartmouth College. Although Pittsburgh had a more competitive basketball team, it was much too close for me. It would have been like staying at home, and although uncertain about many other things, I knew that I had to get away from Ohio. In addition, the University of Pittsburgh offer, as I understood it, was a straight-out athletic scholarship, dependent on my playing basketball. At Dartmouth and Colgate the scholarships were academic grants, which meant I had only to maintain a high grade average. Less pressure, I felt. Dartmouth, I finally decided, was not only too distant but also much too isolated. Finally, Colgate was the choice.

After I received word, in the spring, that my SAT scores were satisfactory, the pressure was off. Assured of excellent grades in all of the college preparatory courses I'd taken and confident that I would again be hired by the Parks Department for a much-needed summer job, I was finally able to join the other graduating seniors in a wild celebratory spree that lasted until the final days of school. Parties and picnics dominated those last two weeks, and during that time I forgot about the racial inequities that had haunted me at South. Even missing the senior prom and spending an evening watching two gory horror movies through a steamy windshield at the drive-in with my friend didn't bother me.

I would be leaving South High near the top of my class as an all-state athlete with a prestigious War Memorial Scholarship to one of the country's best private colleges, and if that didn't work out, there was still a chance to play professional baseball. The social schism that divided Youngstown had not disappeared, but during the last few weeks of high school, I nearly forgot about it. I was headed for a less provincial environment, a university atmosphere where, I was certain, reason would prevail and the petty annoyances of race would fade under the light of higher education.

Katie and Tennessee, along with my sisters and McKay, who had returned from Chicago, attended my graduation ceremonies. And if my father seemed bemused and somewhat in awe of the procession, my mother had never appeared as radiant and proud. I not only was the first of her sons to graduate high school but also would be the first of their children to attend college. For a moment or two, even McKay relaxed the impervious shield or hipster mask that typically cloaked his emotions and pulled me into his arms.

"You did it, my man. I don't know how you put up with these hypocrites all this time, but you did it. You got over." It was the first time my brother had ever expressed unqualified admiration for me or my achievements. Later that evening he took me out for a drink; I'd rarely seen him let his guard down that much and, after we went our separate ways that evening, would rarely feel that close again.

I left South floating on a cloud. A local athletic celebrity, I'd earned the admiration of my classmates, certainly of my family, and was convinced that my reputation and penetration of the race barrier would guarantee me some access to the perks I assumed came with the territory. Within two weeks, I'd been brought back down to earth.

When I inquired about my application for a Parks Department job, I was informed that I'd been turned down. All of the summer jobs for students had been taken. Since my parents had already told me that they could offer only minimum financial aid for college, I was desperate for a summer job to insure that I wouldn't arrive at Colgate penniless. I immediately went to the unemployment office seeking another job. After a week, a spindly, middle-aged clerk matter-of-factly informed me that farmwork was the only thing they could offer. If I was interested, all I need do was report to a designated site downtown, join the itinerant laborers who gathered there, and ride out to the bean fields. A truck would pick us up at

6:00 A.M. each morning. "Bean pickers can earn a good living," she assured me. "The pay is twenty-five cents a bushel, you know."

Memories of Tunica's cotton fields immediately flashed through my mind—endless rows of cloudlike white fluff and, scattered throughout the fields, hunched like contorted scarecrows, dark figures with long burlap sacks draped over their shoulders. I couldn't contain myself; I laughed in her face.

"Is there something funny?" she asked incredulously.

"Yes, you bit—," I started to say, then cut myself short. I walked out—miraculously, I later thought—without pointing out where she might put her bushel of beans.

That summer I finished reading Jean-Paul Sartre's *Being and Nothingness*, did odd jobs for my father and other family members, played for the Buckeye Elks, an all-black team in the city's AA Baseball League, and practiced basketball. I often played with Youngstown University team members and scrimmaged against opponents such as Dusquesne University All-American Tom Stith in pickup games in Youngstown as well as in the Hill district of Pittsburgh. For the first time I got a sense of how tough college basketball might be the following winter.

With the odd jobs, I also hustled enough money for a trip to New York City with Al Bright in August. Leaving with what we thought was sufficient funds for food, a cheap hotel, and cover charges at the jazz clubs we intended to visit, we immediately encountered a disaster. Two hundred miles from home on the Pennsylvania Turnpike, one of the new tires my father had bought for his car blew out. We were not injured in the accident but the cost of towing and purchasing another tire left us nearly broke. Determined to finish the trip, we pushed on to New York.

We parked in Harlem at night and slept in the car, mostly eating in cheap but homey restaurants, where we also washed and changed clothes in the rest rooms. Despite the lack of money, we managed to canvas and roam the streets of Harlem and Greenwich Village. We went to the Apollo Theatre, Birdland, the Village Gate, and listened to Thelonius Monk at the Jazz Gallery. Village coffeehouses afforded a firsthand view of the city's Beat crowd, and we passed through such quasibohemian spots as the Fat Black Pussy Cat.

During that trip, I saw Malcolm X speak for the first time and, standing on the corner of 125th Street and Seventh Avenue, began to understand why McKay had been drawn to the Muslims. His performance was riveting, even though the doctrine was no more acceptable to me then than it had been when McKay explained it earlier.

Al and I returned to Youngstown disheveled and underfed, but I had a good idea of where I'd settle after college. The excitement, anonymity, and freedom of New York City was exactly what I wanted. I knew then that I'd leave Youngstown's steel mills and bean fields behind me.

Two weeks later, I left for Hamilton, New York, with $75 and a used trunk and suitcase, barely enough to purchase books for my first semester.

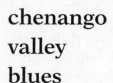

# 12

## chenango valley blues

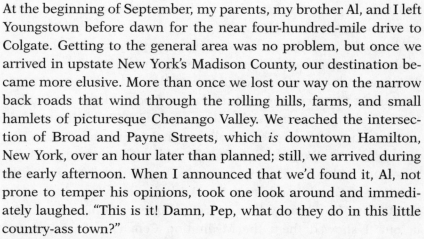

At the beginning of September, my parents, my brother Al, and I left Youngstown before dawn for the near four-hundred-mile drive to Colgate. Getting to the general area was no problem, but once we arrived in upstate New York's Madison County, our destination became more elusive. More than once we lost our way on the narrow back roads that wind through the rolling hills, farms, and small hamlets of picturesque Chenango Valley. We reached the intersection of Broad and Payne Streets, which *is* downtown Hamilton, New York, over an hour later than planned; still, we arrived during the early afternoon. When I announced that we'd found it, Al, not prone to temper his opinions, took one look around and immediately laughed. "This is it! Damn, Pep, what do they do in this little country-ass town?"

My mother, even, chuckled before coming to my defense. "See, there's a picture show right over there," she said, pointing to the village's lone movie, Schine's State Theater. "Anyway, he's here to learn something, not to raise no ruckus."

I didn't know it then, but Al's question was prophetic. I simply laughed it off as we drove down Broad Street, Hamilton's main drag. We passed fraternity row, quiet that day with only a few bare-chested upperclassmen lounging on the porches. It was hard to imagine that during party weekends it could be transformed into the clamorous strip I'd witnessed when visiting in the spring—a raucous party zone where the hoots of beer-sloshed students, the cacophony of competing rock bands, and the squeals of imported coeds cloaked the school's normal serenity and calm.

On the opposite side of the street, for instance, swans and ducks glided through the glistening surface of Taylor Lake or stalked its grassy banks, defying any lone individual to invade their territory. A few students meandered down the Willow Path, which was lined on either side by a regiment of willow trees whose drooping branches and slipper-shaped leaves shaded the winding route through the vast lawn that fronted the university.

We turned onto the campus at College Street. Downtown Hamilton had not impressed my family, but the campus's secluded, rustic setting was better received. It contrasted starkly with Youngstown University, which was located three blocks from the town square and had no campus to speak of. They were only mildly curious, but still I pointed out a few landmarks. I recalled enough from my former visit to guide us through a brief tour and answer some of the questions my mother asked.

Although relatively small, the campus proper occupied about 120 acres of the university's thousand-acre grounds; it was impressive. As we wound our way up the hill toward the dormitories on the narrow drives that twist through the lawns, I pointed out the Student Union and the modern, newly constructed, modular-shaped library, which stood out from the school's mostly Federal and Dutch Colonial structures. We passed the stark, gabled Administration Building—rumored to have inspired eerie likenesses that appeared in the drawings of Charles Addams, a *New Yorker* cartoonist and creator of the *Addams Family* as well as a former student at Colgate. Taking a detour, I showed them the Meditation Center, golf course, and Huntington Gymnasium, where I'd be playing basketball that winter. Finally, at the top of the hill, we parked near the Quad, which was ringed with ivy-covered classroom buildings, freshman dormitories, and the school chapel.

An upperclassman immediately approached and directed us to East Hall and the single room I'd requested. It was the day before the start of Freshman Orientation Week and only a few students had arrived. Those who had shown up—although busily engaged in unpacking, exploring the grounds and dorms, and saying their good-byes—seemed friendly enough. But my mother, who was much more attentive to such matters, had quickly noticed that we hadn't seen a single Negro since we arrived in Hamilton. At one point she pulled me aside to share that observation. I was surprised when she brought it to my attention; I had expected to see *some* blacks at Colgate. Although I suspected that we would be in the minority, I didn't think we would be an endangered species. Still unconvinced, I assured her that the others just hadn't arrived yet.

My new residence was a narrow room with a standard-size bed (into which I barely fit), a desk, and a chair; common bathrooms were down the hallway. The sterile cubbyhole foreshadowed the spartan regimen university administrators had apparently envisioned and, I'd find, was mostly unavoidable at Colgate. With my family's help, it didn't take long to get settled. Almost compulsively I found myself arranging record albums on the desk and bureau, brandishing photos of Miles Davis and Sonny Rollins like fetishes in an attempt to soften the room's impersonal chill. When I'd finished, we walked around the campus for a short time, then drove back to the village, where we ate at the Bluebird Restaurant. Restless and tired, Tennessee was impatient to leave since they intended driving back home that evening. Outside the diner, Katie again drew me aside and, while slipping $10 into my hand, whispered, "You be careful up here, boy. Never know what these folks try to do when nighttime come—and find out where the colored folks live, you hear?"

Afterward, they drove me back to the dorms. Tennessee hadn't spoken, hardly even looked at me since we arrived; he seemed intent on silently casing the campus, alert to any threat. And, I imagined, prepared to confront any challenge arising in this strange outpost. But sitting in the car's passenger seat before they left, he reached out and shook my hand; for an instant, looked directly into my eyes. "You take care of yo'self. Don't let us down," was all he said. Al, on the other hand, had been upbeat as always. He joked and jived throughout the trip as if attempting to assuage a nervousness that, despite my attempt to appear calm and controlled, must have been apparent to him. "Just do your thing, Pep," he offered. "Nothin' to worry about."

They both seemed confident that I could handle the situation. A hug, perhaps too clinging, and kiss from my mother, the only one to step out of the car, and they left.

Katie was still visibly distraught as they drove off. It was, I'm sure, partly because I'd never left home for any extended period of time before; she wasn't prepared for the separation. But something else was on her mind. Her reluctance to leave and the grieved look that settled on her face as the car pulled away, reflected a deeper concern. It was almost as if she felt that she'd abandoned me—left her youngest son, her last child, behind the lines in an enemy camp.

I, too, felt separation pains. But my angst was not fueled by any conscious apprehension about the nervous, mostly nerdy teenagers who filed into East Hall that evening. I jousted with a more generic fear—one derived from the realization that I was suddenly on my own, like the rest of my as yet unknown dorm mates, separated from friends, family, and all the various support systems that previously sustained me. My independence, I discovered that evening, would be accompanied for a time by wrenching anxiety. That concern was more than enough to keep me occupied during my first night at Colgate. And in hindsight, it was probably fortunate that I wasn't more aware of the university's past history; if so, I would have probably been more attentive to Katie's alarm.

Adam Clayton Powell Jr., the controversial Harlem congressman, for instance, attended Colgate in the late 1920s. The lure of Harlem nightlife was too tempting while he attended the City College of New York and he nearly flunked out. But Powell was accepted at Colgate when his father, the well-known pastor of Harlem's famed Abyssinian Baptist Church, interceded and called on his friend George Barton Cutten, a former Baptist pastor who was then president of Colgate. Special allowances were made for Powell's poor grades and Cutten apparently did not mention Powell's race to administrators or faculty. For most of his first year at Colgate, Powell went along with the racial deception, enjoying many of the privileges allotted to white students. He even roomed with a white student, a taboo arrangement at the time. After he joined an all-white fraternity, however, Powell's Negro ancestry was discovered. He was quickly ousted from the fraternity and ordered to find new rooming arrangements; until he graduated in 1930, he was ostracized by white students. For a short time, even the school's four other Negro students avoided him. Harassment and shunning of blacks was not unheard of at Colgate.

The situation, to be sure, had changed. Not counting a few African exchange students, there were now about sixteen Negroes among the thirteen hundred students enrolled at Colgate, and three fraternities had begun accepting blacks when I arrived in 1958; two or three others accepted Jews. The university was struggling to diversify, but there was still more than ample evidence of the attitudes that shaped Powell's experience.

During that first night, however, I was focused on the immediate problem of being four hundred miles away from home and not knowing a soul. During the course of the evening many more students arrived, and while sitting on the steps outside East Hall, I met some of them. By midnight, when parents and girlfriends had departed, almost everyone on the floor gathered and introduced themselves. Some stopped and listened to jazz albums in my room. A few of those initial acquaintances would become relatively good friends during late-night bull sessions where we argued about philosophy, music, and girls. Brad Baker (a musician), Ralph Arlyck (a future independent filmmaker), and Dave Howell (who would become my daughter's godfather) were among the connections that lasted well beyond college.

I was also reassured later that night when I met Phil, a black student from Cleveland who lived on my floor. Altogether there were five Negroes in the freshman class, four of whom would join the 317 seniors who graduated with the class of '62. Before I graduated, I began to think of us more as tokens than a minority. That first year, however, I was so inundated with the peculiar demands of Colgate life that there was rarely time to step back and assess anything.

At South High, I'd floated in and out of mainstream life, essentially a wide-eyed sojourner in that unfamiliar world. Entering was sometimes problematic, but I'd always departed freely, without being mired in its less appealing rituals and mundane daily routines. And always there was a familiar blues-saturated black world awaiting me. That culture, while sometimes chaotic and, by outside estimate, second rate, offered a familiar place to rest and rejuvenate. At Colgate, however, I was completely cut off, immersed in a foreign, white world. Wherever I turned, I was surrounded by alien attitudes and a strange culture: classical music, even Gregorian chants;

deadly silence during required attendance at chapel services, where perfunctory sermons were delivered by dispassionate clergy; bland, unseasoned, and undercooked food such as the creamed chicken on toast that was hurled around the dining hall; and with some glaring exceptions, the smug, overly enthusiastic effusions of a host of mostly pampered, naive classmates who—while knowing nothing about what I considered the real world—knew perfectly well that Colgate was their place and that I was an intruder. The initial shock was devastating. If not for the challenge of my classes, the school's academic life, I would have left after the first three weeks. But although nearly overwhelmed, I was determined to make it through that first year, despite the school's curious demands and my dashed expectations.

The difficulties surfaced the following afternoon shortly after the freshman class gathered in the chapel for the beginning of Orientation Week. The week's activities were intended to help freshmen choose a field of study, introduce us to the school's extracurricular, recreational, and academic resources, and create class solidarity. The aptitude and personality tests, conferences and discussions with advisors, faculty, and upperclassmen were essential for me. I don't think I would have made the adjustment without them.

It was the ritualized hokum associated with creating class solidarity that made me recoil. I knew I had problems the moment we were handed black ties, identification buttons, and purple beanies and told that we had to wear them at all times on campus. If we were spotted without them or failed to memorize the school alma mater and its cheers and fight songs by the end of the week, members of Konosioni, a group of seniors charged with preserving Colgate tradition and indoctrinating freshmen, could exact punishment on the spot with so-called paddles of justice.

No siree, Bob! as my Ohio friends used to say. It wasn't about to happen. The cultural clash was too great. I had avoided taking an ass whipping from Tennessee since I was eleven years old, and I wasn't about to have an overzealous upperclassman force me to submit to a similar indignity because I didn't wear a beanie. I did compromise and, most often, wore the specified knit tie and badge that marked me as a freshman; but the beanie never had a chance.

Besides its lame appearance, the caps had another drawback for me. I'd arrived at Colgate sporting a *do*—the marcelled, intricately waved hairstyle that Al Bright and I not only wore but also fashioned for others in his basement barber shop. Excepting musicians brought in to play at dances or fraternity parties, it may have been its first appearance at Colgate, since most Negroes who attended private Eastern colleges in the fifties were from bourgeois families, for whom such adornment was synonymous with street niggers—a class that they spurned. (That fact, given the origin of most of the other Negro freshmen, may partially explain why I never became overly friendly with any of the blacks in my class.) Since I had a brother and many friends who fit that classification, the association didn't bother me. That aside, I wasn't about to mess up my hair with a skullcap.

Initially, my intransigence provoked frequent confrontations. But after I made it clear that being paddled was not on my agenda, they stopped. Apparently, most Konosioni members also had reservations about street niggers. This despite their wearing white caps and jackets that were vaguely reminiscent of another, more notorious, secret organization that dedicated itself to preserving traditions and, ironically, had begun as a college social club about one hundred years earlier. The connection seemed even more vivid when, at the end of orientation, an effigy of a Konosioni member with a single *K* scrawled on its chest was burned in the Quad.

Months after arriving in Hamilton, the hair problem was eliminated. It became apparent that, unless I journeyed to Syracuse each week and visited a black barbershop in the Central Ward district, trying to maintain the slick look of the fifties hood was impossible. Moreover, since by then I'd dolefully resigned myself to the reality of an all-male school—not only were women unavailable but also, except for so-called townies and a few secretaries and professors' wives, they were not to be seen—primping of that sort became a gratuitous indulgence. By December, like most other students, in addition to an insulated cap and earmuffs, I was wearing several sweaters and the heaviest coat I could find in an attempt to protect myself from the piercing wind that swept through the Chenango Valley as if it had an express ticket from Alaska.

By then I'd realized that I should have visited Hamilton in the winter instead of the spring. No mistake, I'm sure, but I'd been invited in April, when the campus had just started blooming; it was magnificent. On my arrival in September, it was equally impressive.

But fall was a transient presence in Hamilton. A week or so after classes started, the weather began changing. Although temperatures remained in the sixties or low seventies, after a week or so a suspicious chill crept into the air. As I looked up the hill from Whitnall Field and its quarter-mile cinder track, the northern sky had already assumed a ghostly gray cast. Low and ominous, it hung over the Student Union like a shade about to be drawn. Willow trees shivered in the wind, releasing burnt orange or ocher leaves that skipped along the surface of rapidly yellowing grass. Soon, bare, spindly, fingerlike branches would glisten and sag under the weight of icy lamination. Winter, I quickly discovered, was never more than a blink away. During my four years at Colgate, snow fell by mid-October each year; I seldom saw the ground before the beginning of March.

In truth, however, the frigid weather was the least of the surprises that greeted me. I'd spent the summer reading the works of existentialist writers, cramming on Sartre, Kafka, Dostoyevsky, and as many contemporary writers as I could fit in. I'd expected a staid, serious atmosphere in which students and professors explored some of the societal contradictions and enigmas that dogged me. Instead, I soon realized that I'd run headlong into the kind of hail-fellow-well-met, boy's camp atmosphere that I'd incredulously read about in Youngstown. No one requested that we swallow goldfish or attempt squeezing the entire class into a telephone booth; but the pranks and hazing that accompanied initiation into the university tradition were often just as absurd. They seemed to mirror an attitude not far removed from those Oklahoma A&T students who had admitted that their greatest worry was finding a parking spot.

I'd come from the Corn Belt expecting to find a sophisticated, enlightened environment and found more cornball insouciance than I'd ever witnessed in Ohio. While I was searching for answers to personal problems, questioning the sovereignty of arbitrary authority and, more practically, trying to figure out how to pay for the books I'd need that first semester, most of my classmates, it seemed, were already on a holiday romp.

Besides the business of being introduced to the university's academic regimen, classroom expectations, and registration procedures, that first week was filled with songs, contests, and cheers—activities designed to mold group solidarity and demonstrate our commit-

ment to the greater whole. I mouthed the words of the boisterous
cheers and watched my classmates work themselves into a frenzy at
daily chapel gatherings. I joined in the softball games and, reluctantly, helped our side in the traditional tug-of-war—an excuse to
dunk enthusiastic revelers (naive enough to take positions at the
middle of the rope) into Taylor Lake's muddy waters. Once condoned, the rowdy cavorting spilled over into activities that were not
supervised or orchestrated by upperclassmen. So, at dinner, I'd gulp
my food or hover over it protectively as I watched with amazement
when meals at the Student Union turned into food fights: rolls
tossed like grenades, chocolate pudding flung to the ceiling, where
it stuck and dripped onto the heads of the unsuspecting, and Jell-O
or creamed chicken poured into laps or over the heads of the least
assertive or most vulnerable. It was startling to me; I'd never witnessed a food fight in my life. Frequent scarcity in my home dic-
tated that we eat food or save it for someone else—not blithely hurl
it about as if we were playing with mud cakes.

I was thrilled when the week's festivities were capped by building
a huge "bond-fire"; the pep rally that accompanied its lighting was
supposed to signal our unity.

My classmates' fervor and eager response to those college rites
were, of course, not unusual. Isolated and torn away from our roots,
almost every freshman had a desperate need for inclusion during
those first few weeks; all of us wanted to feel connected, to belong.
And, for most of *them,* it worked. Their compliance with freshman
rites, willingness to bend over, fingers to toes, and expose splayed
cheeks to requital by the paddle of justice when they'd transgressed,
for me symbolized their submission to a social hierarchy that was
unacceptable. For many of them that hierarchy was sacrosanct.
Submitting to it was the required homage for establishing contacts,
making the hookups that would eventually put them on-line in a
good-old-boy-network that would extend into the workforce and beyond. At the outset, I suspected that those hookups were unavailable
to Negroes unless we displayed even more obeisance than our white
counterparts, bowed and grinned in the face of aggressive ridicule
that too easily slipped across the line between the joke that it was
supposed to be and the deep-seated disdain for blacks that it too often became. My entry was short-circuited from the beginning. As a
Negro, I was an outsider, whether I liked it or not.

We were, of course, not the only ones. During my second day on campus, I met Walt—a future prize-winning upstate New York journalist. He approached me as we lined up for lunch and asked, "You're Mel Watkins, the basketball player, aren't you?"

Still disturbed by having met only one other black student, I gazed at him and bristled, "Yeah, wasn't too hard to find me, was it?"

He looked around, nodded in agreement, and laughed. "Guess you're right. Anyway, I'm Walt Shepperd."

That exchange and mutual laughter broke the ice, opening a path for a friendship that lasted throughout college and on to the present. The connection was based partly on our interest in basketball. Walt was a fanatic; he loved the game and approached it with as much enthusiasm and dedication as anyone I'd met. His ability, however, never quite matched his enthusiasm. Still, he made the freshman team that year, and as we shared the demands and fatigue of rigorous practice sessions, our friendship grew.

But for me, Walt stood out from most of the white students I initially met in other ways. That, of course, did not mean that I let him slide. When we met I still prodded him with faint digs, responding to his "What's happening?" with, "You tell me, my man. It's your world, you know that." But it was apparent to both of us that he was nearly as uncomfortable in it as I was. Perhaps it was the time he'd spent on city courts in White Plains, New York, competing against black opponents who were unwanted intruders in that well-heeled Westchester bedroom community, but it was apparent that he'd already developed a deep-seated suspicion of his family's complacent bourgeois values; he flaunted his disdain for the inclusive white-bread ethics and conformity that ruled at Colgate. I soon discovered that he was something of a maverick or outsider himself.

During the next four years, however, there was a price to pay. His skepticism and disregard of traditional campus attitudes aroused suspicions. A cynical observer of freshman rules and protocol from the outset, he was dead set on a course that would lead to banishment from the inner circle of campus movers and shakers. That exclusion was based, at least in part, on his continued association with me and other Negroes. As one classmate later pointed out to him, "Well, you must have known you'd be ostracized once you started running with the niggers." By that time it didn't matter. Walt and I, along with a few others, had turned some of the school's peculiar biases and a few students' naiveté and smugness to our own advantage.

It started that first day, when we walked over to the Student Union after lunch. While Walt and I were shooting pool, another freshman walked by and asked to join us. He was a fair player and we sparred innocently for a few games. It soon dawned on me, however, that the pool tables just might be the answer to a problem I knew I'd soon have to face: money. I still had no idea how I'd pay for books or afford any incidental expenses. The $85 I'd arrived with would not go far; that I knew. So, after losing a game of eight ball to our new companion, I suggested that we play for some small stake—say, a dollar a game. My eager classmate jumped at the opportunity. He was, to paraphrase Tennessee, "money wit' a beanie on."

I won only $6 that day, but returning to the dorm later, I realized that I'd discovered a way of supplementing my meager stash. Afterward, whenever studies or basketball practice didn't interfere, I headed for the pool tables. There was no lack of challengers, and when I began spotting my opponents seven balls in games of eight ball, the numbers increased. The ploy, which I'd learned from hustlers in Youngstown, was only a tantalizing deception; with fewer balls on the table, the more skilled player actually had the advantage. After a while, even that inducement was not enough; by the beginning of the second semester almost everyone respectfully declined playing for any stakes. My income source vanished as quickly as it had appeared.

Through Walt I'd also discovered that Colgate had a black market for books. Required textbooks could be purchased at half price from a small group of rebellious freshmen who had chosen to express their defiance in a more larcenous manner. They regularly entered the campus bookstore and acquired whatever book a classmate ordered. With my lack of funds, I didn't allow ethics to stand in the way. I ordered all of my books from them during the first semester.

During the first few months, the proximity of dormitory living revealed some others who, while not totally rejecting the school's orchestrated gung ho attitude, had found it extreme. Phil, the only Negro in my class that I got to know on more than a superficial level, seemed shell-shocked by the rites. Although he went along with them and did not complain, he seemed to withdraw during

those first few weeks—donning a stoic mask that denied all but surface access; for me, at least, it was impenetrable.

Others were less recondite. Brad, with whom I argued continually
about the relative merits of Miles Davis and John Coltrane, had
nearly as much disdain as I. Reveling in the hip vernacular of the
jazz world, he playfully mimicked Louis Armstrong scats and regularly scorned the collegiate hijinks with linguistic riffs that echoed
the tone and rhythms of comedian Lord Buckley's "hipsomatic" dia-
logues or disc jockey Jocko Henderson's radio riffs. "Be-bopsie-do,
how do'ya do? *Yeeaahhhh*, wailin' with the philosophy crew. Sho-be-
doo, bop-bah, what's with these squares and all that hoopla?" It was
jive but funny, and Brad thoroughly enjoyed himself.

Ralph appeared to float above the rites, even as he outwardly con-
formed. His intelligence and playfulness seemed to convey an
amused detachment that trivialized activities he nevertheless embraced without protest. Dave, more serious and perhaps less determined to effectively deflect the weight of our freshman lackey
status, bore the indignities like a cross.

Still, at night in one or another of our dorm rooms, we expressed
our discontent and explored other aspects of our experiences in
rambling raps that often droned on till near dawn. Philosophy, music, religious beliefs, race, careers, and women were all subjected to
the scrutiny of our varying viewpoints: Brad's jazzy irreverence;
Ralph's flip irony; Dave's insistent quest for moral rectitude; and the
shifty, existentially inspired nihilism that shaped my vision at the
time. Just bull sessions, of course, an indulgence we shared with
countless other college freshmen; but they honed our ability to express ourselves and exposed us to some distinctly different viewpoints.

Meanwhile, freshman indoctrination continued into November
and the week of the Syracuse football game. The rivalry had begun
in 1891, and Colgate still held the edge with thirty-one wins against
twenty-five losses and five ties. The Syracuse Orangemen had dominated the contests during the early fifties with such stars as the All-
American fullback Jim Brown, who would become an NFL legend,
leading the onslaught. Still, the game remained a season highlight
for both schools. Prospects for winning were no better in my freshman year than they had been in the recent past or would be in the
near future when Ernie Davis, an All-American halfback, would join

All-American tight end John Mackey to lead Syracuse to lopsided victories. Still, time-honored rituals were observed.

Tradition held that Colgate freshmen build a bonfire at the beginning of the week and light it the night before the game; all during that week Syracuse undergraduates would attempt lighting it prematurely. As freshmen we were charged with keeping all-night vigils to assure that no Orangemen infiltrated the campus and ruined the pregame ceremony. The intercampus games were taken quite seriously. One of the more sinister aspects of the rivalry, particularly if you became an unfortunate victim, was that during that week, each school tried to capture students from the opposing campus and shave their heads, leaving only the initial *S* or *C*. Daily reports were published announcing who was ahead in the race to make unwilling mascots of opposing students. Since I had not yet decided to abandon my do, the thought of such an occurrence created some anxiety for me. During the night on which I was chosen to help guard the bonfire (a duty that I vainly tried to avoid), I was probably more mindful and vigilant of Syracuse invaders than anyone might have suspected.

As it happened, two Negro sophomores, George Davis and Hal Jackson, had managed to borrow a car and chose the Thursday before the game to invite me along on an excursion to Syracuse, which, unlike Colgate, was coed. I had not left campus since arriving in September, and the lure of a chance to meet and talk to women, any woman, outstripped my trepidation about both the dangers of the predicted snow flurries and the threat of an involuntary scalping. My companions, undoubtedly aware of my anxiety, busted my chops during the entirety of the trip.

And at one point I laughingly shared my imagined version of the headlines that would appear the next morning if even an attempt were made. "Yeah, well, if someone comes near me with a razor, you'll be reading about it tomorrow: YOUNGSTOWN NEGRO CUTS SEVERAL SYRACUSE STUDENTS DURING FOILED COLLEGE PRANK." We laughed and jived throughout the trip, although the shit was frankly not that funny to me.

It didn't help when, at the outskirts of Syracuse on East Genesee Street, Hal stopped the car and said, "I'm not sure who you're trying to impress, but if I was you I'd lose that maroon sweater before you get out the car. Otherwise, you're on your own." They howled as I quickly corrected my error and, feeling less natty but much safer, removed the telltale Colgate sweater.

Fortunately, nothing happened. We ventured into the heart of the Syracuse campus and had beers at the Orange, a campus hangout for coeds and Syracuse athletes. Preoccupied with my concern over ritualized haircuts, however, I didn't take advantage of the chance to talk to any coeds, merely stammered something lame to a heavily-mascaraed junior while nervously keeping my eye on the host of orange-lettered jackets behind her. Only later, when we left the campus and drove down to the Ward (the black section of town) and ordered food at Ben's Kitchen, did I relax. Sliced ham, collard greens, and corn bread, a bottle of orange Nehi pop, and the sound of Jerry "The Iceman" Butler were enough to lift me out of the twilight zone of college hijinks. Although miles away from home, for the first time since September I felt as if I were on familiar ground. No fanciful collegiate rigmarole, just a bunch of mostly funky black folks greasing on grits that even Katie would have envied. Although I didn't have an opportunity to return until months later, I'd found where the colored folks lived.

The ride back to Colgate was uneventful. Still salivating from the taste of Ben's soul food, we shucked and jived and I laughingly fended off gibes about freshman ineptitude with the ladies.

"So, young blood," Hal said, "what happened to the young lady you tried to hit on?"

"Yeah," George added, "hear tell back in Ohio you were an operator. Say they use to call you the *doctor*."

"Maybe so," Hal laughed, "but this ain't Ohio. I don't think he earned his New York license yet."

"Hey, I didn't see you seasoned veterans pulling nobody," I said.

"That's 'cause we was waitin' for you, my brother." George laughed. "If we'd gone ahead and took care of business, we'd have had to leave you sittin' out there by yourself. No tellin' what would've happened. I saw two or three football players eyeing your mop as it was."

We were still laughing when they dropped me off at my dorm.

The next morning, the buzz on campus was that we'd won the haircut competition by several heads. There was a flap, however; it seemed that two Syracuse coeds had been captured and kept overnight at one of the fraternities. They hadn't been molested or harmed in any way except that an unfortunate blond had returned with her head shorn—a stubbly *C* the only remaining traces of her formerly flowing tresses. The uproar over the "abduction" of the Syracuse coeds lasted for a few weeks. The celebration of our pregame victory lasted only for a day. On Saturday, Syracuse won the football game 47 to 0.

Still, with the bonfire burning and pep rally on Friday night, the long-awaited end of freshman indoctrination had arrived. For me, one annoying hurdle had been removed, but by that time, several others had arisen in areas that I least expected.

The most immediate was the classroom; from the outset, I was overwhelmed.

On the first day of course attendance, I'd gone to three classes. The assignments for the following day were to read forty or so pages of a dense anthropology textbook and, in required freshman core-curriculum courses, thirty pages of technical exposition for a natural science class that assumed I had far more preparation in physics and biology than my last-ditch efforts at South High had afforded, and another thirty pages for a philosophy-and-religion course. Those initial assignments more than equaled my homework load during any two-week period during my senior year at South. I hadn't even attended the expository writing course that I'd elected or a required Spanish language course, and already I was swamped. Matters did not improve.

For one thing, I had absolutely no interest in the science or language courses. My fascination with the arts and obsession with personal and social problems had led me to naively assume that the sciences were a waste of time; I barely managed C's in that two-semester class and never took another science course at Colgate. I served the required time in Spanish classes, receiving mediocre C's in each of four terms, but I wasn't farsighted enough to appreciate the value of a second language until I'd left college. Even the required core philosophy-and-religion course was disappointing; while I'd been fascinated by existential philosophy and had absorbed it easily, I struggled mightily with Plato, Aristotle, and early European philosophers throughout the year.

During the second term, even my elected introductory psychology class, which I'd eagerly anticipated, was disappointing. Primarily a memorization exercise in the basic principles of psychological mea-

surement and fundamental personality traits—a necessary prerequisite, no doubt, to more creative applications of psychological theory—it touched on none of the areas that I was anxious to explore.
Moreover, our instructor, Professor Reinwald, did not enhance the
essentially dry material.

He was a large, dour, moonfaced man who, in my presence at
least, never varied his stoic expression—as bored as I was, I began
to suspect. Each morning at precisely 7:45 A.M. he walked in and
stood at the lectern going through his notes, then methodically performed a facial exercise to loosen up his mouth. Not a pretty sight
to watch. At two minutes after eight, he locked the door—after
which no one was admitted to the room. For the next fifty minutes
he read from his notes, droning on in a monotonous voice that invited sedation. No questions were allowed, no interruptions tolerated. The last few minutes of class were reserved for student
participation. But when the bell rang, he closed his notes and
abruptly left. I, like many of his captive audience, drifted in and out
of sleep during this less than spellbinding performance. The lecture
that he read, we'd discovered, was little more than a synopsis of the
textbook. We could have read it ourselves.

None of my other classes approached the deadly boredom experienced in that psychology course. In fact, the vitality, support, and
encouragement of some other professors spurred me to do as well
as I did that first year. Despite near failing grades, I developed immense respect for them—particularly their tolerance of my early ineptitude. Near the end of the first semester, for example, while
taking an exam in Professor Terrell's philosophy-and-religion
course, I was forced to ask to be excused to go to the bathroom.
Maintaining only a C in the course even though it was one of the
classes for which I had an actual passion, I was reluctant to ask to
leave the room. Despite an honor system, which could mean expulsion if one were caught cheating, concealed notes and other ploys
had been used to enhance test results. When the urge to piss became unbearable, I simply rushed up and asked to leave. Professor
Terrell granted permission without blinking an eye. After the exam,
I stopped to speak to him.

"I wanted to thank you," I said. "No one has ever trusted me that
much before."

He just smiled and said, "I knew you wouldn't cheat."

The incident left an indelible impression on me. It marked the start of my gaining some true feelings of responsibility toward the school and its traditions. Unfortunately, it happened far too late in the semester to help improve my performance in his class or any others.

There were, I'd discover the following year, several problems. Most important, my lack of application in high school had come back to haunt me. I had almost no idea how to study and prepare for examinations. I'd breezed through the mostly true-or-false and multiple-choice tests at South substituting mother wit for preparation. It had worked there, but I had no clue of how to deal with Colgate's blue-book essay exams. They exposed my weaknesses as glaringly as slick curveball pitchers toy with lunging, fastball-hitting sluggers.

As confounding, I was having a terrible time deciphering classroom lectures. I might as well have been a student who had learned a foreign language solely by reading books; hearing it spoken for the first time baffled me. I knew the meaning of words that I had never pronounced. It was easy to recognize them in print, but they sounded like gibberish when glibly tossed out by my professors. The restricted vocabulary and hybrid Midwestern-and-Southern dialect that I'd become accustomed to in conversation bore little resemblance to their crisp enunciation and urbane accents. Initially, the simple act of taking notes in class was a herculean feat. Those problems, along with the overwhelming quantity of work required, had me reeling from the first day. Sleepless nights were common; four hours' rest was a good night's sleep.

That was before the beginning of the basketball season. The addition of daily practice sessions and, in December, the start of the season, with frequent overnight trips, almost did me in. It was, as blues vocalist Bobby Bland woefully intoned, like "pouring water on a drowning man."

Time-consuming daily practice sessions and frequent road trips during the season shrunk my study time. And since basketball had the longest season of any collegiate sport (practice started in early November and the final game was played in March), the pressure was on for most of the year. And unlike in many other colleges, professors, even avid sports fans, cut no slack for athletes. That reality was indelibly imprinted in my mind during my senior year when my faculty advisor, Professor Fitchen, gave me an F in a required course for fine arts history majors when I arrived five minutes late for his 8:00 A.M. class. It didn't matter that we'd played a game at Lafayette the night before and the team had not returned to campus until 3:00 A.M. It was the third time I'd shown up late—at least one of my other tardy appearances had been for similar reasons—and rules were rules.

During my freshman year, participation in basketball greased my academic slide. I fell further and further behind and finished the first semester with C's in Spanish and in my two core-curriculum courses; I barely avoided failing anthropology, finally receiving a D.

Fortunately, in October I had written an essay on Jean-Paul Sartre and his existential philosophy for my expository writing course. That essay won the Freshman Writing Award and was published in the *Caliper,* the school literary magazine, during the winter. At least my summer reading blitz had not been totally wasted. The award may have even convinced some faculty members that I wasn't the dunce my grades might have indicated. The A that I received in that class kept me afloat. Still, I'd barely escaped losing my scholarship.

Meanwhile, I assured myself, I could partially salvage what had been a frustrating and disappointing start at Colgate with my performance on the basketball court. In the past I'd always turned to it when things started to fall apart. When my social life hit the skids or household chaos on Woodland Avenue threatened to overwhelm me, I'd used it like a drug to bolster my ego and affirm my self-worth. It had always been a given and was, in my mind, the last hope of proving myself.

## 13

## stranger
## in a
## strange
## land

There was a moment in one of our earliest games against the Syracuse University freshman team that is still vividly locked in my mind. A long pass was thrown to me on what should have been an easy breakaway layup. The prior year, in high school or on a Youngstown playground, I would have caught it in stride, might even have showboated, passed it behind my back before going up for a two-handed dunk. Not that evening, however; instead, the ball sailed toward me in slow motion—fluttering like a whiffle ball. Hypnotized by its erratic course, I hesitated; then, feeling a hitch in my stride, lunged forward. Too late. Stunned, I watched the ball slide off the end of my fingers and settle into the outstretched palms of an acne-faced junior in the stands.

It was a prophetic moment. I fumbled my way through most of the remaining freshman games in much the same manner.

It didn't start that way. Basketball practice sessions began well enough, worked like an antidote for the estrangement and alienation I felt during those first months at Colgate. The familiar, leather-grained texture of the ball, crush of shoulders and limbs under the backboard, squeal of rubber-soled sneakers against the hardwood floor, even the smell of sweat-drenched uniforms and clammy bodies that hung over Huntington Gymnasium like a musty veil brought welcome relief from the campus activities outside. I'd leave the gym with a swagger I hadn't felt since Volney Rogers Field, where our team would typically run off ten pickup games in a row, then leave the court and let the losers compete.

For a while there, I felt as if I were back in the zone, in that bubble where absolutely nothing can go wrong, where the hoop looks as wide as a bushel basket and your shot is as dependable as hard currency.

*Boy's jump shot is money in the bank. Go head, Money, shoot it!*

Although magical—nearly as exhilarating and gratifying as an orgasm—the groove was as fragile as it was extraordinary. I'd looked to basketball as a cure-all or instant fix for academic failures and a growing sense of dislocation. Perhaps it was the pressure, I'm not sure, but faltering slightly, I panicked, began dissecting my performance, probing and examining what I'd always taken for granted. The slump quickly became a complete collapse. Confidence deserted me first; then poise and timing followed. The bubble burst and I crashed.

We were not permitted to play varsity ball in the fifties, but with the presence of Bob Duffy, an all-state guard from New York, myself, and two other highly touted players, expectations for our freshman team were high. Largely due to my lackluster performance, however, we had only an average season.

Basketball had become as grueling as my freshman science course, as weighty and burdensome as Professor Reinwald's psychology class. What was once a sure thing, for me, had suddenly turned into a crapshoot. From one day to the next, I never knew who was going to suit up—the confident high school all-star or the bungling, introspective stranger that had materialized in Hamilton. Unfortunately, it was most often the latter. The more I searched for reasons, the less confident I became.

The all-male environment and lukewarm reaction to the sport didn't help. There was little enthusiasm for basketball at Colgate during the 1950s. In fact, even on a national level, it was a minor sport. Televised games, pro or collegiate, were rare. The hype that now surrounds NBA games and the NCAA's Final Four was unimaginable. Hamilton's remote location and harsh weather prevented attendance by fans from opposing schools, and the hundred or so mostly listless students who regularly showed up for our home games reflected the general apathy. Attendance for the entire season at Huntington Gymnasium barely amounted to the crowd we drew for a single game at South High. The distinction between practice and scheduled games quickly blurred. I became increasingly detached and so disinterested that I showed up late for several home games, rushing into the gym after my teammates had warmed up and sat waiting for the opening tip-off.

For me and, I'm sure, my teammates, the presence of coeds would have eased the situation. Like most freshmen, I was frustrated by the absence of the sight and company of women. I didn't realize how much I'd depended on their proximity, their vitality. What is it they say? *Never miss your water till the well runs dry.* A coed school and the potential admiration of female students would probably have driven me to focus more on basketball; the social rewards were, after all, what had initially prompted me to play the game.

But as maddening and frustrating as it was at the time, I'd later come to regard it as a blessing in disguise. I'm certain that given the academic challenges I faced that year, the distraction of coeds would have assured that I flunked out of school after the first semester. I barely made it as it was.

Initially, however, I began second-guessing my decision to attend Colgate, wondered what I'd been thinking the previous year when I'd visited Hamilton. Despite the excitement and gaiety I'd witnessed at Party Weekend, I should have been prepared for the monastic reality of an all-male university in a remote corner of upstate New York. The isolation and social shock affected everyone except, perhaps, those students who had graduated from all-boys prep schools. And even most of them were not quite prepared for the bleak, frigid weather and snow that, from November to February, often made escape from our cloistered retreat a liability.

With no girls and with television (dismissed by highbrows and scholars as an "idiot box" and soon to be labeled a "vast wasteland" by FCC chairman Newton Minow) limited to a few sets where little more than ghostly apparitions could be seen, reading, listening to music, and bull sessions were the chief pastimes. There were few other interruptions in a campus routine that, while perfectly suited for contemplation and study, could and did drive many students to mindless, stir-crazed dalliances, juvenile recreations, and drink.

Mooning, for example, had become a college fad, and at Colgate, students vied to see who could drop his pants and expose his butt in the most unlikely places. Schine's Theater and the bleachers during football games were among the favorite spots. But I'd seen some more-adventurous or irreverent students bare all at the Colgate Inn or inside the chapel. Some football players went further. After a par-ticularly wild drinking spree, a few would punctuate their late-night visits to the diner on Payne Street by loafing out. The sight of an in-ebriated 230-pound linesman's penis lying on the counter was, of course, an unusual occurrence. But even as they called campus se-curity, the seasoned counterpeople responded with practiced indif-ference. Boys will be boys. No need to overreact to the horseplay of a frustrated jock.

Although I sidestepped the food fights and avoided campus hi-jinks such as mooning and loafing out, I joined the others in dous-ing unsuspecting classmates with water balloons (a practice that in the winter amounted to an instant icing that often led to heated face-offs), snowball fights on the Quad, hazardous tray rides from the freshman dorms down the steep hill to the Student Union (on food trays borrowed from the dining hall), and marathon weekend card games. For most freshmen, who were not permitted to have cars and had not yet made the right contacts, the campus could be an austere boot camp where leave was precluded by weather and terrain. The witless diversions, while they may not have altered the social vacuum, at least took our minds off it.

Friendships with upperclassmen who either had cars or access to their fraternity brothers' wheels allowed some freshmen to occa-sionally escape our monkish surroundings. Many upperclassmen, as I would discover, abandoned the campus every weekend—travel-ing to Cazenovia, a nearby girls' school, and Syracuse or, when weather and the typically snowbound roads permitted, to Simmons, Skidmore, Smith, or some other Seven Sisters college. I, like most freshmen, could only watch with envy and dream about those es-capades during the first several months of school.

The hitch was that most of the few black students on campus were on scholarship, and students receiving aid from the university were not supposed to have cars. That fact, combined with white stu-dents' general reluctance to become too familiar with Negroes, helped make our first-year adjustments a bit more difficult than most of our classmates'. As my friend Walt had discovered, too close association with Negroes, in some quarters, meant expulsion from the club. That was particularly so if the association involved double-dating or traveling to another campus in search of dates. Although few students were bold enough to speak out, it was clear that inter-racial dating was a knotty problem for many of them. Their distress surfaced with nervous questions: "Uh, what do you guys do for dates? Are there any Negro girls at Cazenovia?" Or sometimes with overanxious attempts at helpfulness: "Saw a great gal at Oneonta last weekend. A little heavy, but she was real sexy, had a great per-sonality." Their attitudes didn't surprise us or inhibit our behavior, but they significantly added to the problem of exiting the campus on weekends.

In that restricted atmosphere, the lure of fraternity life was blown completely out of proportion. Colgate's thirteen Greek fraternal or-ganizations were the center of campus social life. Acceptance by a frat house, for most freshmen, was not only an important barome-ter of popularity and status but also the key to a successful social life. Rushing started in the fall, when upperclassmen began looking over the incoming class to determine which freshmen seemed best suited for the particular makeup of their frats. In turn, freshmen scrutinized the fraternities, looking for a house with compatible brothers—or, at minimum, a frat whose members would tolerate them. Pressure to pledge was immense.

During the winter, formal rushing began; fraternities hosted cock-tail parties and other gatherings during which prospective fresh-man pledges were scrutinized by brothers. Although the frats were open to all, favorite candidates were glad-handed while marginal freshmen and so-called misfits were given the cold shoulder. For me and other black classmates, the exercise was largely perfunctory; there were, after all, only three houses whose bylaws allowed accep-tance of Negroes. In effect, for most fraternities we were misfits be-fore we ever arrived on campus.

By the time formal rushing began, I'd practically committed my-self to joining Phi Kappa Tau, one of two or three houses known as intellectual, or egghead, frats. My basketball teammate Hal Jackson had pledged there and assured me that, for Negroes, it was the best fraternity on campus. Still, I wanted to check out soirees held by other fraternities. They were, after all, serving hors d'oeuvres and offering free booze. Curiosity was also part of it; I couldn't wait to see how they'd explained their exclusionary codes to freshmen who were banned. Of course, no answers were forthcoming. I ran smack into the same two-faced, surface amiability I'd encountered in Ohio.

> *You're Mel Watkins, right? Helluva ball game you played the other night. Would you like to meet our president? You know, we have a long tradition of recruiting athletes here. Can I get you something to drink? You gotta try these . . . delicious, right? Just make yourself at home. I'll be right back.*

They tap-danced. I nodded and went along with the charade, sometimes, when I'd had a beer or two, escalating the sendup. "You're right, this looks like a terrific house. Why don't you show me the bedrooms? I'm a bit particular about where I sleep, you know."

A tour would follow, all done with a straight face. No mention of restrictive codes or even a straight-out admission that I was wasting their time as well as my own. All I *saw* was polite, if unenthusiastic, forbearance. I'm sure, however, that once I left, moved on to the next house, there was no doubt a mass sigh of relief. Probably some urgent reassurances for legitimate freshman candidates: "Don't worry. Just part of Colgate protocol. There'll be no darkies in this house."

A few fraternities were known for their overt disdain for blacks. I wasn't unaware of the duplicity. By that time, I'd heard an anonymous fraternity member yelling "nigger" as I walked to the Student Union one evening. It would happen on several occasions in years to come. The calls usually came from a safe distance—never to your face, you understand, just disembodied voices ringing out across the Quad or echoing over Whitnall Field—although once, while I was walking to the gym with Walt Shepperd, a lone Delta Kappa Epsilon brother, emboldened by liquor, stumbled to the front porch of his frat, yelled "nigger" several times, and hurled a beer can in my direction. The beer can missed by fifty feet and he skulked back into the frat house as we turned and made a move toward the house. Later that evening I thought I saw him at the game wildly cheering for our team.

Fraternal expressions of discomfort at the presence of Negroes increased rapidly as the civil rights movement intensified during the 1960s. Several years after I left Colgate, Sigma Nu was kicked off campus when someone in the house fired shots at passing black students.

Still, despite the rowdiness and racism, fraternities were the only game on campus. The school's major social events were the year's three Party Weekend celebrations, and although there was a concert, a formal dance, and a few other gatherings, individual frat parties highlighted those weekends. This was particularly so for students who, like myself, could not afford to invite a date to Hamilton.

That fall, however, even Party Weekend was a bust. It started with a mixer that the Freshman Council had arranged with a nearby girls' school. The affair was supposed to be our introduction to the campus social scene. In fact, it was as stilted and deadly as a junior high school sock hop. Wary coeds in gowns clutched one another for support, sipping nonalcoholic punch as febrile freshmen circled them like vultures. While a dozen or so exceptionally attractive young women were rushed and sparkled with eye-fluttering radiance at the shower of attention, most, as uncomfortable as we with this awkward coupling, were more hesitant and reserved. Huddled together in small groups, they shielded themselves behind a wall of indifference. Among the scores of girls invited, there was one Negro coed, and she was surrounded by black and white Colgate frosh.

When I found a Colgate comrade who had the foresight to bring a flask with him, I spiked my punch with the amber-colored whiskey and approached a group of coeds at the perimeter of the gathering. After a few minutes, I managed to pull one aside. The conversation seemed to progress positively. Then she explained that her father was an executive at a New York advertising agency and, in the course of describing what life was like on their New Jersey estate, mentioned that she had met quite a few Negroes. Her favorite, it seemed, was the chauffeur, Ronnie, who was "one of the nicest boys" she'd ever met. A few minutes later, after she asked if I drove, I excused myself. I'd begun to suspect that she was about to offer me a job. After another cup of spiked punch, I left the mixer and returned to my room.

Later that night, I joined Walt Shepperd and Ned, a freshman who was also on the basketball team, to make the rounds at the fraternity parties. As I remembered from the brief glimpse I'd had during my campus visit the previous year, it was here that Colgate students cut loose. In contrast to the stilted formality of the freshman mixer, the frat parties were no-holds-barred, near-riotous bacchanals. A completely new experience for me, they neither resembled the staid, closely-chaperoned dances and sock hops I'd attended at South High nor the funky, dimly lit parties in Al Bright's basement—certainly not the slick, almost self-consciously cool affairs that I'd attended at the New Elms Ballroom.

Each house had its own loud, raucous band that, quality of music aside, pushed the festivities to a fever pitch and kept them there. Beer and alcohol flowed like water, and the revelers, unbound after two months of celibate isolation, did not inhibit themselves. Although I felt as stifled and frustrated, indeed, as horny as my classmates, I held myself in check. Dateless and on unfamiliar ground, I lurked at the fringes of the debauch that first night. Walt and Ned, apparently more at ease in what initially seemed like some orgiastic madhouse to me, occasionally joined the frolic, opportunistically snatching tipsy coeds who had deserted or lost track of their dates and pulling them into a mass of gyrating bodies for a quick feel, a chance openmouthed kiss.

In fact, after they disappeared onto a crowded dance floor at the second house we visited, I lost them. On my own and even more ill at ease, I wandered down fraternity row, pausing at houses where the music caught my attention or some student that I knew waved me inside. And somewhere along the way, I realized that I hadn't seen any other black students that night. There were a few black bands, but none of my Negro classmates. Now, I'm sure they were there; I probably just missed them. Or perhaps they had decided to avoid the entire scene—opted to take their dates to a more discrete, intimate atmosphere. I would if I'd had one. Still, it was surreal. And the more I drank, the more surreal it became.

I moved from house to house, sliding past soused upperclassmen who pawed and groped dates who were equally smashed. Pausing at the bar or pushing my way near the band, I'd hang for a time and listen to music. Curiously detached but nevertheless intently focused, I watched frat brothers pour beer over the heads of gleefully shrieking coeds as they stumbled and sloshed over the brew-soaked floor; smiled as they jerkily shook their off-time fannies, apparently dancing to some personal beat that had nothing to do with the music; or, nudged by other unattached onlookers, gawked when some free-spirited coed lifted her newly purchased Colgate T-shirt to bare still-budding lager-sopped breasts, or sprawled, skirt hitched to thighs, on the beer-slick floor, or, half-dazed and delirious, was led by her date or some other, anonymous frat brothers toward upstairs bedrooms or some private nook at the rear of the house. Finally, tired, more horny than ever, and a bit unstable, I stumbled onto Broad Street and headed back to the dorms, glad to be outside, removed from the temptation.

I didn't want to make a miscue, hit on one of the wrong chicks and overstep the boundaries. The thought had reared several times, but I'd ignored inviting glances from coeds who were apparently alone. I wasn't sure, yet, how to read the signals. Were they just stoned and friendly, or was it a come-on? Almost defensively, I'd cut conversations short and declined slow dances with girls who were too stoned or too brazen. It had been, after all, only a reconnaissance expedition. I needed to get the lay of the land, determine what was and was not acceptable.

It was after midnight when I lurched down Broad Street, light headed and vainly trying to affect the loose, pendulumlike swing of the arms and soulful dip in my stride that would have broadcast: *Yeah, I'm alone and tipsy, but I'm still cool.* Just before crossing the street to enter the campus, I was stopped by the sound of music and screams from a house that I'd previously skipped. The music was blasting loudly enough to drown out the sounds from surrounding houses, and the party had spilled outside to the porch, where a horde of stomping, arm-waving revelers were straining to get in. Echoing the response of those inside the house, they had formed a chorus to the band's emphatic exhortations.

"Throw my hands up and—" the band screamed. *"Shout!"* came the crowd's bellowing response. "Kick my heels up and—" *"Shout!"* "Yeah. Yeaaa, yeaaa—" *"Shout!"* "Come on, now—" *"Shout!"* "Come . . . on now—" *"Shout!"* "Oohhhh . . . all right, now—" *"Shout!"*

I thought the Isley Brothers were actually inside singing their latest hit. The frat house was literally rocking. Mind you, this was the pre-Beatles fifties, and despite the efforts of Alan Freed, most white Americans had not discovered the sound of hard-core rhythm and blues. I was astounded. Although I'd heard a few good bands that night, white and black, this was different. I had to check it out.

Yelling "Excuse me" in an authoritative tone, I pushed pass the crowd outside and made it downstairs, where the band was playing. The bottom of the stairs was as close as I got, since the room was packed except for a small circle in front of the band. Still, looking over the crowd, I could see the band's name scrawled boldly across the bass drum. THE FIVE SCREAMING NIGGERS.

I did a double take, glanced at the all-white crowd, then stared at the bandstand again. No mistake. That was the name. I couldn't believe my eyes—in fact, for a minute, wondered if I'd had too much to drink and wandered off the campus, stumbled into some bizarre nineteenth-century variety show. This was no corked-up stage troupe, however; these brothers were for real. It was an all-black band with saxophone, organ, drums, and guitar, and a leader who not only sounded like the Midnighters' Hank Ballard but also danced his ass off. Actually, there were six, since a busty brown-skinned female vocalist wearing a tight, black sheath stood off to the side. And in front of the band, two dew-eyed, extremely liberated Seven Sisters coeds wearing Bermuda shorts and Vassar T-shirts were shimmying and shaking their butts as if they were go-go dancers at a Jerry Lee Lewis concert.

I was amazed, not only at the group's blasphemous, in-your-face stage name and incredible sound but also at the coeds. For one thing, they could dance. This was a year before the Twist took the country by storm, and despite Elvis Presley, most white kids—still either jitterbugging or doing a stiff two-step shuffle—were somewhat tentative on the dance floor. Excepting performers, the two coeds were among only a few dozen people I'd seen that night whose gyrations even vaguely related to the music being played.

Then there was the erotic interplay between them and the band members. Hard to tell who was jiving whom. "Git it! Git it! Git it!" the guitarist shouted every time the blond dancer rolled her hips in a particularly suggestive manner. "Go 'head, sugar, git down." He laughed, gold tooth sparkling in the lone spotlight. "Shake it, honey, but don't break it . . . never know, somebody might wanna take it."

Damn! What's going on up here? I'm thinking. A few years earlier Nat King Cole was nearly lynched at a Memphis concert after three white female fans rushed up to the stage and touched his hand while asking for an autograph. No observance of that Dixie protocol on this night. In fact, cheered on by onlookers who could do little more than leap up and down in place, the coeds teased and flirted outrageously. One squatted, moving sensually up and down on the saxophonist's outstretched leg as he leaned back, waving his screeching horn like an arched phallic symbol; the other shimmied licentiously in front of the guitar player or challenged the lead singer, shadowing his moves as he glided through funky versions of the Mess Around, Hump, and Mash Potatoes. The crowd, caught up in the near-wanton display, roared with seeming approval.

When "Shout" ended, the band immediately cut to a bluesy rendition of Ray Charles's newly released "What I Say." The two dancers never even paused. Around me, spectators had reached a near-frenzied pitch, swaying en masse to the beat and screaming out the call-and-response verses and orgiastic simulations like a bevy of cloned Raylettes. "Make me feel so good." *"Make me feel so good!"* "Ahhhh, baby make me feel so good." *"Make me feel so good!"* "Baby, shake that thing." *"Baby, shake that thing!"* "Ahhhhhh, shake that thing." *"Baby, shake that thing!"* "Uuhhaahhh." *"Aaahhhhhh!"* "Ooohhhhhha." *"Ooohhhh!"* "Uuuhhhhah." *"Aahhhh!"* "Ohhh!" *"Ohh!"* "Uhmm!" *"AHHH!"* "Make me feel so good." *"Baby, make me feel SO GOOD!"*

I was definitely feeling a surge of *goodness,* since the tall brunette in front of me, who had twice turned to smile, was taking the song literally. With every "uhhhm" and "aahhh," she rocked back, suggestively sliding her pliant if somewhat flat behind back and forth against me. And to my left, a shorter, more cherubic coed had grabbed my shoulder with both hands to lift herself, as she hopped up and down trying to get a better view of the action. The music was cooking, and when the song reached its abrupt end and all six band members started to pack, everyone in that cramped basement howled and begged them to play one more song. They declined— waved off the applause and graciously bowed out, leaving the audience at the peak of excitement.

I lingered for a few minutes, standing off to the side as the band packed and the crowd filed upstairs, watched as the most attractive of the Vassar coeds—a Doris Day look-alike—rushed over and hugged the lead singer before her date snatched her away. On the way out, the saxophonist noticed me and paused.

"What you doin' here, bro?" he asked, laughing. "You with another group?"

I shook my head.

"Nah . . . okay. I dig it."

He gave me another quick once-over, then leaned forward and
whispered conspiratorially, "These ofays is crazy, ain't they, man!"

He winked and slapped my hand before leaving. They marched
out as regally as a group of Marcus Garvey's black brigade, not even
cracking a smile as the few remaining students gave them another
round of applause. When I finished my beer and fought my way back
upstairs to the door, I could feel the eyes of several coeds following
my movements. "Is he with the band?" one whispered. "No, him?
Just a frosh basketball player," her date replied. She turned away.

Unsteadily climbing the hill toward East Hall, I had mixed emotions about the evening. I'd enjoyed myself, all right; was even
turned on at the end. But I couldn't shake the unsettling feeling that
accompanied the pleasurable memories. In part it was the band; I
couldn't get them off my mind. The luminous, tight silk suits, marcelled hair, gaudy jewelry, gold tooth, and brazen, juke-joint sexual-
ity somehow reminded me of Youngstown. They could have just as
easily been playing for a black crowd at the Whale Inn or the Black
and Tan in the Monkey's Nest. And the audacious flaunting of the infamous term "nigger"—I'd been embarrassed by it but, at the same
time, felt strangely released, liberated. I didn't know what to make
of it. Were they just another group of Toms out for a quick buck?
Minstrel Sambos toadying to whites? And if so, why had I suddenly
felt unshackled, unbound? I wasn't sure.

And the two coeds, what the hell was that about? Carefree and totally uninhibited, they'd seemed possessed. They'd shown none of
the reserve or reluctance to intermingle with Negroes that I'd seen
in Youngstown; in fact, they'd seemed indifferent to anyone's reaction, had a look I'd witnessed only in Reverend Rose's church when
sisters got the Spirit. I'd halfway expected them to start rolling on
the floor and speaking in tongues. Down as anyone I'd ever seen.
Was it simply the music? Some primal reaction to the funk and the
throbbing downbeat?

Something was in the wind, and for the life of me I couldn't figure
out what it was. Perplexed and intrigued, I stopped at the top of the
hill and stared down at fraternity row. The parties were still going

strong. And nearby I thought I heard a couple giggling in the bushes behind the chapel. "You better cut that shit out," I yelled in my deepest, most intimidating Negro accent as I passed by. "Don't be gettin' no leg up in here."

By the time I stumbled across the Quad and started up the stairs to my room, I was chuckling uneasily. A nearly forgotten biblical figure from my philosophy-and-religion course had crept into my mind. Should've thought of him during my last exam. In bed that night, however, the name sounded as clearly as the Miles Davis quintet's version of "Kind of Blue," which I'd put on the turntable the moment I stepped into my room. Gershom, yeah, Gershom . . . like him I'd become a stranger in a very strange land.

The next morning, I woke up with a terrible hangover. After spending the day in bed, I decided to go easy for the rest of the weekend. After dinner, I walked to the gym and shot hoops for an hour or so, then stopped by Phi Tau. I wanted to avoid the confusion and temptation of the previous night, and Phi Tau was known for having the most sedate parties on campus. After a few hours of conversation and a beer, I returned to my room. The questions that had reared themselves the night before hadn't disappeared; I'd just filed them away. Changes might well be looming, but the reality of my situation was simple: I was performing badly in basketball, nearly failing, and, come Monday, would once again be a reluctant prisoner in what I'd come to consider a monastic retreat.

Funny how the most unlikely events precipitate crises. But it was only a week or, perhaps, two weeks after party weekend that I reached my lowest point at Colgate. It may not have even been the Screaming Niggers and the curious events of that night—just an aggregate of cultural shocks, dashed expectations, and a frank appraisal of my own mediocre performance. I'd hit rock bottom and was ready to pack up my shit and leave. A faculty advisor convinced me that I ought to, at least, speak to a counselor before I made any rash decisions. Reluctantly, I agreed.

The counselor was cheerful enough. A ruddy-faced, crew-cut graduate student, he still managed to project the avuncular image expected of a college preceptor. In fact, he was too perfect. The pipe, horn-rimmed glasses, and tweed jacket with elbow patches appeared to have come straight from a Warner Brothers movie set. Nevertheless, I stepped into his office and sat down.

"So, what's the problem, Mel?" he began.

"Well, I don't really know where to start. It's the school, the work, the social system . . . I just feel out of place here."

"Wait . . . wait a minute. Slow down for a second. I understand the work problem. Everyone needs some time to adjust here, particularly . . . ah, people who've come from a different environment. We'll get back to that. But . . . what about the school and the social problem? I'd think this would be an ideal atmosphere—a perfect place to get away from . . . well, you know, the city and all that chaos."

"Huh, I don't know . . . I guess I just don't understand these people." *Hesitant now, pausing, since I'm obviously talking to one of* these *people.* "And I'm sure they don't understand me."

"Look, Mel, let me just ask you a few questions. Perhaps we can clear this up."

The downhill plunge started right there. A banal, condescending smile passed over his face as, pad and pencil ready to take notes, he leaned over the desk to begin what, to me, seemed like an interrogation.

> *How did you get along with your parents?*
> No, that has nothing to—
> *Your father, then. How did he treat you?*
> What's that got to do with it?
> *It's okay, you can talk about it. How did your dad treat you?*
> Doesn't matter. That's not what I'm here to talk about.
> *You sure? What did your dad do? How did he treat your mom?*
> (Is this motherfucker trying to play the dozens?) No, man! That's not it.
> *Well, if it wasn't your family, who's causing the problem?*
> It's—it's the society, the whole setup.
> *Wait! You mean to say the society is causing your stress. Are you sure you're not overreacting? Who! Who in the society?*

Unnerved, I stood up, pulled on my coat, and moved toward the door, stifling the urge to yell, "YOU, *motherfucker . . . you and the rest of these deranged, pompous assholes.*" It was bizarre. Either he had no clue or, like some Colin Ferguson precursor in whiteface, had lost track of who he was: *You mean to say my clients are responsible for your problem?* I backed out of the door.

"Ah . . . I don't believe this is going to work. Look, why don't I give this some more thought and, ah, get back to you?"

"Wait, Mel, we can talk about —"

I slammed the door behind me and stormed out of Spear Hall, back to my dorm. Later, lying in the dark with my bags packed, I listened to an Ahmad Jamal jam and tried to figure out how I'd explain quitting school to my parents when I got back to Youngstown.

I had $38, spoils from the eight-ball hustle, which was more than enough for a bus ticket. Skipping basketball practice that evening, I stalked down to the village. After checking the bus schedule at the Bluebird Restaurant, I stopped at the Colgate Inn. Slumped over the oak bar, surrounded by its traditional leather chairs and tables stamped with the university insignia, I drank one rye-and-ginger after another until the hoary, heavy-set bartender spun out of focus, disassembled, and a voice—his, I assumed—prodded, "Time to get back to the dorm, my boy," and cut me off. Stumbling through the inn's lobby, I lurched to the door. Outside, the icy February air yanked me back to near sobriety.

It was on the way back, somewhere around Taylor Lake, when I realized that I'd never be able to face Tennessee if I quit. He'd had fewer opportunities, faced much more difficult circumstances, and survived—sharecropping, the Klan, Bilbo and Crump, as well as pistol-toting Southern rednecks. In comparison, my problems seemed minuscule. Memories of those early checker and tonk games flashed through my mind. The man would probably never speak to me again if I gave up. How many times had he told me, "If you start somethin', boy, you finish. Don't matter how—but you finish it. You wanna be a man, then act like one."

I didn't say a word to anyone at the dorm, just pushed pass a group of frosh tossing a Frisbee in the hallway and went back to my room. After unpacking, I fell asleep or passed out—not sure which. I'd finish the year, no matter how it went down.

### III

Luckily, by this time I'd developed a few durable friendships that proved to be crucial in getting through the remainder of the year. Freshman friends, of course, were no less isolated and confined than I was. Our bonding, to some extent, was based on shared misery.

Most, however, didn't share the peculiar form of cultural and social shock that was unique to Colgate's black students. But except for Phil Jackson, who lived in my dorm and later became a fraternity brother, my contact with other Negro freshmen was limited. I really never became well acquainted with Roger Mitchell and George Mc-Clomb, the two other freshmen who graduated with our class.

Among other things, the nature and demands of our chosen activities set us apart. Like Phil, they ran track and, from the outset, displayed an interest in student government and other campus organizations that did not attract me. In addition, that spring, both of them would pledge at Tau Kappa Epsilon. Given the cliquish nature of fraternity life at Colgate and the absence of any ethnic organizations, there was little chance for any subsequent interaction except in classrooms. Since that did not occur, we remained casual acquaintances. George, an excellent student, was granted several prestigious scholarships during his tenure at Colgate. During our senior year, Roger was elected president and George was vice-president of their fraternity—milestones, I suspect, in the history of TKE. Despite the racial connection, however, we traveled separate paths; acknowledging one another in passing, we focused on individual survival.

Fortunately, I did form some lasting friendships with a few of the school's black upperclassmen. I had met Hal Jackson—a sophomore and member of the varsity track, football, and basketball teams—two weeks after arriving on campus, when he invited me to the gym for a pickup game. Later he introduced me to George Davis, who was in his class.

Both impressed me and, in different ways, temporarily eased my growing anxiety about Colgate. Hal, who was from New York City, immediately reminded me of Aubrey and Steve, the New Yorkers that I'd met in Youngstown when they attended YSU. Like them, he cruised through most social exchanges with a self-assured, cocky attitude that seemed to transcend race. His jaunty, athletic stride, unflinching gaze, and disarming smile razed or neutralized all but the most insistent antagonists. Easygoing and apparently without rancor, but glib as a Tammany Hall politician, he challenged and mocked the slightest suggestion or hint of any subservience or inferiority. Direct challenges and casual or unintended aspersions were deflected with a wink, a smile, and an arsenal of stinging, double-edged retorts that immediately cast the onus back onto the detractor.

"Hey, Jax, *you guys* gonna pull us through that track meet tomorrow?" a relay teammate asked.

"Well, maybe. Fact is, if you get the lead outta your ass, we'd cruise." Hal laughed. "Loosen up, eat some chocolate or something before the race. They say that works, you know."

It was Hal who convinced me to pledge at Phi Tau. I balked at the inane hazing rituals—actually avoided nearly all of them because of basketball practice or simply refusing to participate—but did enough to be accepted. There were advantages. Among other things, Phi Tau had a reputation for having the best food on campus. Pop, the live-in cook, was a campus legend. In addition, Ralph, Brad, and Phil were pledging at Phi Tau. Although I'd lived alone and wasn't sure I'd comfortably adapt to the insistent brotherhood and fraternal living, I figured Hal's gregariousness would help me adjust.

George was not as convincingly aloof or immune to outside agitation. Having grown up in West Virginia and the Baltimore, Maryland, area, he carried himself with an almost studied nonchalance. But the relaxed stance was betrayed by piercingly alert, darting eyes that, like sentinels in enemy territory, constantly assayed the surrounding terrain. His watchful, somewhat wary demeanor was more familiar to me, reflective of attitudes I'd observed in the Midwest. Mindful and moody, he could switch from carefree lollygagging to simmering discontent or explosive outrage at the drop of a hat—the slip of an untutored tongue. Generally, in the company of Hal's jaunty optimism, he was jocular and easygoing.

They helped usher me through that first year. Our several trips to Syracuse provided a desperately needed escape from the rigors of classes and basketball, the monotony of all-male companionship, and the confinement of ice-slicked trails and snowdrifts that sometimes reared as oppressively as the "white death" that D. H. Lawrence vividly depicted in *Women in Love,* a novel that I'd eagerly attempt unraveling in a philosophy of literature course a few years later. Hal, an ebullient optimist with the charm of a snake-oil salesman, and George, a wily country preacher cloaking his razor-sharp intellect with pluckish diversions and down-home aphorisms, did as much as anyone to disperse the gloom and show me the lay of the land during freshman year.

Outside of three excursions to Syracuse—once with Walt and twice with Hal and George—I'd been a virtual prisoner at Colgate until the spring. I'd made only one other attempt to flee the campus with my freshman comrades during that first winter. Despite a driving January snowstorm, Walt, his friend Ned, and I had hitched a ride with a senior who apparently was as desperate to leave Hamilton as we were. He dropped us off on the campus of the State University of New York at Oneonta before going to meet his date. We spent the evening hanging out in the lounge of one of the girls' dorms, striking up conversations with any live female who wandered downstairs. We never did pull any of the coeds, although a few were aroused enough to at least go back upstairs, take the curlers out of their hair, and discard the frumpy robes or sweatshirts that they—resigned to another night with the girls—had been wearing.

It was a blast—as much fun as I'd had all semester. The problem was that we had no ride back to Colgate. Sometime after midnight, when the dorm mother kicked us out, that realization hit us as dramatically as the frigid wind and snow that pounded our faces. The weather assured that the roads were practically deserted; still, we managed to hitch a ride with a truck driver who was traveling north on Route 23. He took us as far as Ambierville or Holmesville, or some other of the small villages between Oneonta and Hamilton. Once there, we huddled in a near-empty diner drinking coffee and making small talk with the employees as we tried to figure out how we'd get back to school.

"You boys from one of the colleges round here?" the counterman asked.

We nodded silently.

"Saw you get outta that truck. Little nippy out there to be hitchin', ain't it?" Again, we nodded. "Well, hate to tell you this, but we close soon. Sure hope you got some long johns on 'cause I ain't seen but two vehicles all night."

A crooked smile flashed across his pockmarked face as he went back to cleaning the grill. Even the waitress chuckled. We looked at one another in disbelief. Seems we were stranded in a town where, as a friend later quipped, people went to family reunions searching for dates.

Before we were asked to leave, which in reality would have meant

throwing ourselves on the mercy of the local sheriff and spending a
night in the can, a car pulled up with two Colgate football players
inside. Slightly inebriated and looking for coffee, they had stopped
at the only diner they'd seen since leaving Oneonta. Relieved at our
stroke of luck, we joined the rowdy pair and crept back toward
Hamilton on the unplowed roads. I didn't venture out of Hamilton
without an assured return ride for the rest of the semester.

That spring, however, Hal, George, and I took off for New York
City and stayed for a weekend at Hal's home, in Harlem. It was not
only much less perilous than the Oneonta venture but also more rewarding.

Most obviously, Hal's family lived on the sixteenth floor of Lenox
Terrace, which was on Fifth Avenue and 135th Street. For a small-
town boy that was, in itself, a major event. The tallest building in
Youngstown was thirteen stories high; for me, skyscrapers were
marvels—symbols of a faster life, larger opportunities. Fantasies of
New York, since I'd first seen the city depicted on television, always
included looking out from a terrace at the millions of lights and
people below. The previous year, Al Bright and I had never gone beyond the first floor of any building we entered. So, upon arriving at
Hal's apartment, I immediately went to the terrace. The view of
Harlem and the brightly lit Triborough Bridge, which at night
spanned the East River like a brilliant, metallic rainbow, was dizzy-
ing. I spent hours just staring out at the view. The Jacksons must
have thought I was crazy, and, of course, Hal reminded me that I
still hadn't escaped my country origins.

"Be careful, sport," he chuckled, "it's windy out there. Try to keep
the hayseed off the neighbors."

Beyond the view from the terrace, Hal also showed me a different
side of the city. Before arriving, I hadn't known that his father was
one of New York's most popular and well-known disc jockeys. I'd
heard of Symphony Sid and Jocko Henderson; despite interference
and static, I sometimes managed to tune in their shows in Hamilton. I'd even heard of Tommy Smalls, or Dr. Jive, as he was called,
but I was amazed to discover that Hal Jackson Sr. was as popular
and well known in New York. Perhaps for that reason, Hal Jr.'s connections in Harlem were widespread.

During our three nights in New York, George, Hal, and I hit
many of the hottest spots uptown. We hung at Small's Paradise, ate

at the Red Rooster, had chicken and waffles at Wells, and listened to music at Jock's. The last, I discovered, was run by the father of a Colgate junior, Mike Jones, a black classmate whom I had not as yet met.

We played bid whist with Hal's thirteen-year-old sister, Jewel, who would, by the 1980s, become chairperson of the National Coalition of 100 Black Women and, in the 1990s, be considered for selection as the executive secretary of the NAACP. The Jacksons' next-door neighbor, the legendary jazz trumpeter Lee Morgan, dropped by that night with his wife, Kiko, a beautiful Japanese woman. After drinking nearly a pint of Southern Comfort, and anxious to demonstrate my wit, I insistently referred to the "inscrutable" nature of her card playing before I passed out. Not much of a drinker at the time, I was apparently even less adept at tactful social interchange.

When I apologized the next morning, they were still chuckling at my feeble attempt at urbane humor; they invited me in for coffee. At least I hadn't offended them.

During the afternoons Hal and I searched the playgrounds for pickup games. I was anxious to meet and play against Jackie Jackson, who at the time was considered one of the city's best playground players. Word had it that he could snatch quarters off the top of a backboard without breaking a sweat. We never ran into him, but held our own in some tough games at the West Fourth Street court, in Greenwich Village, at several school-yard parks along 135th Street, and at the park on the grounds of the low-rent housing project across the street from Lenox Terrace.

On the Saturday before we left, during a bus ride down Fifth Avenue on our way to the Studio Museum, I nudged Hal as a teenager, the tallest kid I'd ever seen, walked by while we were stopped for a light.

"Hey, man, look at that," I said, pointing outside. "Am I losing it, or is he really stooping over to avoid hitting his head on the red light?"

"Could be," Hal laughed. "That's Lew Alcindor, from Power Memorial High School. He's about seven feet tall and they say he's gonna be better than the Stilt. I don't know, but . . . think we can get him to Colgate?"

I was still gawking as the bus pulled off. New York was, in more ways than one, bigger than life.

When our ride, one of Hal's fraternity brothers, picked us up Sunday afternoon for the trip back upstate, I was reluctant to leave. Except for five days at home during Christmas vacation, it was the first time that I'd escaped Hamilton's closeted atmosphere for any sustained length of time. Speeding up the Thruway toward the Tappan Zee Bridge, I promised myself that I'd be back. Soon.

The city took my mind off of my dissatisfaction with Colgate. And although it was March and most of the snow had melted, it took only a day or two before the doldrums set in and that cornered feeling returned. Still, the worst of it was over.

The basketball season, which had seemed interminable to me, had ended. And with more time to study, I was able to catch up in most classes. Gradually I was learning how to approach course work and becoming more attuned to the rhythm and cadence of my professors' speech. Although my grades were only slightly above average, I wasn't burdened with the anxiety of knowing that one slip might mean failure and expulsion.

Moreover, the social and cultural isolation had slackened. Hanging with the upperclassmen George and Hal not only afforded access to trips to Syracuse and contact with a coed scene but had also, even within the confines of the campus, provided exposure to less whitewashed attitudes and viewpoints. And friendships with Walt, Dave, and my three fellow Phi Tau pledges—Ralph, Brad, and Phil—gave me a base of camaraderie in my own class. Mere acceptance in a fraternity, in fact, conferred a kind of superficial status in that provincial, extremely hierarchic campus world. Phi Tau, for example, had a reputation for attracting many of the school's brightest scholars; its pledges, whether they liked it or not, automatically were assumed to be good students. That identification, unless proven otherwise, came with the territory.

The casual conversations and associations developed with Phi Tau brothers during brief visits to the frat house that spring helped improve my study habits. Encouragement and tips on how to study were offered freely. Moreover, the diminished instances of bias I encountered among those students affirmed my belief that, while not exact, there was a clear correlation between racism and ignorance. That and the allure of Pop's cooking drew me to the frat house more frequently.

Colgate had not changed significantly but I'd found a niche and

was increasingly discovering how to navigate its icy, often hazardous waters. I became even more adept during the spring Party
Weekend.

After my bizarre experience in the fall, I'd avoided fraternity
bashes at the winter Party Weekend. It was the height of the basketball season, and still struggling on the court and in classes, I tried to
avoid the temptation of going on a drinking spree. Nor did I want a
repeat of the encounter with the Screaming Niggers. I still hadn't
quite figured that out. Instead, I only briefly ventured down the hill
to fraternity row. I stopped at one or two houses early in the
evening—for a few hours, at least, brushed shoulders with some
women and reminded myself that the world was not as off-line and
unbalanced as four months at Colgate might leave one to believe.
Afterward I returned to my room and studied. My dorm mates
razzed me, of course, but I didn't care. I felt I was doing the right
thing—saluted my self-control. The restraint kept me out of trouble
and probably helped my grades, but it certainly didn't lessen my desire for companionship or build my ego.

By spring, however, basketball was done and I was getting a better handle on my classwork. I'd also become much more aware of
the particular nature of the house party scene. Knew which frats
hosted the hippest parties, where to find the rowdiest sets. Unfortunately, the jumping parties were held at Sigma Nu and DKE, the so-
called jock houses where disdain for Negroes was least veiled.
Those parties and the school's ranking as runner-up in alcohol consumption among American colleges would make Colgate a close
second to Dartmouth as the model for the film *Animal House*. Although other houses were less tolerant of the beer-slinging, butt-
groping near orgies for which those frats were famous, the same
single-minded quest for sex energized their parties. It was simply
cloaked by a surface nod to decorum.

I didn't avoid Sigma Nu and DKE, even after the beer-can-tossing
incident. I'd never sensed any imminent threat since, as I said, campus bigots usually kept their distance—delivered slurs from one
hundred yards away and from out of the darkness or whispered behind your back. I'd become accustomed to the hypocrisy. Moreover,
these were jock houses, and although basketball didn't have the status of football, I got some respect simply because I was an athlete.

Still, whenever I dropped by one of those wild frat parties, I worked at affecting a more menacing appearance. Sometimes it paid to work the stereotypes. Standing erect, shoulders back and chest flexed, with a slight scowl curling my lips, I mimicked the cold, imperturbable stance of a Youngstown hustler. I never quite duplicated it but, at nearly six feet four and 205 pounds, in that preppy environment, it took little more than sunglasses, a swaggering gait, and a curt manner to conjure up images of the street nigger that, for many, loomed in their minds as disturbingly as exaggerated fantasies of gargantuan Negro sexual organs. No one bothered me.

That spring, however, I spent very little time at the wilder parties. On Friday night, I checked them out to see if any truly funky bands were playing. Finding none, I moved on to less feral grounds. Looser and less anxious about grades, I got caught up in the festive spirit. Dropping the defiant shield, I laughed and joked, danced with a few brothers' dates at Phi Tau, then joined Walt and Ned to cruise a few other houses. Near one o'clock, I left them. On the way back to the dorm, I stopped at Sigma Chi, the only fraternity on the campus grounds. My freshman friend Dave had pledged there, and outside the jock houses, they had the liveliest parties on campus. Still, I'd intended staying for only a few minutes.

The party was jumping, so it took a while to find Dave. When I did, he poured me a drink and we talked for a minute or two before one of his new fraternity brothers pulled him away. I turned my attention to the bandstand. An Italian group dressed in flaming red jackets was pumping up the crowd with their own original tunes as well as some wildly upbeat versions of rock 'n' roll hits such as "Rock Around the Clock," "Maybe Baby," and "Whole Lotta Shakin Goin On." I finished my drink and was pushing my way toward the door when someone grabbed my arm.

"Where you going?"

I turned to find a thin brunette with a narrow, angular face and striking deep-set, green eyes peering up at me. "Well, I was on my way back to the dorm," I said.

She didn't let go of my arm. "You know, I saw you dancing earlier at one of the other houses. I was going to come over and say hello, but you disappeared. I'm Jordan, from New York. Who are you?"

"Ah . . . Mel. I'm a freshman here."

"Mind if I leave with you? I'm tired of all this . . . think it's time to call it a night."

I looked around to see if there was a date lurking nearby. No one in the vicinity seemed concerned.

"Don't worry, I'm alone." She smiled, half pushing me toward the door.

It was a typically cool spring evening in Hamilton, and, outside, she crossed her arms and hunched her shoulders. "Brrrrrr, it's getting chilly out here."

"Yeah, and you didn't come prepared."

She was wearing only a light sweater and shorts. Lean and small breasted, she had the figure of an athlete—a far cry from the era's preferred, busty, cherubic look. Moreover, even when she smiled, there was an intensity, an almost ethereal spark in her eyes, that contrasted starkly with the sportive but frivolous expressions that most Party Weekend dates wore like emblems. She was free spirited, but there was a determined air of independence about her. I wasn't sure if it was unpredictability or madness, but I was intrigued.

"Where you staying?" I asked.

"At the Inn, with the rest of the imported dishes." She laughed and turned abruptly, as if headed down the hill, toward town.

"Hey! Wait a minute, Jordan. Mind if I walk you partway?"

Turning back toward me, she did a pirouette before stopping and raising her arms. "Thought you'd never ask." She laughed, bowing slightly at the waist.

I threw my jacket over her shoulders and we started down the hill. It turned out that she was a dancer and a junior at Hunter College. Her blind date had met her at four that afternoon and, by six, was smashed. When he tried to pull her into a frat house bedroom, she'd pushed him away and gone back to her room at the Colgate Inn. Bored and alone, she'd decided that her trip to Hamilton shouldn't be a total loss and ventured out to see what a Colgate party was like.

"The Sigma Chi house seemed safest," she said, since it was so far away from the rest of the fraternities.

"You haven't seen much of the campus, then?" I asked.

She shook her head, no.

"Well, why don't you let me show you around? You've already ruined my plans to turn in early. Come on, we're not all macho sex deviants."

For the next hour or so we walked around campus and talked: strolled down the willow path and sat on a bench near the lake, went back to Phi Tau and filled paper cups with scotch—the first I'd ever tasted—then climbed back up the hill and paused at the Meditation Center. She couldn't shut me up. It was the first time since Christmas, when I'd seen my East High School friend in Youngstown, that I'd talked to a woman alone.

"Let's stop for a minute," she said, looking up at the sky as we crossed Whitnall Field on the way back to town. "It's gorgeous, isn't it?"

I stopped and looked up. A half-moon was peeking through a typically overcast Hamilton sky, and now and then a cluster of stars lit up behind the clouds. It wasn't that beautiful to me—dark and mysterious, perhaps, but "gorgeous" was a stretch. Still, when she sat down yoga-style on the grass, I joined her. A few seconds later we were embracing. And shortly afterward, lying on top of my jacket with the sound of rock 'n' roll music drifting from fraternity row and giggling couples passing close enough to occasionally force us to muffle our cries, I had my first intimate encounter at Colgate. There was no pretense of being cool or restrained, just the raw urgency of trying to get a nut. Afterward, spent, we lay there for a half hour, giggling and ignoring passing couples who passed within a few yards of us. It was after four when we got back to the Colgate Inn.

"Why don't we meet for brunch tomorrow?" I suggested after we kissed good night. She stroked my cheek and nodded her head before twirling through the door and up the stairs. I think I actually trotted all the way back to campus and up the hill to my dorm. And although I slept fitfully and was awake in less than five hours, I had never had a more satisfying night's sleep in East Hall.

When I arrived at the Inn to meet her for brunch, she wasn't in the lounge as we'd agreed. After a ten-minute wait, I asked the desk clerk if he'd ring her room. "No need," he said. "She checked out this morning. Are you Mel?"

I nodded. "Then this message is for you," he said, giving me a suspicious once-over.

I stepped outside before opening the envelope. "Dear Mel," it

said. "Sorry, but I had to leave. I couldn't face running into Jerry
again. Glad I met you, though, you were delightful. Don't hate
me.—Jordan."

I was stunned and, naturally, disappointed. I'd spent much of the
morning dreaming about a repeat performance and working out
plans to find a more secluded spot somewhere on campus. Despite
the setback, when I returned to my room, my estimate of Colgate's
social life was considerably brightened. That night I made the
rounds on fraternity row again, but found no one as exciting or willing as Jordan. I met a few disenchanted coeds, but the encounters
went no further than playful flirting and amicable chitchat. Still, the
previous night's encounter had somewhat balanced what had been a
totally disappointing year.

The last month and a half of school sailed by as I focused on my
class work. I finished the semester with a slightly improved, 2.4
grade average. At least, I told myself, I'd made it through the year.
But after finals I was still unsure about returning the next year.
Hedging my bet, I packed my trunk and stored it at Phi Tau. If I returned I'd be set. If I didn't, I'd pick it up or have it sent back to
Youngstown in the fall.

The evening before I was to leave for summer vacation, I took a
walk around the entire campus, pausing at Taylor Lake, the Student
Union, and Huntington Gymnasium before meeting freshman
friends at the Colgate Inn. We toasted the successful completion of
our first year, and while everyone cheerfully ruminated about the
prospects for the coming year, I tried to conceal my uncertainty
about the future.

The following afternoon I took what I thought might be my last
look at Colgate University and the village of Hamilton. Later, I
piled into the car with a group of four boisterous students to begin
the ride to Pittsburgh. My companion in the backseat, a soon-to-be
junior, immediately opened a can of brew. At the intersection of
Broad and Payne, he unbuckled his pants, snaked them down over
his hips, and hoisting his butt up near the rear window, mooned
the campus just before we pulled away on Route 12B. We were
headed back to the heartland.

# 14

## fly away home

My parents picked me up in Pittsburgh and I drove the sixty-five miles to Youngstown. The previous September, no one could have convinced me that I'd be anxious to return home. But the city's modest skyline with the Home Savings and Loan Building's clock tower rising above surrounding structures, even the silhouettes of blackened factories outlined against the evening sky, and the steel mills' jutting coke-plant stacks were welcomed sights. Temporarily, at least, I'd escaped from semivoluntary exile in Hamilton. That thought alone kept a smile on my face for the first few weeks.

My mother was as proud and glowing as I'd ever seen her; so, it seems, were the neighbors. The day after I arrived Katie insisted that I go and say hello to the Baskins and Mitchells, the sedate, middle-class families who lived across the street, and to Mrs. Hicks and Big Six, who lived next door. These were people who had watched me grow up, in fact helped discipline me whenever I went astray; they were as pleased to see a kid from the neighborhood succeed as she was. Typically, Tennessee didn't say much, but the smile that lit his face was an even louder signal. And by the next evening, the rest of the family had dropped by to greet me. All during the summer, whenever someone stopped by the house, Katie would find reason to introduce me and announce that I'd just returned from college.

Since, for the first time since I could remember, our house was nearly empty, I didn't feel cramped or confined that summer. McKay had left town and was living in Chicago or Detroit, or, perhaps, Toledo; no one really knew which. My brother Al and both my sisters had moved out of the neighborhood with their families and owned their own homes. Only my parents and my brother Herbert remained.

From the moment I arrived, there were a thousand questions about school. How'd I liked it? How'd I done? And with my family, I skirted most of them. I wasn't proud of either the 2.4 grade average with which I'd finished or my performance in basketball. I'd averaged about ten points a game but played poorly. I also didn't want to let on that I wasn't sure about returning in the fall. My only real achievement had been winning the Freshman Writing Award, and that had no impact in my household. The essay might as well have been written in Arabic; they had no idea what it was about. Had they read it closely, they would have discovered that Sartre was an atheist, and then, surely, dismissed it. Once, my mother did attempt reading part of it to Tennessee. She barely got to the second page. "Man can never be said *to be* at any one moment . . . his being always escapes him and exists somewhere in the future. . . . It is only a vague possibility toward which he projects himself . . . "

At that point, Tennessee got up and poured himself a glass of cold water. "Hold it, hold it right there," he laughed. "That's plenty for me. But let's see here, boy. They teach you anything 'bout playing checkers? Come on over here and set up the board. Let me show you somethin' 'bout them *pos-a-bilties*."

Their reaction didn't surprise me. Funny, though, how things work. I'd spent only one year at Colgate, but already, in my mind, the university's logical, reasoned, measured perceptions and focus on tangible reality had begun warring with the sly, covert sensibility that had been shaped by Miss Aggie's tales, Tennessee's delta blues, and Katie's cat bones. It had also widened the gap between me and my parents; the more they encouraged and pushed me toward college, the further I moved away from their Southern roots and down-home folk culture. That growing chasm was partially responsible for my ambiguous feelings about returning to Colgate. I wrestled with the decision throughout the summer.

I had gotten the Parks Department job that I applied for in the spring and, within two weeks, started working at nearby Grant School playground as a counselor. The job kept me occupied. Working with young kids was as gratifying as it was relaxing. My partner, Delores, a pretty black college student who had graduated from South High the year before me, was responsible for the girls. In addition to setting up equipment each morning (swings, teeter-totters, and such), I was in charge of activities for the boys. Essentially I played all day, organizing softball teams, then coaching or umpiring in games with other playgrounds, advising my eager eight-to-fourteen-year-old wards on everything from shooting a jump shot to playing dodgeball, checkers, or ringers—a variation of horseshoes in which points were scored by sinking washers in metal cups that substituted for spikes. I lost myself in a carefree world of athletics and childhood games, couldn't have been more relaxed. It was the perfect tonic for the pressure and cultural shock I'd experienced the previous year.

After work, there were more sports. I returned to the pickup games in Mill Creek Park and, magically, found my own game. Perhaps it was just the familiarity of my old stomping grounds and the lack of pressure. I'm not sure, but the shot, the timing, and the poise reappeared. Basketball was fun again and I excelled. Playing in a benefit game with a group of Ohio and Pennsylvania college All-Stars at Pittsburgh University that summer, I had an outstanding game, scoring in double figures although I played less than a half.

I also played baseball for the Buckeye Elks. I wanted to keep all options alive. Although I wasn't sure if the offer was still available, in the back of my mind professional baseball was still an attractive alternative choice. My performance that year, however, partially curtailed those thoughts. Hitting wasn't a problem; I had one of my best years as a batter. It was in left field that problems arose. A simple pop fly hit my way, a play that would not have vexed a Little Leaguer, inexplicably became an adventure. It happened three times, and never in practice—always in a game situation. I didn't know if I was running on my heels, losing my vision, or, perhaps, my mind. But as I approached and circled underneath the elusive sphere, the ball would dance in the air like a feather, hovering and taunting me, before dropping. Mystified, on two occasions I missed it entirely.

Dropping an easy pop fly is always an embarrassment. But when

I was playing for the all-Negro Buckeye Elks team with its ram-bunctious, signifying fans, it became an invitation for outright ridicule. "Sit yo' nonplaying ass down!" one of the least abusive fans screamed. Another came down to the bench and offered me a big hat. "Havin' some trouble out dere, boy. Why don't you try this?" He laughed.

I survived. Much of the invective could be deflected with a timely base hit later on, which I got on at least one occasion. Still, I couldn't help wondering: whatever happened to Marvelous Mel? Discovering that my newfound gracelessness had pursued me to the baseball diamond, I relegated minor-league ball to a very low priority.

Work and sports took up most of my time that summer. And usu-ally exhausted after returning from a workout, I was most often content to sit at home and read or watch television. My social life was nonexistent.

Three weeks after returning, I'd met my East High friend, who had just graduated, for what turned out to be our last drive-in tryst. My absence had strained the hot but fragile relationship we'd had a year earlier; I'd seen her only at Christmas since the previous sum-mer, and although she'd written, I couldn't send letters to her home. Frustrated and tired of the imploring, the wrestling, even the pas-sionate petting sessions, I issued an ultimatum. Essentially, it was either put out or end it. It was, of course, not that cold. In fact, I'd tried my best we're-no-longer-juveniles, times-are-changing, saving-yourself-for-what? rap. It didn't work. She politely informed me that she was going to college in the South next year anyway—Furman and John Wesley were being considered—so maybe it was best that we cut it off. I'd started the car before she even retrieved her blouse from the backseat. When I dropped her off at her car, she said she'd call, but we never talked after that night.

Naturally, I was disappointed. But later I realized that she was probably right; it was just as well. The relationship had been doomed from the moment we began sneaking around instead of facing up to her parents and the social consequences. Moreover, that summer I needed to be alone. And after we split, I withdrew into a contemplative shell.

Al Bright and I did not have much of a chance to hang out that summer. He worked as a laborer in the steel mills and an apprentice sign painter, waiting for acceptance in a local barbers' school until a chance meeting with industrial bigwigs at the National Junior Achievement Conference in Bloomington, Indiana, steered him to Youngstown University that fall.

I did occasionally hang with Huck, my next-door neighbor's son. I was still not much of a drinker, but at Colgate I'd been forced to at least learn how to imbibe well enough to avoid getting smashed on a few beers. Huck put my newly developed capacity to the test. We'd sometimes cruise in my father's car for hours, bullshitting while drinking Thunderbird or Ripple. He had just returned from a stint in the army and had been stationed in Germany for several months. His exotic tales about the sights of Munich and his wild escapades with free-spirited fräuleins immediately captured my attention and sense of wanderlust. And while I was amazed that he had returned and settled so easily into what I considered an ordinary job, as a driver for a beverage distribution company, I couldn't conceal my envy of his adventures in Europe.

We also shot pool a few times and stopped once or twice at nitty-gritty dives such as the Forty Club, on East Federal Street, or the Ritz Bar, on Wilson Avenue, a slightly more upscale hangout. Huck would sometimes rap with the seasoned, mostly older, and generally bawdy female habitués, trading innuendoes with dedicated barflies who, although seemingly only one shot away from passing out, never refused a drink. There were also some truly fine women—a few as stunning, flirtatious, and elusive as the sexy factory worker Dorothy Dandridge played in *Carmen Jones*. Their hip-hugging dresses and wily come-hither smiles commanded my attention. But they knew, as well as I did, that I was out of my element. They'd peeped the ingenuous collegiate I'd struggled to disguise with hip attire and a cool front as quickly as if I'd been wearing one of those telltale Colgate freshman beanies, shot me down before I could get a word out. "See somethin' you like, sugar?" they'd tease, brushing my cheek with lacquered fingernails before gliding away.

"Don't get too excited, honey. You too young and tender for me to surrender," one laughed. "Y'know I'm a keeper . . . come on back when yo' pockets git deeper."

Huck and I cracked up. I, at least, was much too green for them. Still, I watched with fascination as those sleek brown-skinned foxes worked the clientele with calculated precision, separating tipsy steelworkers from their paychecks as expertly as a team of medical students might dissect a cadaver.

Mostly I sought solitude, perfectly content to stay at home or to drive aimlessly around the city trying to once again get in touch with the feel and rhythm of my hometown. Crime and gangland activities still dominated the headlines. And as I soon discovered, the area was just beginning an economic plunge that, by the mid-seventies, would bring on a complete collapse of the steel industry. During the previous year steel production had fallen 25 percent of capacity and state unemployment claims had risen to the highest level in history. The U.S. Department of Labor announced that the city was among the twenty most depressed in the nation. In addition, a harsh winter with snow and rain setting off the worst flooding in fifty years had inflicted severe property damage on local businesses and residential areas. No one seemed overly disturbed, however; apparently convinced that the economic plunge was temporary, residents confidently assumed that the prosperity they'd enjoyed since World War II would soon return.

Most seemed more concerned with the activities of Otto Stankey, an oddball bird exterminator who was imported from Kansas City to rid the County Court House of an annoying roost of starlings who had downtown pedestrians ducking and dodging their droppings whenever they approached the building. Stankey and the mysterious black box that he moved from place to place along the building's ledges drew a substantial crowd during that summer. The starlings ignored him.

Negroes were as lackadaisical and sanguine as most everyone else. Despite increasing agitation for an end to segregation in the South, the city's hotels and motels, many of its restaurants and movie houses, and a large segment of its public and private recreational facilities were still segregated. There were few overt complaints. Nor did the disproportionate number of their own members among the newly unemployed seem to alarm most blacks. There was still an eerie feeling of living in a time warp. The city had not changed much. But I had, and although I was still unsure where I would go in the fall, each day convinced me more that I would leave Youngstown.

Fortunately, things were quiet at home. My parents had apparently reached some kind of détente. Although they argued occasionally, their tiffs usually ended with uneasy laughter and sarcastic joking that reflected my mother's ambivalent feelings more than any mirth. They slept together, but I couldn't even imagine the tension that must have wracked any physical contact they shared. Tennessee had not drastically changed his behavior, but he had mellowed. Perhaps it was just his age. In his late fifties, he hung out less and rarely demonstrated the explosive violence I'd previously seen. Still, it was Katie who had made the concessions, dampened her expectations, and accepted his adulterous wandering. Only occasionally did the rage that simmered behind her reluctant compromise show itself.

Instead, she turned her attention to my brother Herbert, coddled and shielded him from the outside world, particularly those women who, in her view, sought to misuse him. He still worked with his twin brother, Al, and lived at home. Although he was self-sufficient, there was just enough of a slur in his speech and a hitch in his gait to mark him as a target for hustlers, male and female. Sometimes to his annoyance, Katie watched over him like a suspicious lioness tending a young cub, forcing him to leave part of his money at home before leaving, calling or going out to find him if he strayed too far or stayed out too late. In a sense he filled the emotional void that Tennessee had left. During the remainder of her life, almost all of her affection and caring would be focused on him.

That summer, I too received that near-obsessively-doting attention. My mother treated me like a visiting dignitary. I would have steak or lamb chops when everyone else had hocks and greens. And whenever she could, she'd slip me money without Tennessee knowing it. "No, you take that, Mel," she'd insist when I tried to turn it down. "Save that little money you making at the playground. I know you didn't have enough to get along last year. I want you to have just as much as them other boys."

But since I was content staying home, her overzealous concern about my whereabouts was rarely a source of irritation. On Woodland, I mostly read, which she wholeheartedly endorsed, or watched television with her while she reminisced about the South—a period of her life that she increasingly viewed more fondly. During those talks, I drew closer to her than I would at any other time before or after. Sensing her heartache and dependency on me and Herbert, for the first time I glimpsed the price she had paid for the liberty Tennessee insisted upon.

The only discomfort I felt from her intense concern was its effect on the decision I was trying to make. It became obvious that my going back to Colgate, finishing college, was crucially important to her. Even as I marked time, put off my decision, the weight of her expectations began to bear down on me.

That summer, in mid-July, the United Steelworkers of America went out on a nationwide strike. Their action closed the mills for four months and put some smaller Youngstown factories permanently out of business. It also left my father and brother Al out of work and disrupted the calm that had settled over the household. Money was again short, and Tennessee was forced to intensify his various hustles to make ends meet. Since he was home more often, tension increased around the house; after a week or so, my mother's nervousness was palpable.

On the heels of the strike, during the first week of August, my parents received an urgent call from the Ohio State Highway Patrol. My brother McKay had been shot and was in critical condition in a hospital outside Akron. The next morning, they left to see about him.

When they returned, two days later, my mother was a wreck. Another of her seed was imperiled and she wore her concern and distress like a hair shirt. Tennessee, as usual, revealed nothing; the cold stamp of fatalistic acceptance masked any reaction. It was days before I got the details of the story. McKay had apparently fled a gas station without paying for fuel and led a patrol car on a wild twenty-mile chase before he pulled over. Then, according to the officer, he had reached toward the glove compartment of the car, presumably to get a weapon; one shot was fired, and McKay had been taken to a hospital with a bullet wound in his arm and neck. Fortunately, it had missed all major arteries, and forty-eight hours later he was removed from the critical list. After he regained consciousness, however, McKay insisted that when the officer approached the car, he raised his hands and didn't move. The bullet, which pierced his left forearm before entering his neck, seemed to validate his version. No gun was found in his car.

I never visited McKay in the hospital, never saw him before he was transferred to a cell and, later, due to inconsistencies in the officer's story and seeming contradiction by the physical evidence, charged only with petty theft. The incident rattled me, however; indelibly emphasized the perils of an option I'd been considering.

I'd begun to see college and the staid, conventional, working-class lives my other brothers and sisters had chosen as a cop-out, a tacit submission to the hypocrisy of the race game or, at least, an admission of one's abject powerlessness in dealing with it. In part, I admired McKay's lawlessness and Tennessee's rebellious allegiance to the Negro netherworld of gambling and hustling. Their responses, in many ways, seemed perfectly rational reactions to the madness surrounding them.

In turn, the prospect of eluding mainstream society's deceit and self-righteousness by dropping out and leading a vagabond life in New York still loomed as an attractive option for me. Despite magazine and newspaper articles that attacked the so-called Beat Movement—even writers such as Allen Ginsberg, Norman Mailer, and LeRoi Jones—the coffeehouse scene in New York with its poetry reading and jazz remained an appealing attraction for me. They were, at least, expressing their disaffection and discontent. As important, many seemed to have abandoned some of the racist beliefs that dominated the rest of the country. My first year at Colgate had made the Beat scene seem even more appealing.

McKay's scrape with the law, however, brought a sudden dose of reality to my fantasies. Negroes who stepped outside society's prescribed social roles found themselves on more hazardous grounds than their white counterparts. Almost all of the writers and dissenters who became associated with the Beat scene suffered some vilification and harassment by the press and the authorities. But as LeRoi Jones discovered during run-ins with the law in Greenwich Village years later, crackdowns by authorities were much more swift and violent when dissenters were black. Slipping from mere dissent to lawlessness was even more hazardous. McKay's latest encounter reminded me that the path he'd taken often led to disaster—could lead to millimeter-narrow brushes with death.

Still uncertain about returning to Colgate, I began looking for other options. It was during this time, in August, while trying simultaneously to get my head together and minister to Katie's distress, that I first discovered James Baldwin's *Notes of a Native Son*. I immediately put down Sartre's *Anti-Semite and Jew*—I would come back to it—and devoured that collection of essays. The lead essay, "Everybody's Protest Novel," led me to borrow and read Richard Wright's novel *Native Son*. But although I was impressed by Wright's graphic depiction of the besieged Bigger Thomas, it was Baldwin's subtle, more nuanced analysis of America's race problem that intrigued me.

That book accelerated my interest in writing more than anything I'd previously read. Every time I put it down, I immediately reached for a pen and pad, anxious to see if I could evoke my own experiences with even half the lyricism and power I sensed in his writing.

I must have read the final essay, "Stranger in the Village," twenty times. I kept finding sentences, paragraphs that for me perfectly described the racial "conundrum" on which he focused. Phrases—"it was impossible for Americans to accept the black man as one of themselves, for to do so was to jeopardize their status as a white man" or "the American vision of the world is dangerously inaccurate, and perfectly useless"—leapt into my mind at the most curious times: while umpiring a softball game, driving, or, sadly, camping under a pop fly while in the outfield.

For the next two weeks, I buried myself in Sartre and Baldwin. I went to work, came home to dinner, and if there was no scheduled baseball game, went to my room to read. Around midnight, about the time Herbert stopped watching television and went to bed, I'd go back downstairs and spend a few more hours reading or writing. I was convinced that Baldwin's *Notes* and Sartre's *Anti-Semite and Jew* held answers to many of the questions I'd been asking. I had not yet discovered them, but I was certain they were there. It was apparent, however, that both the Frenchman and the American black man saw the concept of race as a fabrication, an emotion-laden mirage—utterly useless beyond its narrow anthropological use as a system of classification of large masses of people.

This mother lode of ideas notwithstanding, the summer was quickly coming to an end. I had to decide what I'd do in the fall. In retrospect, I'm not sure if it wasn't the summer's reading combined with the memory of "nigger" echoing across the Quad at Colgate that shaped my decision. Or perhaps it was the photograph of my brother Al in a leather jacket, white scarf, and rakish pilot's cap that had sat on my mother's bureau for as long as I could remember. (I later discovered that it was a staged photo. The Tuskegee airmen notwithstanding, most Negroes in the air force during the forties never got near a plane.) It could even have been Huck's tales of Germany and the liberation he felt in Europe, or even some unconscious remembrance of Miss Aggie and Dancer's magically flying away and disappearing without anyone knowing where he'd gone. Whatever the motivation, near the end of the month I decided to join the air force.

I borrowed Tennessee's car and, on August 29, drove to Cleveland and marched into the air force recruiting office. An incredulous expression flashed across the face of the stern, crew-cut officer who sat behind the desk when I entered. He had that hard-nosed, Midwestern-farm-boy gaze that I'd seen a thousand times, and initially I had some anxiety, thought he assumed I'd been sent to sweep up the place. "I'm here to sign up for officer's training," I blurted out, probably too insistently. "I want to be a pilot."

He didn't flinch, which, to my mind, was a victory. And while I nervously gave him a rundown of my background and explained why I wanted to join the service, he assumed a stone-faced professional stare. "The thing is," I concluded, "I have to know immediately. College starts next week."

"You're sure about this? Sure you want to quit college?"

I nodded.

"Okay, here's the deal," he said. "There are some tests you have to take to see if you qualify. We'll know by this afternoon."

I was directed to take several written tests and given a rudimentary physical examination during the morning. About noon they told me I could go out for lunch for a few hours and come back in the afternoon to see how I'd done.

I had a hamburger and Coke at a nearby diner, then walked around downtown Cleveland, window-shopping and killing time. I was tense. It was a big move, and still, I didn't know how I'd explain the choice to my parents. It would seem stupid to them and, at the very least, quixotic to most others. But besides the allure of speed and flying, I felt officers' training school in the air force was the quickest way to get out of the United States and see if Europe was as liberating as Huck had described, or even as marginally less repressive as Baldwin and other expatriates had suggested. Being a pilot, I thought, would be not only an exciting career but also one that would take me to the far-flung, exotic places I'd read about.

Anxious to get the results, I returned to the recruiting office in about an hour and a half. It was another hour before the officer got back to his desk. In his absence I'd sat reading the *Cleveland Plain Dealer,* for the first time noticing how rapidly hostilities were escalating around the world. The only good news on the front page was that Hawaii was still celebrating its annexation as the fiftieth state. Otherwise, the news was grim. Castro was making waves in Cuba. India had sent troops to the Tibetan border to resist Chinese communist aggression, and communist North Vietnamese forces were overrunning the American-backed Royal Laotian Army in the northern provinces of Laos. No United States soldiers were involved yet, but the situation was getting sticky. My romantic vision of the air force had not included the possibility of war; it gave me something to think about while I waited.

When the recruiting officer returned, he called me into his cubicle. "Passed everything without a problem," he said, cheerfully. "You're in if you want it. The thing is ... your vision. Pilots gotta have twenty-twenty vision. Your left eye is only twenty-forty. Won't keep you out of the air force, but it means we can't put you in the pilot's seat. You'll have to shoot for navigator. What'd'ya think?"

"Uhhhmm ... damn, I don't know," I stammered. For minutes I sat there, eyes closed, shaking my head. It was only a small difference, I knew. But somehow the shift was devastating; it wasn't the air force career I had envisioned. For me it was the difference between steering a car and being relegated to backseat driver.

"Look," he said, "you have until the beginning of next week to make a decision, right? Why not think about it for a few days and give us a call on Monday or Tuesday?"

"Yeah ... maybe that's the thing to do," I mumbled, lost in my own thoughts. I stood, shook his hand, and left.

In the car, my decision had been made practically before I got out of downtown traffic and began driving past the sprawling estates of Shaker Heights. I cruised back to Youngstown in a near daze. My bold plan to flee both Youngstown and Colgate at the same time had been thwarted; I'd have to find another means of taking flight. Like it or not, it seemed I was headed back to Hamilton. For the time being, it was the best opportunity I had. I'd just have to devise a way to deal with it.

Six days later, Katie and Tennessee drove me to Pittsburgh, where I met my ride back to New York. I'd saved over $250 during the summer, so at least I wouldn't be broke after the first week. Moreover, I consoled myself, it could be worse. A few days earlier I'd read that, after a year of being shut down, the Little Rock, Arkansas, schools had been ordered to reopen and the National Guard had again been called out to protect a handful of black students trying to attend Central High. What the hell. If they could defy a mob of rabble-rousing rednecks armed with clubs and baseball bats, I could certainly deal with a few preppie bigots screaming "nigger" from out of the darkness.

# 15

## spotting
## the
## spades

I arrived in Hamilton with a much more positive attitude that fall. There was some apprehension about the weather and the isolation, but I was braced to contend with it and determined to improve my grades. If I had to be there, I'd make the most of the situation. I expected that fraternity living would be less hectic than my experience in East Hall, but I was still surprised to discover how much it eased the hurdles I'd anticipated. During the first weeks of my sophomore year, Phi Tau emerged as an oasis.

It took a few weeks to get used to rooming with another student. But as it turned out, my roommate spent much of his time practicing for the wrestling team or cramming at the library. We seldom bumped into each other and I usually had the room to myself. It helped that I was a night person while he was up at the crack of dawn. Even when he was studying at his desk, it was easy for me to find isolation and space to read in the living room or lounge area; late at night, the dining room was nearly always deserted. We got along without problems, and as long as I didn't wake him climbing into my upper bunk and he didn't wake me when he bounded out of bed in the mornings, we seldom disturbed each other.

On the other hand, I resented the kitchen job I'd had to take to make up the difference between the cost of room and board at the university's facilities, which my scholarship covered, and the higher fee at Phi Tau. For one thing, although his cooking was superb, the house chef, Pop, was a bona fide eccentric. While he could be warm and humorous when he set his mind to it and would advise or aid any house member who had a problem, more often than not he seemed intent on affirming his reputation as a grizzled old curmudgeon who ruled his domain like a despot. Known to chase unwanted brothers out of his kitchen brandishing a cleaver on occasion, he subjected nearly everybody who worked with him to a continuous stream of abusive, if sometimes hilarious, banter. Pop's unsettling presence aside, I never did adjust to waiting tables or bussing pots and pans after meals. Although frat members rarely assumed a superior attitude toward the guys who worked the kitchen, I didn't adapt well to the servile position. Once I donned the required white apron, I became as surly and uncivil as Pop. After a while, most frat brothers learned that it was best to leave me alone while meals were being served. The annoyances of my fraternity job, however, were balanced by other advantages that Phi Tau offered.

Most important, the frat's studious atmosphere positively affected my class work. Besides the incidental discourse that developed naturally during meals or loafing in the lounge area, there was an overall sense of intellectual competitiveness between frat brothers. Of course, we had our share of rambling bull sessions reminiscent of those held in the freshman dorm. But most often, the input of more serious upperclassmen upgraded the rap sessions. Typically, no one got involved if he was the least bit hesitant about his knowledge of a subject. Those heated debates, with topics ranging from philosophy and English literature to politics and current affairs, were like practice sessions to me. They geared me up for classroom exchanges and, whether I participated or just listened, kept me on my toes.

I'd returned to school more focused, and prompted by the intellectual environment and comfortable atmosphere, I settled easily into my courses. I also began rethinking my tentative choice of a field of concentration. Initially I'd leaned toward psychology. But it was a second choice; there was no creative writing major at Colgate. Since I'd read some Freud and had devoured Sartre's *Existential Psychology*, I assumed that psychology would continue holding my attention. It held the additional promise of unraveling some of my personal problems and shedding some light on the racial issue. My experiences in the introductory psychology course and with the school counselor, however, had dampened my enthusiasm and shattered any illusions I had about examining the psychology of racism. Significantly, the ideas of such black psychiatrists as William H. Grier and Price M. Cobbs *(Black Rage)* or Frantz Fanon *(Black Skin, White Mask)* were unavailable at the time. By the end of my sophomore year, I was fed up with the Psychology Department; I narrowed my choices to philosophy and fine arts history. Finally, I chose the latter; it seemed a perfect way to get a grasp of history and the evolution of world culture and the arts while taking as many writing courses as I could.

The new environment and my more determined approach worked; I moved from near-failing grades as a freshman to the dean's list in the first semester of my sophomore year. The previous year had shaken my confidence, left me thinking that perhaps I couldn't cut it at college, so making the dean's list was an ego boost that I sorely needed. During the winter, however, when the demands of the basketball season were added to my kitchen duties, my grades dipped just beneath that level. Still, I'd found an academic niche and an approach that suited me. When outside activities interfered with class work, I'd concentrate on the courses that most interested me and skate through the others. While my grades were only average in required language and core-curriculum courses, I maintained a dean's list average in fine arts history and elective philosophy and English courses during the four years at Colgate.

As I suspected, fraternity life as an upperclassman completely transformed the social scene. Many fraternity brothers had cars, and if we were disposed, rides were available to several nearby girls' schools each weekend. I used those opportunities sparingly that year since I was dead set on bringing my grades up and usually strapped for money. Just knowing escape was possible, however, was a tremendous relief. And on one or two occasions, I got away for evenings at Syracuse and Skidmore. Still, the most obvious benefits came during Party Weekends.

Since I was struggling to make ends meet, inviting a date to campus was out of the question. Instead, I took a job as the house bartender during those weekends. Mostly it involved keeping tabs on individual bottles that fraternity brothers left in my care and, after opening a keg, slinging beer to anyone who asked.

In addition to making some much-needed extra money, there were more enjoyable perks. As I'd discovered the previous spring, there were usually a number of coeds who came to Colgate on blind dates. Many found that they couldn't stand the weekend partners with whom they'd been matched. Most of those unattached coeds drifted from house to house during the course of an evening, and the one place they were sure to stop was the bar. It was, I quickly discovered, the perfect spot to meet any disenchanted visitors. By the end of most evenings that year, I had two or three restless and dateless young women to choose from.

There was a problem. Fraternity bedrooms, like the freshman dorm rooms, were off limits for dates after eight o'clock; the penalty upon discovery was expulsion. Although many fraternities regularly ignored that sanction, my Phi Tau brothers were sticklers and would check to make sure no one was jeopardizing the house's good standing. There was always the possibility of finding a secluded spot on the grounds if the coed was adventurous and inclined toward after-hours dalliances. But not all were as daring as the Hunter College dancer I'd met, and at fall and winter parties, when snow had usually fallen, that option was hard to sell.

For the less daring but still willing, arrangements were not difficult if they were staying at a motel outside of Hamilton where night clerks were unconcerned about who went in or out. But many campus visitors were housed in professors' homes or the Colgate Inn, which made entry to a single woman's room a challenge and test of ingenuity. Colgate students had devised all manner of gimmicks to divert the attention of the Inn's desk clerk when entering and, later, stealthily exiting before dawn. Some, I'm told, had even managed to infiltrate professors' homes—a risk I was unwilling to take. Of course, many of the abandoned dates were not looking for any sexual connection. Alone and disappointed, they simply wanted companionship, someone with whom they could hang out and talk. Many times they were far more interesting than their more libertine counterparts. The bottom line was that, despite my never having a date, Colgate's all-male environment was not much of a problem that year. I met scores of diverse, interesting women. Race seldom emerged as formidable hindrance.

In fact, on the second night of the fall Party Weekend I met an attractive blond who caught my eye while she was dancing. With her long hair, dark eye shadow, and svelte figure, she looked as though she'd just stepped out of a William Burroughs or Jack Kerouac novel. I was intrigued; she was the most interesting woman I'd seen all evening, and when she came to the bar, I immediately struck up a conversation. Her name was Faith.

"There's no Hope," she laughed slyly, "but I do have a sister named Charity."

She had ditched her date and, as it turned out, was looking for company. We talked and, when I closed the bar, left to hang out at another house. Although only an eighteen-year-old high school senior, she was extremely bright; she also admired many of the same writers and jazz musicians that I did. She was leaving early the next morning, but we exchanged addresses and numbers when I walked her back to her room just before dawn; we agreed to write and try to get together later in the year.

The following semester, during spring break, I contacted her and made a date. I arranged to stay at Hal Jackson's apartment, and we drove to the city in his year-old Corvette. Scholarship students weren't permitted to have cars, so Hal was forced to stash the Corvette off campus at a gas station about four miles outside Hamilton. We had to hitch a ride to the car before getting started. I'll never forget that drive to New York that night; it was wild. Hal cranked it up to over 130 miles per hour while we flew down the Thruway, and about forty miles outside New York, we heard John Coltrane's classic, newly released version of "My Favorite Things" for the first time. The next evening he drove me to pick up Faith in Rowayton, Connecticut, an exclusive village outside of Stamford.

When we arrived, I was surprised to discover that her mother was Kay Boyle, a well-known writer whose work I knew from a short story anthology that I'd read. With my budding interest in writing, I was as interested in talking to her as I was to the daughter. A gaunt, imposing woman, whose piercing eyes seemed capable of penetrating steel, she was as gracious as she was intelligent and, as I quickly discovered, wary. That night, she was particularly concerned with checking me out and assuring that I got Faith back by eleven o'clock. Since we intended listening to jazz in New York, that didn't seem possible, but I insisted that we'd try. We had dinner in Greenwich Village and listened to a jazz group at the Village Vanguard. Afterward, largely through Hal's risky but expeditious driving, we made it back to Rowayton about midnight. Faith's mother wasn't overly disturbed. She made tea and we talked for a half hour or so before she went to bed. Hal and I left shortly afterward.

I'd had a terrific evening with Faith, and the brief conversation with her mother had been fascinating. She was the first literary luminary that I'd ever met, and although her comments about the responsibilities of a writer, the unconditional necessity of truth and honesty, were sobering, her encouragement fired my passion. When I returned to campus that Sunday night, I began keeping the journal that she had advised was absolutely necessary for anyone who wanted to write.

The Colgate social scene, I was quickly discovering, was not as stifling as I'd suspected. It could, if worked cautiously, lead to some rewarding connections. There were, of course, also some bizarre encounters.

Earlier that spring, I'd agreed to join Ralph Arlyck on an expedition to Skidmore College, where he had met several coeds. We met the girls that afternoon and, after lunch, decided to rent a car and drive back to Colgate. Later that night someone suggested that we drive to Syracuse for dinner. All went well until Laura, a petite sophomore with jet black hair and a mischievous glint in her eyes, insisted that she wanted to learn how to drive. We were just tipsy enough to agree to the idea. Outside of Hamilton, on Route 20, she took the wheel with me sitting in the front seat giving instructions. She drove admirably on the open highway but, when we got to Cazenovia, the traffic apparently unnerved her. Just as we were pulling over to change drivers, a car pulled out from the curb and Laura back-ended it. There was only minimal damage, but the middle-aged woman whose car had been hit was furious. She leaped out onto the street and began screaming and waving her arms wildly.

Since Laura did not have a driver's license, I quickly tried to switch seats with her. While we were attempting to make the exchange, however, she stepped on the gas pedal again and our car plowed ahead, ramming the other car a second time. At that point I managed to slide behind the wheel. But the other driver noticed, and when a skinny young police officer arrived, she insisted that, no, I wasn't the driver, it was the girl.

"Look, lady," I whispered to her, after I'd stepped out of the car. "She doesn't have a license and it's a rented car. Just say I was driving and the insurance will take care of any damage."

She wasn't buying it. In fact, my plea sent her into a rage. I wasn't sure if she was just distraught over seeing the dent in her fender, stupid, scrupulously honest, or insulted because a Negro had asked her to bend the truth. Bottom line, however, was that not only were we involved in an accident with an unlicensed driver but also a hysterical woman was fingering me as a felon who was attempting to cover up the truth.

Apparently Cazenovia was short on excitement since, following the accident, a crowd gathered. Our cars were in the middle of the street and traffic had stopped. It seemed that the entire student body from the local girls' school as well as a good proportion of the town's residents had come out to view the commotion. Finally, after about twenty minutes of confusion, we admitted that Laura was the driver. She and I were taken across the street to the Cazenovia jail.

Ralph, who found the incident more amusing than I did, was standing to the side with the other coed, laughing during most of this brouhaha. But when we were led away, he and Laura's friend accompanied us. After a few minutes of questioning and confirming that Laura wasn't licensed, the policeman, who looked like a boyish high school sophomore, told us that unless we had bail money she'd have to be locked up overnight. I was reprimanded for my part in attempting to obstruct justice and, much to the dismay of the still-livid female driver, told I was free to go. We, of course, didn't have bail, so I was concerned about the situation. Ralph, Laura, and her friend appeared unfazed.

For good reason, it seems. Before being locked into the jail's only cell, Laura was allowed a phone call. Her parents weren't at home but someone assured her that her father would get back to her immediately. "Don't worry," she said. "Dad will take care of it."

Damn, I thought, so this is how white folks are treated by the law. At that point even I relaxed. Ralph and the other coed went across the street to have dinner, and for an hour or two, I sat on a stool outside the cell, talking to Laura. I wasn't allowed inside with her, the officer said, but he didn't mind if I stayed and kept her company. He even allowed Ralph to return with a pizza and wait with us. So, with her on one side of the bars and me on the other, Laura and I finally had dinner.

By the time the phone call came and bail was arranged, all of us were chuckling, even the young cop. Having seen the police in action on several occasions in Youngstown, I was amazed. Either the officer had enough previous experience with college students to find the entire affair humorous and not out of the ordinary or, as I did, he recognized the irony of holding a cute, young white coed in the lockup while her Negro date sat outside the cell gobbling pizza and laughing at the absurdity of the law. When Laura was released, we headed for a motel, where we howled about the incident until the next morning. During the rest of the weekend, I drove.

As it turned out, Laura and I dated for nearly a year. And the following fall, she came down for a Party Weekend. It was the only time during my four years at Colgate that I imported a date for a party. Money remained a problem, but I'd found ways to get around the social obstacles I faced at Colgate during my sophomore year.

I also came to terms with basketball during that year. Once I realized that it no longer conferred the social status that it had in high school, I lost much of the fire that had previously driven me. Increased interest in the academic life and the growing sense that I wanted to be a writer further dampened my enthusiasm. I enjoyed the game, but it had been eclipsed as the primary gauge of my self-worth. It simply was no longer the obsession that it had been. Still, I played with as much eagerness as I could muster and rarely experienced the sense of futility that had plagued me during my freshman year. During the three years of varsity ball, I averaged eight rebounds a game and shot over 45 percent from the floor while averaging just under ten points.

Some other of my teammates and I did, however, harbor some resentment toward Bob Duffy, who we sometimes sarcastically referred to as Gatling, because of his predilection for shooting. I still remember a thirty-foot, left-handed hook shot that he heaved during a close game while I stood unguarded under the basket. Several times during the eighty or so games we played together my irritation reached a point where I refused to pass the ball to him; an ill-advised tack since he was a guard and handled the ball most of the time. He was, however, a superb athlete. Ambidextrous, he could drive or shoot with either hand—an ability that was not common during the early sixties. Moreover, he was a dedicated, well-conditioned ballplayer who did not smoke or drink, something that I and most of my teammates could not say of ourselves. In retrospect, since we were often overmatched against bigger, more talented teams, it's difficult to fault him for exploiting the situation to showcase his own talent. If I had been in his shoes, I might have done it myself. Moreover, it worked. After graduation in 1962, he went on to play for the New York Knicks and Detroit Pistons.

By the spring of my sophomore year, I'd devised ways of dealing with nearly all the problems I'd wrestled with as a freshman. I had basketball, my class work, and the social scene under control. For most of the year, I'd easily handled the routine, day-to-day campus rituals. Since I lived off campus, getting to my classes was more difficult than the previous year. I had to walk past the lake and Student Union, then up the sometimes treacherously slippery hill that we'd slid down as freshmen before reaching the classroom buildings. Once there, however, I felt totally at home; most important, I'd begun to pick up on the professors' speech patterns, and note taking was no longer an exercise in translation. I had only one writing course that year, but the literature, religion, and philosophy courses I took challenged and held my attention. I was particularly impressed by Professor Balmuth's logic-and-scientific-method course; it explained and laid out the principles of thought processes that I found useful throughout college and afterward. Balmuth himself, a small, compactly built man with a no-nonsense demeanor and riveting stare, seemed to personify the integrity of the commonsense principles he taught.

I also had my first class with Professor Alfred Krakusin that year. He was a small, nervous man whose bristling energy was evident the moment you stepped into his classroom. His passion for art was also palpable, and during heated class lectures, he not only vividly evoked the era in which a work was created but also compelled students to feel the emotions that had inspired classic paintings by Rembrandt, van Gogh, Degas, Picasso, and others. He, more than any other teacher, influenced my decision to choose fine arts history as a major. Few professors at Colgate demonstrated as much passion for the subjects they taught; none were as candidly revealing about the passions that shaped their academic interests.

During my last two years at school, he became a friend whose advice I depended upon. Sensing that he, too, was battling his own personal demons, I was less reluctant to discuss social problems that I never broached with other professors. Although I attended only three more of his classes, I'd often stop by his office to discuss my writing or, on occasion, meet him at the Bluebird Restaurant for coffee, where conversations ranged from civil rights to the process of creating facsimiles of classic statues that he was working on with the Rockefeller Foundation in New York. I was shocked several years after I'd graduated when I discovered he had died from a self-inflicted gunshot wound.

Outside of classes that year, I forced myself to become more involved in campus and fraternity life. Despite the demands of basketball, I partied and drank more, pushed myself to adopt a more carefree attitude. But despite the frivolity, there were always small, subtle reminders that the other black students and I were oddities in that rarefied atmosphere. Television reports of the racial ferment in the South, for instance, would draw a curtain of awkward silence over the lounge if I happened to be sitting in the room with a group of fraternity brothers. Pretense and avoidance reigned. And I abetted it by directing conversations either to lighter, frivolous subjects that didn't touch on race or to more abstract, general topics that transcended it. It was as easy and much less cumbrous to emphasize similarities than dwell on apparent differences. Even so, it was sometimes trying. But, scorning sentimentality of any kind, I cloaked my concern with a mask of remote, ivory-tower indifference, hoped that the glib, ironic distance that I'd assumed would quiet or, at least, veil the underlying stress that still persisted. The sign I'd tacked to the door of my room at Phi Tau—I CRIED BECAUSE I HAD NO SHOES, THEN I SAW A MAN WITH NO FEET . . . I LAUGHED—signaled the direction I'd taken.

### III

Shortly after returning from New York and the chance meeting with Kay Boyle, however, that cavalier posture collided head-on with the lurking suspicion that something was unresolved and still pending.

The inevitable collision occurred about three weeks before the end of the second term. I'd gone to the Phi Tau dining room to read the final chapters of Proust's *Remembrance of Things Past* for a French literature course. But I was preoccupied, and my gaze kept wandering over to Taylor Lake, which was visible through the large picture window at the front of the house. Finally, I opened my by now dog-eared copy of Baldwin's *Notes of a Native Son*. Final exams were two weeks away, and I should have been studying. Instead, I kept riffling through the pages, scanning the underlined passages.

I couldn't shake my preoccupation with the race issue that night. And the more I thought about it, the more alarmed I became. I was overcome by a queasy, guilt-ridden feeling that the entire year had been a sham. Was I slipping into some unholy alliance that required eradicating self in order to fit in at Phi Tau, becoming too comfortably acclimated to a world in which I remained an outsider?

Now, I'm sure, the question was triggered by events that I'd read about or seen on television during the previous few months. Little Rock's Central High School was still in the news, and in February student sit-ins had started in Greensboro, North Carolina. Similar demonstrations quickly spread across the South; riots followed several of those protests. Later that month, a bomb exploded at the Little Rock home of one of the black Central High students. And eight Negroes were shot during a disturbance that broke out after an attempt to integrate a beach in Biloxi, Mississippi. In March, a thousand Negro students had gathered in protest on the steps of the capitol building in Montgomery, Alabama, and after local authorities forcefully dispersed them, Martin Luther King Jr. appealed to President Eisenhower to intervene. A few days later, a gang of white Houston youths had beaten a lone Negro and carved "KKK" into his chest. The Sharpeville, South Africa, massacre, in which fifty black Africans were killed, punctuated racial problems here and abroad.

Being safely cradled in the isolated, placid surroundings of a private, near-all-white college while the furor intensified was a bizarre, unsettling experience. Not that I had any impulse to rush to the South and join those nonviolent protests.

"If anyone thinks they cannot be orderly," a Montgomery protest leader had warned, "they can help us more by staying at home." Given that decree, I knew it was best that I kept my ass out of the fray. I would have been a definite liability, for myself as well as other demonstrators. I had no illusions about being able to react passively when attacked. When it came to self-defense, my allegiance was with the eye-for-an-eye approach that the Black Muslims espoused and Tennessee exemplified.

Still, my near-seamless absorption into the vagaries and frivolous routines of fraternity life suddenly seemed heretical. Images from the past flashed through my mind: the child with her innocent, Shirley Temple smile screaming "Nigger!"; Al Bright being led around an empty swimming pool by a lone lifeguard; a savage mob hurling eggs and brandishing clubs at black teenagers in Little Rock; McKay attempting to banish his disillusionment by shooting poison into his arm in our darkened Woodland Avenue living room; the enthusiastic reception given the Five Screaming Niggers; the insistent grilling and inane questions of the college counselor. And in front of me, a passage from Baldwin's *Notes* leaping off the page: "One may say that the Negro in America does not really exist except in the darkness of our minds."

Who the fuck were they, then? Who was I?

Whose tune should I be dancing to anyway? The bouncy rhythms of an Irish jig? The foot-stomping, hand-clapping exuberance of an African jig? The somber, ritualistic tom-tom meter of a Native American fertility dance? Perhaps, even, some purely American hybrid composition that combined all those ancestral strains? Or was it more cut-and-dried, as simplistic as almost everyone seemed to have concluded—was *I* actually the *jig* that everybody apparently assumed I was?

I slammed the book closed, leaned back, and stared across at the lighted Willow Path. A few minutes later I got up and walked over to the campus. I sat on a bench near the lake. It was after one o'clock, and the area was deserted. Only the sound of swans gliding through the water and an occasional squawk—a protest, I assumed, over the invasion of territory that, at this hour, should have been theirs alone—interrupted the calm. My mind, however, was afire; passages from Baldwin and from Sartre's *Anti-Semite and Jew* rushed through it, colliding with images from Aichinger's "The Bound Man." The crash of Baldwin's personal testimony and Sartre's analysis, my own conviction that we chose who we wanted to be, shaped ourselves, thundered in my head.

I lit a cigarette, leaned back, and tried to get a grip.

Sartre had pointed out the fallacy of basing one's identity on spurious social roles and Aichinger had vividly portrayed the futility of either accepting or struggling against outside boundaries or definitions. Baldwin had articulated similar ideas, finally suggesting that deliverance was possible only when the white world relinquished its false image of the Negro. Perhaps, but given the extreme reaction to Negroes' request to be seated at dime-store lunch counters, that possibility didn't seem likely. Nor did it solve the problem of how to proceed in a society where madness and the elevation of myth to the status of reality obstructed your pathway at nearly every turn.

An hour or so later, still with no clue to the dilemma, I walked back to the house. I had a glass of juice, picked up my books, and headed toward my room. In his own bluesy, lyrical way, I mused, Baldwin had come closest to an answer when he suggested that Negroes were black only so long as America thought it was white.

And in a flash, with that quirky, reverse logic that sometimes steers us, it came to me. The fear that had gripped the child and the consternation that had wracked the young mother on that lawn in Youngstown when I'd naively deflected her daughter's accusatory scream of "nigger" was no accident. It had shaken something in them, frightened the child and caused the mother to momentarily question her own assumptions. Was that it? Had Baldwin turned it around?

Nearly fifteen years later, accompanied by the Dial Press publicity director, who happened to be from Youngstown, Baldwin and I would explore the idea while guzzling Johnnie Walker Black at a midtown Manhattan bar. But that night my thoughts raced uncontested through my mind. Why wait for America to change its mind, to admit that race was the useless, outworn concept he'd suggested it was? I had no control over that. And who would willingly abandon a classification that worked entirely in their favor, kept so-called Negroes scurrying around attempting to prove that they weren't something that, in reality, never existed, or worse, slyly persuaded them to accept the spurious distinction and appeal for equal treatment despite it? Visions of the nameless hero of Ralph Ellison's *Invisible Man* flooded my mind—*Hope him to death but keep this nigger running*. No! The responsibility was mine. They were no more white than I was black; I had to alter my own perception; had to do it myself.

And suddenly, the solution seemed simple: *they were white only so long as I thought I was black!*

"Yes!" I shouted, then quickly looked around to see if I'd awakened anyone or if some frat brother, bent on an all-nighter or plagued by insomnia, hadn't been wandering around the house and heard my outburst. No one was about, and I laughed softly. For another half hour or so, I walked around the dining room savoring the insight and chuckling to myself. Finally, near dawn, I went to my room; I didn't want anyone to witness my glee just yet. But I was giddy with excitement when I climbed into my bunk that night. The implications of the thought kept surging through my mind.

I didn't know how I'd eliminate all the subtle gestures, defensive speech mannerisms, and expectations of denial that had become near second nature after twenty years of reacting to society's daily slights and accepting the offhand assumption that color or race had some inherent special meaning. It would be difficult to suppress my by then knee-jerk reactions to those situations. Nor did I expect the transformation to immediately affect much outside myself. Certainly the taxi driver who had passed me by only a few weeks earlier as I flailed my arms on a New York street corner wouldn't have cared. The change would primarily affect me. It would reverse the game—eliminate my complicity and put the onus on whoever was determined to sustain the pretense.

Lying awake in the dark, I couldn't help laughing aloud even as my roommate stirred in the bunk beneath me.

It would be, I thought, like implementing the premise of Schuyler's outrageous satirical novel *Black No More*. Instead of a magic potion that changed Negroes' physical appearance, however, a change of attitude was all that was required—total abandonment of the concept of race. Just ignore it and move beyond its ambiguous pseudoscientific implications. My mind swirled with wild speculation about the ramifications if the approach were enacted en masse. A national crisis would be precipitated, for instance, if Negroes began marking "Other" on the census questionnaire; after all, four out of five blacks had some trace of Caucasian or Indian blood anyway. We might also, at capricious intervals, boycott chicken, chitterlings, and spare ribs, or all garments with even a hint of red dye; eat lo mein or pasta bolognese for a month or two (it was just as cheap); wear Vatican white, no matter how down and dirty we may have gotten the previous night. Not give them up, you understand; that would be denying the *culture*—fleeing elements of a lifestyle that had been cleverly portrayed as low or inferior. No, what I fantasized about that night were temporary "whiteballings" that would demonstrate that choices of food and clothes were not the consequence of some inherent racial destiny but simply culturally shaped preferences. Of course, the image of thousands of frustrated A&P and Kroeger supermarket managers standing beside stacks of rotting hog entrails wondering, "Where are the niggers?" did fire my imagination.

More significantly, all that was really needed was for every one of those phantom Americans who under Mississippi's one-drop-of-Negro-blood classification ("50 million souls," according to Schuyler's 1930 estimate) were legally black to stand up and affirm their Negro ancestry, thereby exposing the absurdity of the issue.

"Hey, Mel," my roommate mumbled, "you all right?"

"Yeah . . . I'm just dandy." I laughed. "Sorry, go on back to sleep."

Fanciful speculation aside, there was as little hope of such across-the-board desertion of the pretense then as there is now. As Schuyler had humorously documented, too many people were firmly locked into it for psychological as well as economic reasons. Entire industries had grown up around it. They fed from the segregation trough on both sides—black civil rights leaders and middle-class businessmen, race-film producers and minority directors of government agencies prospered as much as racist labor unions, white race experts and academic specialists. Then there were those 50 million or more presumed white souls and their offspring who, as a 1990s comedian would suggest, might *look* at their family trees but would never, ever *shake* them—too much chance that a nigger might fall out.

I didn't harbor the illusion that my personal revelation would find general acceptance among other Negroes. For many, identification with the illusory social role was too strong, fear of reprisal and, perhaps, of the responsibility of shaping their own individual identities too threatening. Already, I'd begun to discover, there was an insidious attraction to the role of victim. No matter that social circumstances might in fact corroborate the stance, that enervating self-indulgence was as debilitating as assuaging one's frustration with drugs. It was a diversion that, with profuse outside encouragement, had immense appeal. But I was determined to avoid it. As I saw it, *mentally* abandoning the racial label yielded the same benefits as the Black Muslim's insistence upon pride and self-reliance— but without the religious mumbo-jumbo and self-imposed isolation that resulted from the attempt to turn the racial myth around and reverse its values. I swore that night that I'd never willingly segregate myself again. Moreover, while I extolled the culture that had grown out of it, I'd ridicule and undermine the myth at every turn.

The next morning, although I slept only about two hours, I bounded out of bed. And during the last weeks of school, even as I prepared for finals, I kept pondering the idea, questioning myself. At the end of the term I was still convinced I was right. The only rational way to deal with an illusion that had become a social reality, for me, was to ignore it. Like the bound man, I was determined to unshackle myself, even if the consequence was ostracism by those— white or black—who relied on racial identity to define and, to my way of thinking, nearly always restrict themselves.

For the remainder of the term, I put those thoughts on the back burner and threw myself into studying for final exams. Once, at the village supermarket after I'd brought about eight items to the checkout counter, I was tested. When I casually dropped a $10 bill on the counter in front of the clerk-owner, it set him off for some reason.

"You people get into college and suddenly think you own the world," he shouted. "Don't *throw* money at me!"

He pushed the bill back toward me as if he expected me to pick it up and hand it to him. At first I bristled and was about to respond. But I caught myself before I exploded. *Don't react—it only reaffirms the illusion.* "You people?" I calmly repeated.

"Yeah, you know what I mean," he said.

"No, I don't think so, my friend," I said, smiling. Picking up my money, I turned and, laughing, walked out. Left his shit on the counter.

"Come back here," he yelled. "You can't leave this stuff here."

I walked over to the smaller grocery store across the street and picked up the items I needed before returning to the house. Other than that, there wasn't much opportunity to test my new resolve. I was much too preoccupied with cramming for exams, particularly a psychology course that I'd ignored all during the semester.

A week before I returned home, however, I discovered that Hal Jackson was leaving Colgate; he would be transferring to Marquette in the fall. (He later earned his law degree there and eventually became a judge in Milwaukee.) His departure and, despite the relative ease with which I'd fit in, my need for more isolation, however, convinced me that the frat house was not the best place to find myself, develop a new attitude. I'd also grown more and more frustrated with the kitchen job that I was forced to take in order to live and eat at Phi Tau. Although I kept dining privileges at the house, before leaving I arranged to move into the special quarters set aside for scholarship students in my junior year. I'd save money on room costs and apply that to the extra charge of eating at Phi Tau next year. Before Hal left that spring, we hitched a ride out to the Madison gas station, picked up his Corvette, and drove to Syracuse. Hal introduced me to Hank, the service station owner, and we discussed the possibility of my leaving a car there next year. Since he was a sports fan and Colgate booster, there was no charge other than having him service the car. I assured him that I'd see him in the fall.

I had no idea how I'd do it, but when I left the fraternity, I knew I'd need a car. I had to get away from the closeness of frat house living, but I didn't want a return to the complete isolation of my freshman year.

### III

In Youngstown that summer, I was determined to relax and focus my attention on the decision I'd made in that fraternity dining room. I returned to Grant playground as a counselor, which meant that there was no pressure at the job. I played basketball and baseball; at night, I usually relaxed and read. It was a perfect time for me to catch up on the works of authors that weren't included in the Colgate curriculum.

I devoured W. E. B. DuBois's *Souls of Black Folks* and Richard Wright's *Black Boy*, and later in the summer found time to read more of Dostoyevsky as well as Norman Mailer's *The Deer Park* and *Advertisements for Myself*. The latter included "The White Negro," the controversial essay in which Mailer forwarded his view of how hipsters, rebelling against the fifties' rush to conformity, were lured by the freedom of the black lifestyle. It was also the first time I'd seen any writer draw an analogy between Negro life and existentialism; I read it feverishly, even though I was put off by Mailer's superficial analysis of Negro life. Those books not only fueled my desire to write but also increased my determination to step outside the rigid bounds of racial categorization that Wright so vividly described. Outside of work and sports, books and the journal I kept in my spiral notepad consumed nearly all my time.

Nothing much had changed with my family. Katie and Tennessee had not grown closer, but they had learned to coexist without overt fireworks. It had become primarily a marriage of convenience. Tennessee most often went his own way, and my mother still lavished her affection on her children and a growing brood of grandchildren. McKay had recovered from the gunshot wound but was still behind bars. And since by then my sisters and brother Al had left the neighborhood and their children were no longer constant visitors at our house, Herbert remained the near-obsessive focus of her attention. He was happy to see me return and divert some of that concern.

During that summer, I discovered why Eugene Gant, Thomas Wolfe's most famous character, had concluded that "you can't go home again." Not to say that there weren't many warm, comfortable moments with my family.

I laughed and lollygagged with my sister Doris and her husband, Leroy, about politics, the Negro problem, and sports. Leroy continued to insist that I should assert myself and take more shots in basketball games. "You oughtta try and make the pros." He laughed. "Damn the coach. Look out for yourself!"

I also stopped in at my brother Al's house and talked with him and his wife, Julia. She was intent on separating herself from the apathy that seemed to have engulfed most Youngstown Negroes, and whenever I even hinted at being dissatisfied with college, she'd get on my case. "You better stay up there and get an education, Pepper," she'd warn. "Just look at all these poor niggers out here. None of 'em got a pot to piss in and no idea about how to get one." It was largely her determination and thrift that inspired my brother to move out of Youngstown. Despite the bombings, cross burnings, and milder protests that had greeted Negro families who moved into white neighborhoods within the city or attempted moving into nearly all-white suburbs, they acquired a sprawling ranch-style house in the exclusive suburban community of Boardman. There, they assumed, their children would at least have an opportunity to avoid the influence of the rising crime rate and drug epidemic that increasingly plagued Youngstown's Negro community.

There were also stops at my sister Cherrie's house, where I rapped, drank, and invariably shared some of her excellent cooking with her and the rest of the family. Although Cherrie was in some ways more supportive than all my siblings, at that time I always had a disquieting sense of foreboding when I visited. It was not my sister or her husband, Billy, but their oldest daughter, Levern, who stirred the misgiving. It was something I'd noticed while in junior high school—a predilection for manipulation that caught my attention primarily because I was often the target of her schemes. She seemed to revel in playing people against one another, sometimes for her own gain and, at others, seemingly for the pure joy of it. When I'd begun jotting down notes and observations during high school, there were as many entries for her as there were for my brother McKay.

Early on I had dubbed her "Walter Winchell" because of her knack of seeking out and, when the time was right, readily dispensing information about others. For me it meant concealing my whereabouts as well as any personal possessions from her. Still, like some precocious eight-year-old sleuth, she would track me down no matter where I went. She had established a direct pipeline to my parents, and most times, when I attempted avoiding their scrutiny, she would promptly assume the role of willing informant. She was relentless, an unshakable nemesis, so there was always an edge to our relationship. But it was more than just a personal conflict.

Later, in high school, when most of my activities were beyond her eagle-eyed snooping, she remained a frequent entry in the journal that I began keeping. There was a certain wildness and disrespect for authority about her that, to me, seemed unchecked. She had always been bright, but the quick wit was most often used for deception. "Slick and clever," I had written, "she erroneously assumes that her glibness will protect her."

During the summer of 1960, that disaster seemed to loom even more prominently. She was having problems in school and had fallen in with an older, cockier, and more irreverent crowd. Once or twice I tried to talk to her about getting her act together, but she was beyond consultation. Refusing everyone's advice, she was gradually sucked into Youngstown's netherworld of miscreants and felons, began a downward spiral into a world of violence and crime that, some years later, ended in a fatal car crash as she and her boyfriend fled the police. She was the first. Later, a few others among my nieces and nephews and their children would madly plunge down a similar course, flailing against the gloom and stagnancy of that stratified, dead-end society and succumbing to the lure of drugs, easy money, and fast living. Despite their move to the suburbs, even Al and Julia's youngest son would fall prey to the trap.

Outside of visits with my brothers and sisters, I generally stayed at home. Not only did I want time to myself, but I'd also decided to save money for purchasing a car. I'd talked to Tennessee about it a few weeks after arriving and he promised that if I had $200 by the end of the summer, he'd help me out by matching it. Since I was taking home only about $50 a week, it put me on a tight budget. But I was determined to save the money; staying home had an added incentive. It also meant spending more time with my mother, and during those times I noticed a subtle change in her behavior.

Katie had always been nervous and cautious. That protective instinct led her to carefully gird herself against presumed threats, whether real or, as with her fear of hexes and spells, in my estimate imagined. During the two years since I'd left for college, however, her suspicious nature had intensified. Growing up on Woodland Avenue, we had seldom locked the doors, and I often slept outside on the front porch on hot summer nights. But that year Katie had taken to latching and bolting all doors in the evening. At night, when we sat and talked or watched television, she was skittish and jumpy. Any strange or sudden sound—a car slowing down in front of our house or an animal squealing in the backyard—drew her attention. Periodically she went to the living room window to peer out and assure herself that no one was lurking on the porch. When I borrowed my father's car and went out, she invariably issued ominous warnings about the dangers of the streets.

"Make sure you lock the doors and roll up them windows," she'd say. "Man got stopped by them hoodlums last month. Just pulled him out and took his car. And don't drive up Hillman. That's where they all hang out." Her anxiety, I discovered, was a barometer of changes that had occurred in Youngstown during the two short years I'd been away.

The strike that had shut down the steel industry the previous year had been settled. Tennessee and my brother Al were back at work, but mills were functioning far below capacity; many workers were forced to accept part-time positions, and twenty thousand were unemployed. Youngstown was being referred to as "steel's sick city" in the national press. In 1960, crime would also increase by 31 percent over the previous year. Gangland activities accounted for some of that rise, but street crime was increasingly becoming a serious problem. And much of that problem was concentrated on the south side, which had become nearly all Negro.

The passive acceptance of de facto segregation that had reigned during my adolescence and teens was coming to an end. It was one thing to accept second-class citizenship when the economy was thriving and everyone had money in his pocket, but another entirely when a large segment of the community was out of work with no prospects of employment. The black community's simmering discontent erupted in minor disturbances that disrupted the city's traditionally unruffled racial calm. Drugs, too, were much more in evidence. Across the street and a few doors down from my parents' home, a drug house had opened. Heroin, pot, and speed were sold, and a continuing stream of customers went in and out. With the drug use came an increase in house break-ins, muggings, and robberies. Most of those crimes were inflicted on the law-abiding residents of the black community.

Katie had some reason for concern. The rapid transition of Woodland Avenue and the rest of the south side was most threatening to Negroes of my parents' generation. It was part disillusionment and part shock at witnessing their own sons' and daughters' rejection of the fragile lifestyle they had constructed in the shadow of bigotry. For my mother and many others of her generation, the turmoil surrounding them signaled defeat and retreat. They withdrew behind locked doors and savored memories of more-tranquil times. Katie, for instance, drifted into romanticized reveries about the South, erasing uglier experiences and focusing on the fact that at least she did not have to hide from the onslaught of enraged black youths, particularly her neighbors' children. For Tennessee and those accustomed to the street, there was no problem. It was a familiar situation and, armed and ready, they glided through it without blinking.

Nor was it frightening to me. The streets of Harlem had seemed far riskier; in comparison, the increased crime in Youngstown was minor. I was more disturbed and frustrated by other things. Again, that summer, I occasionally hung out in local bars and cabarets, hoping to find some spot frequented by Negro professionals or college students. I was looking for blacks who, like Aubrey, Hal, George, or some of the black coeds I'd met at Skidmore or Syracuse, shared my interests. Either there were none or I simply couldn't find them.

I felt as estranged in Youngstown that summer as I had at Colgate when I first arrived. There were a few clubs, like the Ritz Bar, that featured jazz groups during the week; the clientele was mostly older but I'd still sit, listen to music, and sometimes strike up a conversation with whoever was near. But—my mind flooded with the ideas of Baldwin, Sartre, Mailer, Schuyler, and Wright—I felt as out of place with the finger-poppin' crowds in the loud, boisterous, insistently down-home black bars as I would have, had I been admitted, in white joints where Elvis, country and western, and pop rock reigned. By the first week of August, I'd given up the hunt.

On rare occasions when I borrowed Tennessee's car and went out, I'd visit my brothers and sisters or simply look for a quiet restaurant to eat, read, and have a cup of coffee. Bored, I began to amuse myself by studying white people—scrutinizing their features and physiques to see if I could spot anything that supported Schuyler's theory about 50 million Negro deserters. Walking along the street, shopping in downtown department stores, or sitting in a restaurant, I'd look for clues: lips that were a shade too full, nostrils that flared a bit too broadly, butts that rode too prominently on the hips, or hair with that unexplainable extra kink in it. I jokingly called it spotting the spades.

When I spotted someone suspicious, I'd stare at them with a knowing grin in an attempt to get their attention, and if I could, greet them with a hearty "Hey, bro!" or "Hi there, sister!" Nine times out of ten, the response was a blank stare, a look of confusion and tentative "Hello," or, sometimes, an angry scowl. Those reactions, of course, revealed almost nothing, since the object of my scrutiny might have been unaware of why I'd been staring or what I'd meant by "bro," trying to conceal their identities, or simply reacting to the discomfort of being stared at and addressed by a stranger. They may even have assumed that I was a bit loony. Who knows? I got no points for them. But now and then there was a suspiciously defensive look that said, "Who, me?" and occasionally that surprised gasp and wide-eyed, guilty stare that told me, *Damn. Got a witness!* Those I definitely counted.

Aside from the kids at the playground, family visits, and those frivolous amusements, the summer was a bust. I couldn't wait to get out of Youngstown's stratified, highly restrictive social scene. A week before I was to return to Colgate, I withdrew my savings from the bank and went to Tennessee with the agreed-upon $200. Three days later we had found a black 1957 Ford Fairlane that I liked and my father okayed. We had it checked by a mechanic who owed my father a favor, and the next day I signed the papers.

Finally I'd be completely independent at Colgate. With my own ride, I could escape anytime I wanted. I was thrilled.

I left for Hamilton a day early. I had to pick up my things at Phi Tau, drop off my books and belongings at my new residence, find someone to drive the four miles to Madison with me, then bring me back after I'd left the car with Hank. Of course, I didn't mind. I left town with the frenzy of a man who had just been released from prison.

Except for Christmas vacation the following year and spring break in my senior year, I would not return to Youngstown until after I graduated.

# 16

## down in the basement

My new residence was in the basement of Andrews Hall, one of the freshman dorms that was set away from the Quad, just beneath a rolling hill at the top of which stood the observatory and the president's house. When I first stepped down into that cellar dwelling, I was shocked. I had expected the space to be cramped, but the narrow hallway and lack of headroom caught me by surprise. The top of my head scraped the ceiling as I walked back to the building's northeast corner and my room. But ducking beneath the doorsill and entering, I found that except for its height, the room was spacious enough. It was, in fact, twice the size of my freshman dorm room. Still, initially there was a sense of claustrophobia. The cement walls gave the space a dank, closeted aura. And the exposed heating pipes running across the ceiling made the short trip between the bed and desk hazardous in the dark. Learning to stoop and dodge those impediments at the right moment was the first adjustment I had to make.

There were three other students living in Andrews Hall's basement in my junior year, Rico and Peter, both football players, and Steve Block, a nonathlete whom we affectionately called Stumbling. In one way or another, we were all loners. Stumbling was the most social minded of the other three. He regularly took off for Oneonta or one of the other coed schools on weekends. At Andrews, however, he kept to himself. I seldom saw him during the week. Rico and Peter, on the other hand, rarely left the basement's confines except for classes and football practice. Although they sometimes joined me or my friends for card games or rap sessions, they were extremely reclusive. Rico went so far as to cook most of his meals on the hot plate that he kept in his room and had a thriving business selling hot grilled-cheese sandwiches to the rest of us.

It was quickly apparent that at Colgate we were all outcasts, since anyone who was not an active member of a fraternity was considered something of a pariah. Even the students who lived in Kendrick, Eaton, or Dodge houses, the formal upper-class dorms, were casually referred to as "geeks" by frat members. The basement of Andrews had even less prestige. In addition to being outside the fraternity social scene, we had the stigma of not even being able to afford regular campus accommodations.

There was, however, a sweet irony in all this for me. I'd left the fraternity voluntarily—well, nearly so: continuing to live at Phi Tau would have meant taking out student loans that I hoped to avoid. And that year I maintained contact with the frat house as a boarding member. More important, living outside the house allowed me to avoid much of the idle socializing that in-house living demanded. Not that there was any overt stress between me and my frat brothers. Quite the opposite; I'd begun to feel that I was becoming *too* comfortable, too at ease among a mostly privileged crowd for whom the outside world's racial strife seemed meaningless. While the civil rights movement and my own identity crisis intensified, most of my fraternity brothers confidently and rightly assumed that their place in society would not be jeopardized.

It was much easier to deal with my vacillating reaction to the civil rights movement (as a supporter who nonetheless disagreed with the tactics) in solitude than while surrounded by a house filled with gregarious frat brothers who often subtly or unwittingly triggered racial discussions that I wanted to avoid. Even in Phi Tau's comparatively enlightened atmosphere, there were many white students who seemed unable to talk with Negroes without turning the conversation to race. It often reflected genuine concern, although sometimes appeared to be no more than an attempt to exorcise guilt or demonstrate some superficial compatibility. A discussion of base-ball would too often lead to some admiring mention of Willie Mays or a political discussion to the "terrific job Ralph Bunche had done"—as if my attention would wander if we strayed too far afield of the Negro problem. It was irritating even if, after a while, it be-came humorous—particularly since I was still checking to see which of my classmates had quietly slipped across the color line. There were a few likely suspects.

As I quickly discovered, idle chitchat and intrusive socializing were not a problem in the basement. At Andrews, while an open door meant the occupant was willing to socialize, a closed one was like a DO NOT DISTURB sign. And most often, doors were closed. It was perfect for me. Even its slightly tainted reputation was attractive since it confirmed the alien status that Negroes were generally ac-corded in mainstream society during the early sixties. I looked on it as a training ground of sorts. There was little inkling of the immi-nent changes that would soon break down many traditional racial barriers and ease access to the mainstream world.

The superficial similarity between my cavelike existence and the plight of Dostoyevsky's nameless underground man or Ralph Elli-son's invisible man did not, of course, escape me. In fact, it added a kind of edgy portentousness to my dank quarters. I'd eagerly return from dinner at the frat house or basketball practice knowing that I could find the kind of solitary deliberation I desperately sought. And while never as mockingly cynical as Dostoyevsky's hero or deter-minedly withdrawn and solitary as Ellison's, I wallowed in the ironic aptness of my subterranean residence.

I hadn't chosen to leave the fraternity house to become a hermit, however, and in that regard also, Andrews offered advantages. There was a side entrance, which was next to my room. Outside, once you passed behind the adjacent dormitory, a twenty-five-yard expanse of grass lay between that building and the student parking lot. Access to a car that year meant that after dark I could drive back to campus and spirit a coed into the building without using the front entrance, which was lighted and easily visible from the win-dows above or the drive in front of the dorm. One window in my room also opened to that side of the building, and if too many of the basement doors were open, it provided an alternative route. In fact, when climbing into the room through the window, my date and I literally fell into the bed; foreplay was unnecessary. On those occasions when I did bring visitors to campus, I was always a little leery the next morning when I had to remove my car. I, of course, had no campus parking sticker, and theoretically, if I'd been caught I could have lost my scholarship. I figured it was worth the risk. And, after Fred Vero, the campus cop, spotted me as I tried to ease my car out of the lot one morning and simply winked and looked the other way, my concern was considerably lessened. Apparently, Vero sympathized with the plight of scholarship students who were stuck on campus without wheels and had decided to give us a break. Still, I seldom abused the privilege and nearly always returned the car to its Madison hideout.

I was usually able to convince a Phi Tau brother or a basketball teammate to drive out and give me a ride back to town. In fact, despite an average season, the basketball team was in fairly good spirits that year, largely because of two upset victories against heavily favored teams. One came in an unscheduled meeting with New York University. In February we were supposed to play Holy Cross as part of a doubleheader at the Utica Memorial Auditorium; Syracuse was to face NYU in the other game, which was to be televised nationally. But a massive storm had dumped nearly two feet of snow in the upstate New York area, and traffic was virtually halted. We made it to the arena only because a farmer stopped and towed our stalled team bus through the snow-clogged roads. Although NYU had arrived, the Syracuse team was stuck at the airport. To fulfill the TV commitment, we played the National Invitational Tournament-bound NYU team. We shocked almost everyone by beating them 80 to 75. It was Colgate's only appearance on national TV while I was there and one of the most satisfying games of my college career.

But basketball was no longer a priority; I was much more interested in my courses and getting away from campus. The Ford allowed me to leave whenever I chose. During the next two years there were frequent trips to Skidmore, where I went out with Laura and, later, Kathy, an attractive and extremely intelligent black coed who later became an independent filmmaker. There were also excursions to Oneonta, Bennington, Simmons, and Smith with Walt and George Davis or sometimes Ned or Warren Davis, a black student in George's class. Although we often got no further than light conversations with hastily arranged dates in campus hangouts, we occasionally found more willing companions. As important, I was exposed to a diverse group of socially conscious, committed young people on those trips. I gradually discovered a social scene that was entirely different from the narrow provincialism I'd experienced in Youngstown. In part, I'd been correct—something was in the air. And the Northeast was changing much quicker than the rest of the nation. Many of the college students I ran into during that time (including a select group at Colgate) were among the volunteers who risked their lives and joined masses of Negroes in the sit-ins and freedom rides that began sweeping the South in 1961.

Syracuse was the most frequent destination when I left campus during my junior and senior years, however; only an hour away, its proximity made it particularly appealing when basketball games or impending exams made longer trips impossible. Although fraternities, sororities, and most other social organizations were segregated, there was, at least in comparison to Colgate, a sizable black student population. Moreover, it was known as a party school; its black students upheld that reputation. They had bonded together and formed their own informal social group. John Mackey was its honorary "chancellor" during those years and Sylvia, his girlfriend and future wife, was "keeper of the lists." Nearly every weekend there was either an organized party or, at least, an impromptu gathering with dancing and lively, rise-and-fly bid whist games, during which losers were loudly dissed when they lost their place at the table.

The parties, which were sometimes broadcast in the school newspaper or the bulletin board at the Commons or one of the campus coffeehouses, were usually announced under the simple heading MEMBERS—LET'S PARTY. No one was excluded, but only the hippest white students showed up at those affairs. One frequent visitor was Felix Cavaliere, who would quit college, move to New York City, and after a successful stint at the Peppermint Lounge, rise to rock stardom as a member of the Young Rascals. He voluntarily appeared at many sets and astounded some of us with his odd habit of continually sipping a nonalcoholic, concentrated-lemon-juice concoction from the bottle while he played piano.

Hal and George had introduced me to the nucleus of the Syracuse crowd during my sophomore year. Both occasionally dated Syracuse coeds, and the inroads they made eased my acceptance into the scene. Walt Shepperd also hung out with us and, during his senior year, hooked up with Valita, a black coed from an old-line Washington, D.C., family. They would marry a year after graduation despite the objections of both their families. The school's black football stars, of course, were kingpins at most gatherings. John Brown, Art Baker, John Mackey, and Ernie Davis had taken up where the recently departed Jim Brown left off. But the hip black coeds who arrived on campus were not automatically enamored of gridiron success. Students joked that year about Ernie Davis's initiation into the scene.

"Hey, what's happening, baby?" he was said to have asked a coed soon after arriving on campus as a freshman.

"Definitely not you, honey," was the curt reply.

Davis's status improved, and, presumably, much warmer receptions were extended once he became an All-American, certainly after he became the first Syracuse athlete as well as the first Negro to win the Heisman Trophy, in 1962.

During my junior year, George was hanging out with Loretta, a smart, attractive sophomore who would later become a lawyer. That association was beneficial to me in several ways. For one thing, Loretta was an excellent dancer, who helped pay her tuition by working part-time as a go-go dancer. In fact, she was partially responsible for the dance craze that swept the university in 1961, when she began demonstrating the Madison (a line dance much like today's Electric Slide) in the lobby between Flint and Day Halls, two of the largest girls' dorms on campus. When the New York Knicks' broadcast analyst Marv Albert, then a student announcer on the Syracuse University radio station, mentioned the happening, a crowd gathered. Soon nearly four hundred students were strutting to the music of Motown's Martha and the Vandellas. The police were called in to quell the disturbance, but by the time they arrived, several hundred Syracuse coeds had picked up the fundamentals; a small piece of black cultural life had slipped into the campus mainstream, and during the next few years, the Madison would become more popular at white fraternity and sorority parties than it had ever been at the smaller, black parties on campus.

Since Loretta was at nearly all of the affairs, I also picked up some dance steps from her. It was at those parties—with the always-present mixture of Catawba Pink (a cheap, carbonated wine), club soda, and fruit juices fueling my spirits—that I put to rest a lingering hesitancy about dancing that had bedeviled me since my non-watermelon-eating days in high school. Inspired by Loretta's uninhibited interpretations, I quickly became adept at the Pony, Mash Potatoes, Monkey, and Boog-a-loo. By the end of my junior year, I'd even mastered a few of Jackie Wilson's turns and James Brown's slides and splits. I thought I was bad until I challenged the Five Screaming Niggers' lead singer to a dance-off at a Colgate frat party. After I'd finished my James Brown imitation, while holding his drink in one hand he did an acrobatic double split, rose slowly from the floor, and without breaking stride segued into something he called the "pop." He never spilled a drop of his bourbon, and I never challenged another professional performer.

It was also through Loretta that I first met Patricia Marsh. A sophomore, she was one of Loretta's best friends, and although I'd seen her at parties, it wasn't until George and I played whist with them that we met. I was immediately bowled over.

Pat was one of the most beautiful women I'd ever met. Model thin and nicknamed "Tweety" after the cartoon character, she was fiery and competitive, but with just enough of a hint of softness in her eyes to create an aura of mystery and dampen the brash impression she sometimes left. She was stunning and I was hooked. Initially it was to no avail. She was dating the Syracuse football team's star fullback at the time and was definitely off limits. It didn't keep me from trying, of course. And that year, desperate to get her attention, I almost blew my chances. I'd heard she was from Jamaica and, thinking I'd impress her, cornered her at a party and began lacing a casual conversation with an admittedly shaky Caribbean accent. A minute or so into my reggae rap she laughed and, before walking away, said, "No, Mel. Jamaica, Queens. That's in New York."

Still, she had my attention, and undaunted by my geographical faux pas, during my senior year I made every effort to tighten up that relationship. That spring, however, I discovered that I'd gotten a summer job in New York through the university's work-study program. I immediately called the Youngstown Parks Department and informed them that I wouldn't return that summer. There was no question about where I wanted to spend my vacation; I had my bags packed three weeks before the semester ended.

## III

I started work as a copyboy at the *Daily News* in June. And as I'd expected, there was an aura of excitement and urgency about the newspaper business. For the first few months, whenever I could get away from the frantic but pedestrian duties of running copy from one desk to another or hustling some late change to the composing room, I'd haunt the Associated Press tickertape, trying to get a glimpse of developing news reports before anyone else, or hang around the newsroom and watch the reporters. I was fascinated by the speed with which they took information from field reporters and turned it into a printable story.

The *News,* I quickly discovered, was one of New York's most hawkish and conservative tabloids. Coverage of the sit-ins and freedom rides that were spreading across the South, for example, was minimal, but the paper's editorials regularly warned of an imminent Third World War and urged President Kennedy to end the communist threat with military intervention in Germany and Cuba. Still—even though I much preferred *New York Post* columnists such as Max Lerner (whose books I'd read in college) or Harry Golden, Earl Wilson, and Murray Kempton—I tried to meet Dick Young, Edward O'Neill, Ted Lewis, and other *News* writers. Although I bumped into a few of them in the hallways and delivered copy to their desks on occasion, I never had a chance to talk with any of them during that summer.

My job wasn't at all glamorous, but it was an exciting time, and nearly every day provocative stories seemed to break on both the foreign and domestic scene. In April the Soviet Union had put the first man into space, and a month later Alan Shepard made the first United States space flight. In July the United States sent a second astronaut into space. Tension had been building in Berlin as thousands of East Berliners scrambled to get to the western sector. And at the end of August, the Berlin Wall was erected. After the failed Bay of Pigs invasion of Cuba, in April, relations between the United States and Cuba continued worsening, and by August Castro was challenging our right to maintain the naval base at Guantanamo. Although rarely reflected in the *News's* pages, Negro protests escalated that summer and violent attacks on blacks increased. Even the local sports scene was hot, as the New York Yankees' outfielders

Mickey Mantle and Roger Maris challenged Babe Ruth's home run record; Maris would break the mark, hitting his sixty-first homer on the last day of the season. It seemed to be a journalist's dream. And although I was merely a runner, shifting papers from one desk to another, I couldn't avoid getting caught up in the frenzy.

For me, even the commute from Harlem to the *News*'s East Forty-second Street office was rousing. The crammed subways, bustling crowds, and fast pace of the city were magnets for me; after a month, I knew that I'd move there after graduation. I also knew that I'd have to make much more than the $50 a week I was earning at the newspaper.

Even living on Harlem's Morningside Avenue in one room of a railroad flat, it was difficult to make ends meet. In fact, living in that room was a huge concession. If finances had permitted I would have moved out after the first night.

The building was still impressive from the outside; even the lobby, with its marble floors and gigantic pillars, had a certain grandeur that harked back to better, more opulent times. But it sat directly across the street from Morningside Park. And while Columbia University was just over the hill, on the other side of the park, Morningside was considered one of the city's most dangerous parks. My landlord, a retired city employee of about sixty-five, warned me not to go near it at night. The building's tenants seemed to live in constant fear of the drifters, addicts, and hustlers who hung out and, during the summer, apparently slept there. Older men and women who, I imagined, must have been hell-raisers during the glorious days of the Harlem Renaissance cowered behind the lobby's pillars if an unfamiliar face appeared when they picked up their mail or ducked on the stairway if they heard footsteps. The apartments themselves were fortresses; each had four or five locks on the door. That precaution made no sense to me; although it may have kept intruders out, it required three to four minutes to open the doors—more than enough time for a lurking mugger to get to his prey. Still, with caution, I figured, I could deal with the street danger. There was, however, a more formidable problem for me.

The seven-room flat in which I lived was kept relatively clean; at least the kitchen and landlord's rooms were. There were, however, three other tenants, and if their rooms mirrored their appearance, I'm sure they would not have passed a sanitation inspection. Despite the landlord's tidiness, as I found out the first night, the apartment was overrun with roaches. Apparently the dumbwaiters in most apartments hadn't worked for years, so tenants had taken to throwing their garbage into the air shaft that sliced through the middle of the building. It was a breeding ground for rats and cockroaches. I was on the fourth floor, and already the garbage was stacked above the windows of second-floor apartments. That, by the way, is why I almost moved out on the second day.

Mind you, this was not a mere clutch of pesky insects; the building was completely infested. I had never seen anything like it. In fact, I had never seen a roach—not in Youngstown or even in the basement of Andrews Hall. And I hadn't seen one when I moved into the New York City apartment the first day. But that night I awoke to find the walls covered with them. It might have been wallpaper, except that it or they were alive and moving. I panicked when I turned on the lights and saw them scurrying back into hiding. I didn't go back to sleep that night. It was only after I checked the papers the next day and found that no rooms for comparable rents were available that I decided to stay. Still, for weeks I had nightmares, woke up imagining myself being attacked and flailing at the covers with a magazine or newspaper. After a time, however, I was able to shut it out and console myself with the thought that I'd be out of there within two months.

Rent was only $7 per week, but even at that, I was left with just over $30 for food and recreation. With a budget tighter than a Thom McAn shoe, I was somewhat restricted. I couldn't frequent many of the places that I'd visited with Hal Jackson the previous year. I saw Hal nearly every week, since we played basketball in a White Plains YMCA league with Walt Shepperd that summer. But there was no hanging out at Jock's or the Red Rooster. In fact, after buying gas for my car and accounting for subway tokens and lunch at work, I had very little left for food. Generally I ate at a mom-and-pop soul food restaurant at the corner of Eighth Avenue and 124th Street or made do with twenty-five-cent hot dogs or hot sausages from pushcart vendors.

But if I ate sparingly, I gorged myself on Harlem's culture that summer—at least that part which my meager salary and time allowed.

Much of my time was spent roaming the streets in the evenings after work or on Saturdays and Sundays, observing and listening to speakers that gathered at 135th Street or in front of Michaux's Bookstore near 125th Street and Seventh Avenue. Black Muslims, evangelists, communists, black nationalists, Baptists, socialists, and Africanists could be heard on most evenings or weekend afternoons. Nearly all of them were entertainers as well as forceful speakers—knew that, to hold a Harlem crowd, style was as important as the message. The harangues were spiced with anecdotes, riddles, and jokes; most could silence a critic as readily as I'd seen Redd Foxx quiet a heckler at the Apollo Theatre.

"Hey, brother!" one shouted at a too-vocal observer. "You with that loud-ass purple jacket on. Why don't you shut up? I don't come on yo' job and throw no dirt back in the hole you diggin'. And why don't you change your clothes befo' you blind somebody?"

Some, like Malcolm X, whom I saw several times, were spellbinding. Eyes flashing like beacons, forefinger jabbing the air like an accusatory pointer, he alternately admonished and gibed, flagellated and tickled, as he hammered home a separatist ideology that he would later recant. He was mesmerizing, even if I could not buy the philosophy in its entirety. Others, less artful and articulate, nevertheless lured crowds with invigorated recall of the single element that bound most everyone in the audience except the white policemen who always seemed to be present—the vivid memory of some direct encounter with racial bigotry.

The reaction of the audience—which ranged from hustlers and winos to blue-collar workers and churchly sisters, from the unemployed to businessmen or clerical types who, like myself, had just returned from a downtown job—varied. Some laughed and jeered, caught up in the superficial novelty and diversion of the rap and unmindful of the message, while others joined in a chorus of "Amen's" and feverish yells of "Tell it like it is. Teach, brother. Teach!" Some, like myself, hung at the edge of the crowd and either nodded their heads in tacit agreement or listened out of curiosity, then moved on.

With little money but plenty of time at my disposal that summer, I also haunted the Studio Museum, Michaux's Bookstore, and the 135th Street Library (now the Schomburg). Although I was a fine arts history major, it was during that time that I was first exposed to the works of black artists such as Jacob Lawrence and Romere Bearden. I couldn't afford to buy any books at Michaux's, but I

browsed and scanned works such as Alain Locke's *The New Negro,*
J. A. Rogers's *Great Men of Color,* and Zora Neale Hurston's *Mules
and Men.* Less pressured at the library, I must have become an annoying presence as I spent hours perusing their collection of original source materials, histories, and biographies of black Americans.
I even visited the Abyssinian Baptist Church in hopes of seeing Colgate alumnus Adam Clayton Powell Jr. make a guest appearance in
the pulpit; but Powell, who had recently assumed duties as chairman of the House Committee on Education and Labor, was busy in
Washington trying to strike deals with the Kennedy administration
on behalf of the civil rights movement. Still, the church was magnificent. As I quickly discovered that summer, Harlem was a vast
repository of a history that I'd ignored or been denied, of a rich cultural tradition of which I'd previously only scratched the surface.

At night, even with limited funds, I found that there were other,
less heady treasures to explore. The Baby Grand, where the comedian Nipsey Russell appeared, was just around the corner from my
Morningside Avenue single room. For a $3 entry fee and the price of
one drink, I frequently found a spot in the gaudily appointed inner
room and, squeezing in among the mostly downtown crowd of
tourists and celebrities, sat through an entire cabaret show. Typically, it featured a jazz combo, vocalists, an exotic dancer, and Russell's hip, acerbic social commentary. "He who turns the other
cheek," he'd quip, "will get hit with the other fist." Or, "I used to say,
'We've always had integration in the South—now we just want it in
the daytime.' " The mixed audience would roar with delight, even
though the midtown sojourners beat a hasty retreat to the row of
limousines lining the thoroughfare after the show. Still, Harlem at
that time was not the racially exclusive enclave that it would become later in the decade. Whites still walked the streets in compar-
ative safety. The Baby Grand and the Apollo Theatre, which was
farther down 125th Street and regularly featured the sixties' best
black performers, were magnets for those who lived outside the
community.

Admission at the Apollo was only $1.25, and for that price you
could sit in the theatre all day, watching several shows if you
wished. And on Saturdays I often did just that. There was no better
entertainment value in the city. I was even fascinated by the huge
mural that ran the length of the lobby and depicted a galaxy of leg-

endary black performers. Count Basie, Sammy Davis Jr., Bessie Smith, Duke Ellington, Ella Fitzgerald, James Brown, Bill "Bojangles" Robinson, and Dinah Washington were all pictured there. It was a shrine to a performance legacy that, at that time, had not received full recognition. During that summer I saw bills that ranged from gospel shows to the Motown review, with the Temptations, Supremes, Smokey and the Miracles, or the Four Tops; there were also blues shows with T-Bone Walker and Bobby "Blue" Bland, and jazz shows that featured Ramsey Lewis, Nancy Wilson, the Cannonball Adderley Quintet, and comedian Flip Wilson. Older vaudeville and black-circuit comics such as Mantan Moreland, Dusty Fletcher, and Pigmeat Markham were also regularly featured and were among my favorite acts. Pigmeat's "Here Come de Judge" routine, with him as the irascible magistrate, always knocked me out. "The judge is mean dis mawnin'! I'm goin' start by givin' myself thirty days—next case!"

My weekly budget always included a buck and a quarter for the Apollo Theatre.

On other nights, although I couldn't afford the pricey jazz clubs, I'd sometimes hang out at smaller, neighborhood bars, many of which showcased excellent music. Usually it was performed by one of the organ, saxophone, and drum trios that were popular in black bars during the fifties and early sixties. My favorite spot was the Dew Drop Inn, which sat between an abandoned movie house and a drugstore near the corner of Eighth Avenue and 125th Street. It was one of hundreds of so-called three-for-one bars that served three shots of whiskey for a dollar; once you got to know the bartenders and they ditched the false-bottom shot glass used for transient customers, it was a bargain.

I discovered the place a few weeks after arriving in New York, and by the end of June, I'd become a regular. When they discovered that I was a college student, the bartenders, Bee and Florence, began calling me "Ivy" and the other regulars picked up on it. It was a comfortable joint, filled with unusual characters, and for a few dollars I could sit there all evening, bullshitting and hitting on the women who paraded through on weekends, or listening to the funky mix of jazz and blues served up by the trio that played in the lounge while making entries in my journal. No one seemed to mind.

Bee was a lithe, dark-skinned, thirtyish beauty who exuded sex and came on to every male who entered; hinting at after-hour trysts, she toyed with lonely, middle-aged customers and regularly wheedled $10 tips from barflies who didn't appear able to afford a subway ride home. Then, just before her shift ended, she inevitably got a phone call. Afterward she'd smile and explain that her daughter was waiting or that her mother was sick; any excuse would do. Before sashaying out the door, she'd pause to kiss each of the evening's pigeons on the cheek. The next night, many of the same customers returned for an encore. I always wondered who the phone accomplice was or if there was anybody at all.

Less manipulative and therefore less handsomely rewarded, Florence was a buxom woman who tried to disguise her jolly, somewhat vulnerable personality with a scowl and a wall of heavy makeup. It didn't work. She was really a sweetheart and a sucker for a sob story. Most evenings she became mired in conversation with some down-and-out wino, junkie, or dejected husband whose wife had supposedly deserted him. Often it was she who gave the customer a few dollars.

Two of my favorite regulars were Stuart and Rodney; on slow nights, I'd sometimes spend the entire evening talking to them. Stuart was a single, balding, and slightly overweight post-office worker who had a jones for Bee. He must have spent half his salary at that bar. And although, as far as I could tell, he never got anywhere with her, it didn't seem to dampen his spirits. He jived and jousted quip for quip with her, always left a generous tip, and accepted the nightly dismissal and good-bye kiss with a smile. He had grown up in Harlem and loved to talk about its history, however; so I'd listen with rapt attention to his stories about Adam Clayton Powell, Daddy Grace, and the heyday of Harlem nightlife. Quick witted and funny as hell, he had a comeback for every situation. When a busboy sounded on him for being Bee's patsy, for instance, he quickly shut him up with, "Yeah, like you the soul of wisdom, mu'fucker. Why don't you put that damn broom down? We know you don't know nothin' 'bout no machinery."

Rodney, on the other hand, was a fast-talking, good-looking hustler. Although he was only five seven and extremely sensitive about his height (he would not talk to me if we were standing), he prided himself on being a ladies' man and, in some ways, reminded me of my brother McKay. Born and raised in Boston, his accent and boyish looks along with the tie, V-neck sweater, and sports jacket that he customarily wore led many to believe that he too was a college student. The surface refinement was a front, however; as I discovered later, Rodney was actually a pimp who had a reputation for viciously controlling his "ladies."

It was through him that I met Candy. She was a beautiful twenty-two-year-old with a chocolate complexion and the wide-eyed smile of an ingenue. The smile was utterly misleading. Although not as hard or manipulative as some of the other women who hung out at the bar, she was thoroughly streetwise. I'd seen her and a girlfriend at the club a few times at the start of the summer, but although interested, I never had a chance to talk with them.

"Stacked like a mama-jama," Rodney observed when he noticed her. The following evening he approached her. Later that evening, after Rodney left, she approached me. That's when I discovered Rodney's true hustle. Apparently he had tried to recruit her for his stable. She'd brushed him off, and for the rest of the night we sat and talked. She lived in Newark and was married—unhappily, obviously, since I'd seen her flirting in the club for the past three weekends. Her husband was a small-time hustler who, she said, was out partying in Newark every night. She had gotten tired of sitting at home. A high school graduate, she was smart as well as beautiful. I talked too much about college and Ohio, and spent too much money that first night, but we hit it off. At the end of the evening, she said she'd be back next weekend.

She kept her promise, and after a drink at the bar the following Friday, we left her girlfriend and took a drive through Central Park, into midtown Manhattan, then back up to Harlem. Before returning, we parked on a quiet street on the Upper West Side and climbed into the backseat of the car. That night began a five-week affair that was confined to the Dew Drop Inn, the backseat of my Ford, or, sadly, my tiny room, where we were forced to keep the lights on to avoid an invasion of roaches. Fortunately, Candy had a good sense of humor.

At the beginning of August, however, she disappeared, just failed to show up one Friday, and for three weeks I didn't see her. I had no idea of what had happened. Although I'd driven her back to Newark a few times, dropping her off two blocks from her house, there was no way of contacting her. By the third Friday I'd given up. I was disappointed but I assumed she had forgotten the summer fling and gone back to her husband.

On my last weekend before returning to Colgate, however, Candy returned to the bar. She approached me tentatively, and when I saw her up close, I was shocked. A long, still-puffy scar ran from high on her left cheekbone to just below the corner of her mouth.

"What happened, baby?" I asked when I sat next to her at the bar.

"My husband slashed me," she said resignedly. "He suspected I was runnin' around on him."

We rapped for two hours that night and I tried to convince her that she should leave him. Walk out. "And do what?" she said, staring at me. "Where would I go? Yeah, I could get a job as a receptionist or maybe even as a secretary and have some sloppy, middle-aged honkie hittin' on me every day. I don't need that. Ain't nowhere for us to go."

"Anything's better than staying at home and being abused. And you could move up once you started a job. You're smart enough to do whatever you want. This shit's going to change, baby. It's already started, just look at what's happening—"

"Bull! They ain't giving us a thing and they don't intend to—not unless we come across with something they want. And for a black woman it's sex. At least he's taking care of me—puttin' a roof over my head. That's more than I can say for most niggers out here!" She laughed and ordered another drink. "Look at you. You're a senior at some high-class school and still you livin' in Harlem in a roach-infested room and hanging out in this joint. How many of your rich white classmates you think stuck in the ghetto fighting bugs and rats this summer?"

I, of course, had no answer. I was due back in Hamilton in a week and had already started packing my things. The conversation stalled because, finally, I couldn't provide the solution she indirectly requested, couldn't take care of her and couldn't take her with me, even if I'd wanted to. I couldn't even state the obvious—that she had to stand up for herself. It didn't matter that there was some truth in what she was saying. As long as you played the role of victim, accepted it as some inevitable destiny, racial heritage, you were hopelessly trapped. Predators—whether enraged spouses or manipulative white folks—approached with salivary relish. The way

I saw it, she had to abandon that role, put it down and move on. Nobody was going to do it for her.

When the standoff became unbearable, I drove her back through the tunnel to Newark. We parked at the usual spot a few blocks from her house. A kiss and a few more minutes of silence, then she opened the door and walked away. Her tears were still on my cheek as I turned the car around and drove back to Manhattan. I never saw her again.

Four days later, I left the city and drove back to Hamilton.

# 17

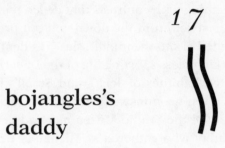

## bojangles's daddy

The first semester of my final year seemed to pass in a flash. Although the sudden, unexpected end to my affair with Candy left me despondent, the summer in New York had focused my attention on a single goal. I knew that I wanted to become a writer. The city's frenetic pace, the buzz of the paper's newsroom, the contrast of Harlem's rich culture and underlying squalor, and the unique characters I'd met were irresistible; my journal was filled with notes and detailed descriptions.

I approached that semester with more zeal than I'd ever felt at Colgate. In addition to four required courses in fine arts history, I'd received permission to take a special-studies writing course in which I'd have to write a novella. I had also signed up to audit a course in the philosophic aspects of literature. I'd receive no credit and the course required attending all classes and taking the exams, but the reading list included works by T. S. Eliot, Thomas Mann, Kafka, Nietzsche, and Sartre. The academic challenge inspired me, and I gladly spent most of my time hunched over my desk in my basement retreat.

Perhaps more important, the summer in New York had cemented my views about the race issue. Submersion in Harlem's day-to-day routine had opened my eyes to the diversity and richness of so-called Negro culture. Unlike the narrow confines of black life in Youngstown, Harlem was teeming with contrasts that defied the notion of a monolithic black lifestyle. From the down-and-out predators that haunted Morningside Park to the middle-class residents of Lenox Terrace, from the working-class sporting life of the Dew Drop Inn to the more sophisticated habitués of Jock's and Small's Paradise, or from the raucous, often neominstrel performances at the Apollo Theatre to the sobriety of the Studio Museum crowd or the intellectualism of the dissenters who gathered at Michaux's Bookstore, I'd found that Harlem life was as diverse as, or more diverse than, mainstream American life. Even as I buried myself in the study of European artists and writers, Baldwin's observation kept rearing itself: *The Negro in America does not really exist except in the darkness of our minds.*

It seemed evident to me that the bond that united me and all these multicolored folks was not some primal racial identity that defined character and behavior but the externally imposed experience of repression. I was convinced of it. What was truly amazing to me was the richness of the folk culture that had emerged despite the oppression. That culture, which, as I would later discover, was a unique manifestation of African and American influences and a seemingly indomitable spirit, had sustained America's erstwhile black folks and shaped their contributions in art, athletics, science, dance, literature, and music.

I was astounded that I hadn't recognized it before. Mainstream condemnation and trivialization of Negro culture had jaundiced me—distorted my vision. I'd at least partially bought into that oblique view of Negro life as deprived and second rate. Sure, I'd come to see that jazz and rhythm and blues were infinitely more expressive and richly textured than the pop tunes that dominated the airways in Youngstown. But I'd looked upon most other aspects of black life in my hometown as tawdry and limited.

While Youngstown clearly did not have the diversity of a New York City, the cultural treasures had been there all along. The Muddy Waters and John Lee Hooker blues that Tennessee hummed or tinkled on the piano or wore thin on the record player (and I'd unwittingly dismissed as "country") were no less creative than the Dizzy, Bird, and Miles tunes that I'd been introduced to by McKay. Then there were the joyous hymns and gospel shouts my brother-in-law Leroy and his group had sung in our living room (sometimes nearly making the incredible imaginable) and the wit, humor, and ironic, roundabout intelligence of the most outrageous liars—Pines from Governor Oates's barbershop and Big Six from next door. Not to mention the flair and élan that the best-dressed hustlers could impart to a precariously cocked maroon stingy-brim lid and fly crimson English broadcloth vine or the prophetic wisdom with which Miss Aggie dressed her tales. It had all been there—draped in down-home, country garb, perhaps, but no less creative for all of that. I had simply been too shortsighted and ill at ease to fully embrace it.

Those thoughts shadowed me that fall, but I didn't resign myself to hibernation and obsessive pondering. I'd come to think of race as a fraudulent concept that was as binding on its white originators as it was on its intended victims. I needed to move outside that definition. It had been an enigma, a confounding riddle for me. But that fall, determinedly if somewhat romantically, I resolved to change that by becoming a racial outlaw—lampooning simplistic black-white racial distinctions and exposing the notion as the insidious joke that it was.

So, despite the concentration on class work and the necessity of playing basketball, I also started to adopt the approach I'd watched Aubrey, Steve, and Hal employ. I became a puckish agitator, twitting the self-righteous but altogether confused assumption of superiority and entitlement that occasionally surfaced even in those classmates who strove to shuck their racist backgrounds.

Walt's friend Ned was one of my targets. He was a frequent visitor to the basement, where, that year, Walt had joined our underground corps. And although Ned partied with us and in some ways may even have admired me, it seemed then that he could not shake a bias that had somehow become entrenched in the course of his decidedly Aryan upbringing; I would, in the dark recesses of his mind, remain a nigger no matter what transpired during our personal encounters. Still, when stranded on snowbound weekends, we hung out together, amused ourselves viewing Walt's television set or, as when we played pinochle for twenty-four consecutive hours while repeatedly listening to the Marvelettes' "Please Mr. Postman," gambled and mocked our entrapment. During those times I'd prod his scantily concealed bigotry with casual assertions of the superiority

of Negro League baseball players such as Josh Gibson when compared to major-league stars such as Mickey Mantle or with allusions
to conquests, fabricated or real, of blue-eyed damsels from nearby
colleges. Eyebrows lifted, face growing taut, he would fidget in his
seat and attempt dissembling his ire with nervous laughter.

"You okay, my man?" I'd offer, as, head thrown back in sham
mirth, he eyed me suspiciously. It was little more than jest for me,
and, I'm sure, he knew I was intentionally pushing buttons; racial
taboos, however, disallowed any shared laughter at the sendup.

Inspired, perhaps, by Loretta's mass dance teach-in at Syracuse, I
half jokingly announced to my fellow basement dwellers that I
would start a dance school that fall. "I'm tired of seeing you turkeys
tripping all over yourselves." I laughed. "Time you learned how to at
least approximate some rhythmical continuity." I meant it as a joke,
although that evening I halfheartedly went through some steps of
the Madison and tried to point out that, when doing the Twist, the
hand movements are counterpoised against a weight shift to the opposite hip. I cracked up watching the aptly named Stumbling and
two burly football players bungling their way through some fairly
elementary steps that night. Actually, we all had a ball; they showed
some improvement and everyone ended up laughing their asses off.

I'd forgotten about it by the next morning, but during the week
Rico jokingly asked when the next class was being held, and apparently through Walt's mentioning it to a few others in the campus
store and cafeteria, word had gotten around. That weekend the Mel
Watkins School of Funky Dance was born. Twice a week, for a small
donation, classmates were invited to join in some rudimentary instruction in the Boog-a-loo, Mash Potatoes, and Twist. I was definitely no Alvin Ailey and it was more fun and diversion than
anything else, but the sessions progressed enough so that a black
freshman friend was called in to assist in the instruction. Walt even
began promoting the effort with a unique endorsement. "As a graduate of the Mel Watkins School," he ironically vouched, "I'm getting
all the white coeds I can handle and I ain't even black."

Almost everyone who attended those spectacles left laughing, and,
at least I like to think, a few even learned that, despite Arthur Murray, the pelvis did not have to remain stationary on the dance floor.
The classes ended in November, however; basketball practice began
and there just wasn't enough time. Still, it was apparent that the

winds were shifting. When I arrived at Colgate, only a few of the most progressive coeds had been willing to flaunt custom and get down with black dance and rhythm and blues; three years later I was giving lessons to eager classmates who had previously disdained the dances and the "primitive" culture that had inspired them.

At fall Party Weekend, I discovered even more evidence of the shift. The Five Screaming Niggers had returned, and although I still hadn't come to terms with that phenomenon, I was intrigued by them. As expected, they were playing at one of the jock houses, and by then I'd come to suspect that the frats who hired them had sinister motives. In part, I took it personally. Was it just a clever way of framing us all—including Colgate's score of Negro students—in the same picture? Were they trying to suggest that the Screaming Niggers were what all of us were about? A bit paranoid, perhaps, but I wasn't sure. Anyway, donning sunglasses and affecting my most belligerent expression, I drew myself to maximum height and busted into the party.

While just as frenetic, the scene was a bit different. Instead of a few adventurous coeds putting on an exotic display while almost everyone stood agape at the perimeters, it was an all-out bash. Everybody was dancing, or trying to find some space to cut loose. The band was playing "Work with Me, Annie," a mid-fifties Midnighters' R&B hit that was banned from radio when it was originally released; Georgia Gibbs had released a more acceptable pop version with less suggestive lyrics, called "Dance with Me, Henry," a year or so later. That evening, however, there was little evidence of a desire to sanitize anything. The screaming, gyrating mob of students let it all hang out. Even some formerly reserved classmates had joined the debauch; ripping off their T-shirts and pouring brew over themselves, they substituted a maladroit shimmy and pogo-stick-like, in-place bounding movement for recognizable dance steps. A kind of Chubby Checkerish, bourgeois, antifunk pallor still lingered, but it was about as down and dirty as a white party was likely to get in the early sixties.

Caught up in the music, I pushed my way through the throng and managed to grab a beer at the bar. Less than a minute later, a pudgy brunette whom someone should have advised not to wear tight Bermuda shorts rushed over and pulled me onto the dance floor. It was packed, so as she swayed and undulated to the music, letting

out high-pitched squeals timed to the heavy bass beat that punctuated the chorus, her pendulous breasts slapped into my stomach.
Fortunately the song and the set ended in a few minutes. "Now,
don't you go anywhere, sugar," she cooed in what appeared to be a
Southern accent. "I'll be right back, you hear." I immediately moved
to an obscure spot in the corner of the room.

Although many of the revelers left, the band members still lingered. The lead singer was surrounded by a clutch of coeds and Colgate students, seemingly absorbed in conversation. The saxophonist
was rapping to the female vocalist, and judging from his protective
posture, she was his old lady. The guitarist and piano player stood
near the bandstand smoking cigarettes; the other band member had
disappeared. Perhaps, I laughed to myself, somebody had decided
to give the drummer some.

A few minutes later, I caught the eye of the gold-toothed guitarist,
yelled at him, and walked over to join them. I was determined to
satisfy my curiosity about the name, and since I'd talked to the guitarist before, I decided to ask him. "Hey, Professor," he said, "see
you still here, huh." He laughed and slapped my hand. "Now, you
didn't come out'cher tryin' to challenge nobody to dance, did ya?"

"No, my man." I smiled. "I got better sense than that. He's the
champ."

"That's all right, you was bad. Just need a little mo' practice. Anyway, what's happenin'?"

"Not much, just gliding on through here." I paused and gulped
some of my beer. "Somethin' I need to ask you though, man. What's
up with this name? You guys are bad, could be playin' at the Apollo
or somewhere. What the hell led you to choose that name?"

The piano player broke up immediately, almost spilled his drink
as he bent over laughing. "Go 'head, my man," he said to the guitarist, "you tell him." He walked off toward the bar.

"Well, it's like this," the guitarist said, pausing, pulling his shoulders back, and flashing an askance grin that reminded me of the
stance and look my cousin Charles Ernest assumed before he
swelled up and prepared to fashion some huge lie or impart a bit of
folk wisdom. "See, we was hackin' around, bustin' our asses and
gettin' nowhere when we had one a them regular names. Couldn't
get booked nowheres. Then I come up on this idea of shockin' folks.
You know, give 'em a little jab, somethin' to remember you

by . . . like Sugar Ray. Since then, we cain' even keep up with the work. Play all the big schools through the year, then we take off in the summer and go down South for a little vacation."

"But 'Screaming Niggers', my man? That's a little, well, embarrassing, isn't it?"

"Sheee-it." He laughed. "Ain't nothin' embarrassin' about it. Call ourselves 'Snow White and the Five Clouds' and they still be callin' us niggers when we leave outta here. And what you think they call you?" He stared for a minute, then lit another cigarette. I just smiled. "Nah, don't make a bit a difference."

"Yeah, you right about that. But, dig it, with King and all those people fighting for equal rights down South, don't you think we should be trying to get rid of these jive labels and stereotypes?"

He cracked up then. I thought he was about to start rolling on the floor.

"And what you think they goin' call 'em after they sit down to eat, get a seat on one a them buses?" he asked when he'd stopped laughing. "How long you been up here in the country . . . 'way from home? The thing is, we doin' 'bout much as they are to straighten out the shit. You been here befo', seen these kids shakin' they ass and tryin' get down, get with the black thang. Lemme tell you somethin'. I'm near 'bout twice yo' age and I'm from the South, know them honkies near 'bout as well as I know my own kin. This music, that funky beat, is what's goin' change it. These little broads runnin' round here is ready to integrate right now. Know that for a fact." He paused and smiled. "We just helpin' along. Meanwhile, if it take billin' ourselves as Screaming Niggers to get 'em in here . . . what the hell? We done done our job. Up to you educated, college *Negroes* to do the rest."

The bandleader called out to him at that point and he looked over at the rest of the group. They were about to start a new set. "Hey, Professor," he said as he reached into his jacket and pulled out a flask of Jack Daniel's, "why don'cha have a sip of this good stuff 'fore I get back on the stand? That beer make you dance funny, boy."

I took a slug of the bourbon and handed it back to him; after taking a belt himself, he slapped my hand and returned to the bandstand. The rest of that night is still foggy to me. I do remember dancing with several coeds; a few of them were gorgeous. But the pudgy Southerner also tracked me down again, and I know I spent a great deal of the evening trying to fend off her tipsy advances. Once, after she'd trapped me for a slow dance, she pressed herself close and whispered into my ear. "You know, my daddy is still a bigot, sugar," she tittered, slurring her words. "We treated you-all badly but that's all in the past. No reason we can't be as fra— friendly as we want now. You don't mind, do you, sugar?"

I think it was shortly afterward that I stepped outside with a musician from another band; I know that we found a deserted spot in the darkness of the parking lot and lit a joint. Too many beers later, as I vaguely recall, I stumbled back across Whitnall Field, stopped to throw up, then groped my way back up the hill to Andrews Hall. I woke up the next morning with a tremendous hangover. Happily, I discovered that the pushy Southern coed was not lying beside me.

I stumbled through much of the morning glancing at a paper on Matisse that was due on Monday and trying to remember exactly what the guitar player had been trying to say. That night, instead of returning to the frat parties, I drove to Syracuse with Walt. By that time he was dating Valita, the attractive light-skinned coed that he'd eventually marry; I was hoping to run into Pat. I did see her at the small party we attended, but despite dancing a few times, I made no immediate headway. She seemed vaguely interested, however, and even though she declined my offer to drive her back to her dorm, she suggested I call her next week. Although Walt was thrilled about his relationship with Valita and couldn't be quieted, I didn't say much during the ride back to Hamilton. Besides being a little despondent over not progressing faster with Pat, I found that the previous night's events were still rattling through my mind.

The relationship with Pat improved noticeably during the last month and a half of the semester, however; I had a few dates with her, and finally she agreed to come down to Colgate for winter Party Weekend. I was floating, so much so that it was two weeks before the end of the term when I realized that the novella I was supposed to write for my special studies course was only half done. I crammed those final weeks, rarely leaving the basement except to eat or attend basketball practice. Still, when exams were over, I hadn't finished the project. My professor, Atlee Sproul, gave me an extra four days to complete it.

While the campus emptied for semester break, I was confined to my desk, where I frantically scribbled out pages of the novella. Walt, who had decided to stay at school during the break, agreed to help and would come over and type up the finished pages at the end of the day. I spent the night before the work was due writing furiously and handing pages to him. He typed and proofread them. At about ten o'clock the next morning, two hours before the deadline that Professor Sproul had set, I finished. After handing in the novella, which was titled *Weak Vows, Excess Prices* from a line in a Baudelaire poem, I slept for nine hours. That night, Walt and I drove to Syracuse, which was still in session. We partied until dawn.

A few days later I found that I'd gotten one of the few A's that Professor Sproul had ever given in that course. It was particularly gratifying, since the story had deep personal meaning. It focused on the conflict between two brothers, much like McKay and myself, who had taken separate paths—one to a street life as a hustler and the other to college—and end up as rivals for the same woman. The characters and Harlem setting were also heavily indebted to observations I'd made during the past summer. The experiences I'd had at the Dew Drop Inn with Candy and Rodney were mirrored in the work nearly as much as my relationship to McKay. Eight years later I published part of *Weak Vows* as a short story in *Black Review,* a paperback literary anthology that I edited. It was printed under the pseudonym Franklin Jefferson Jackson, a tribute to all those Negroes (such as my twin brothers Herbert Hoover and Al Smith) whose parents had burdened them with the names of presidents and Oval Office aspirants. The positive notice that story received was even more satisfying for me than generally admiring reviews of the anthology.

The final semester at Colgate began more promisingly than I'd hoped. I was cruising through the basketball season with no problems; while not expending that much effort, I'd come to terms with the unenthusiastic fans and lack of shooting opportunities. Mostly I played as if it were an intramural league and generally enjoyed myself. Professor Sproul's high estimate of the novella I'd written, along with his encouragement, had strengthened my resolve to pursue a writing career when I graduated. And in February I expected Pat to spend Party Weekend in Hamilton.

Having been dismissed from an ancient-architecture course the previous semester for being late on three occasions, I had to take eighteen credit hours that term, but I wasn't overly concerned. In fact, I was looking forward to the academic term since my classes included Professor Arnold Sio's "The American Negro"—the only course offered at Colgate that directly addressed the race problem.

During the first few weeks, I quickly discovered that Professor Sio's views reflected the era's conventional perception of Negro life. Although not as inflexible or rigid, his perception of the "Negro problem" mirrored ideas presented in Gunnar Myrdal's *The American Dilemma,* a sociological study that viewed blacks primarily as passive victims and their culture as "a distorted development, or a pathological condition, of the general American culture." We were, of course, assigned Myrdal's work and essays by other like-minded sociologists. But we also read W. E. B. Du Bois and the Negro sociologist E. Franklin Frazier, as well as fictional works by Richard Wright, Ralph Ellison, and James Baldwin. The direction the course took was far afield of my subjective thoughts on the race issue, even of my interpretations of works by Ellison, Du Bois, and Wright, which I had already read. Frustrated by what I thought was a distorted view of blacks, I nevertheless approached the course with fervor during the first few weeks. I hoped that, as the class progressed, I'd have a chance to express my contrary views.

The rousing finish I'd anticipated during that final semester, however, suffered a serious setback early in February. During a game in which we routed Bucknell 85 to 66, I drove to the hoop for a layup and was taken out from underneath by an opposing player. I landed in the third row of the wooden bleacher seats at the end of the court. There was no immediate pain, so I continued playing. I finished what would be my last game for Colgate with twelve rebounds and fifteen points. Afterward I drove to Syracuse for one of the Members' Saturday night parties.

It was not until two days later that I discovered I'd been injured. After practice on Monday, while Walt and I were walking back up the hill toward the dorms, I felt an excruciating pain in my side. Thinking it was a minor ailment, perhaps something I'd eaten, I tried to ignore the pain. A moment later, however, I buckled over and collapsed. I had never felt anything like it in my life. Walt helped me back down the hill and across Broad Street to the school infirmary. The doctor was not there, and although the lone, wizened nurse was sympathetic, she informed me that there was nothing she could do until he returned.

She escorted me into a waiting room and I went completely berserk. Yelling and cursing in pain, I practically tore that small, antiseptic cubbyhole apart. Cabinets, bottles, the examining table, everything that could be moved was turned over and thrown against the walls. The frail nurse was apparently afraid to intervene. Probably thinking I was going mad, she locked the door and tried to coax and calm me from the other side. The doctor—a benign, avuncular type whose granny glasses hung precariously from the tip of his nose—finally arrived an hour later. When he saw that the room was a complete wreck, he immediately gave me a sedative.

### III

For the next six weeks I was confined to the sterile corridors of Colgate's modest infirmary. Its ivory-clad nurses and bleached-white walls were nearly all I saw. It was probably unnecessary, since I was probed and treated for nearly a month for a nonexistent infection. Afterward, doctors discovered that I had been suffering from internal bleeding all along. It was, they submitted, probably the result of an injury sustained during the spill I'd taken in the Bucknell game. No one really ever made a definitive determination. Meanwhile, I had two minor operations and was bedridden the entire time. Misapprehended again, I later mused. Ironically, the fiasco mirrored the so-called Negro problem—an externally produced contusion insistently perceived and misdiagnosed as some mysteriously elusive organic malfunction. Obviously, not the way I'd anticipated spending my final semester at college.

Walt and a few black undergraduate friends visited often during my convalescence, bringing news from outside as well as assignments from my professors. Under the circumstances, it was virtually impossible to keep up with course work. I missed nearly half of the class lectures and wrote none of the papers that were assigned during the first half of the term. Although I worked whenever possible, a sedative-induced drowsiness limited the focused time I was able to expend on studying. If not for more pressing worries about health, I'm sure that the anxiety about graduating would have been overwhelming. As it was, I simply did as much as I could and, with no television and an inadequate radio, most often settled into a contemplative haze.

I had, of course, missed Party Weekend, and Walt had informed Pat that I'd have to postpone our date. The Monday after the party, however, I heard that the Five Screaming Niggers had returned to Colgate. But they'd performed only one night. Apparently the festivities had escalated beyond the usual riotous clamor and the revelers had become overly incited. In the middle of the group's third set, not only had someone made a too-aggressive pass at the sexy singer but another drunken student had also poured beer into the saxophonist's horn. A brief scuffle had ensued, during which a knife was pulled and two students had received superficial wounds. The Five Screaming Niggers apparently dropped their happy minstrel guise, took their money, packed up, and left.

Now, despite doctor's orders to avoid it, my first impulse was to laugh. And since one of the black underclassmen who had begun hanging out in the basement brought the news, I did allow myself to at least chortle mildly. After all, on the surface, the incident was outrageously funny, particularly since no one was seriously hurt. I was surprised that the mayhem hadn't taken a more sinister turn. Lying there imagining the scene, I couldn't help wondering how the students must have felt when, after being mistreated, those self-proclaimed niggers rebelled and revealed themselves as something other than the exotic clowns they'd pretended to be. *What's wrong with our niggers? Have they gone crazy?* My freshman friend had to restrain me even though, when I'd shared the speculation, he cracked up.

Later, when alone, however, I tried to view the incident more soberly. It was, I thought, the price of the ticket—the inevitable result when, for small immediate gains, you take on a role that was little more than someone else's illusion. Sooner or later it boomerangs and, like a bad joke, comes back to haunt and ridicule you.

During my stay in the infirmary, I had plenty of time to ruminate. Either moving hazily in and out of a drugged stupor or alert but bedridden and bored, I could do little else except read course assignments or stare out across the street at Huntington Gymnasium and the adjacent ski slope. Much of my reading involved assignments for Professor Sio's course on the American Negro, and that prompted more thoughts on the race issue.

The more I thought about it, the less surprised I was that the Screaming Niggers had been feverishly embraced by white college students at Colgate and elsewhere. In a sense, the guitarist was right. The fact was, they were not only helping to introduce powerful, emotionally charged music that roused their mostly white, middle-class collegiate audiences but also exposing that audience to the unique cultural yield of a distinctly African American heritage. And mainstream absorption of that culture—as it had at the turn of the century, when such black vaudeville performers as Williams and Walker (billed as the Two Real Coons) revitalized American popular entertainment, or two decades later, when jazz and such Negro dances as the Black Bottom and Charleston set the twenties to roaring—would accelerate blacks' struggle for equal rights. Fact, however, as Miss Aggie would have quickly pointed out, did not always reveal the truth. While the Two Real Coons' early-twentieth-century act may have hastened mainstream acceptance of Negro performers and recently freed slaves, by the early sixties a group called the Five Screaming Niggers was as outdated and recidivistic as the Cakewalk and blackface makeup. Many of those students, while eagerly yielding to the pulsating lure of the music, were simultaneously affirming their condescending, romanticized, mostly distorted view of Negroes. For many of them, the Screaming Niggers remained caricatures, confirmed members of an alien class who, however talented, encouraged and happily acceded to the role of amusing, one-dimensional exotics. They may have come bearing a valuable gift, but cloaked in the fantasy they unmindfully shaped, it was mostly squandered.

Even the coeds who enthusiastically reached out to dispense favors, a phenomenon the guitarist had acknowledged with a furtive wink, often demanded an extremely high toll. My experience with the young Southern belle had given me a taste of how insistently those favors could be tendered and how determined the bearer could be, even when spurned. And during the late sixties and seventies, those formerly taboo invitations would increase. "Guilt pussy" was readily available but usually came at the cost of either the pretense or actuality of reducing yourself to a cipher—affecting, if only for a moment, the guise of the misused, deprived, and pitiable pariah the mainstream envisioned or *becoming* the statistical casualty or enraged victim whose presence they eagerly endorsed. You merely had to assume the role of the wrongfully treated, angry nigger and demand some redress or slyly suggest that you were being rejected because you were black. The downside was that, when you accepted the designation and the favors (whether an easy lay or a quick buck), began acting out the part, you were most often forced to abandon your birthright as a complex, multifaceted human be-ing—an individual. Moreover, just as the gold-toothed guitarist had found at Colgate, sooner or later someone would take you at your word. The role invited the traditional disdain America had accorded its prime scapegoats and whipping boys since slavery.

I didn't ignore my other course work, but lying in the infirmary that winter I often pored over the sociological and psychological reports, novels, and biographical accounts that were assigned for the Negro class. And after the second operation, about a week be-fore I was released, I was thoroughly convinced that the class, the *study* of the so-called Negro, except for Baldwin and Ellison, was misdirected. We were examining *symptoms* of the root social prob-lem—studying the behavior of a group of people arbitrarily lumped together and indiscriminately maligned while drawing conclusions based on a false premise. Yet no one questioned the premise.

The hordes of multiethnic people I'd met in Harlem and Youngstown, I had found, were as diverse as any other segment of the population. They would, without outside coercion, have classi-fied themselves according to their varying individual likes and dis-likes. It was externally imposed isolation, housing restrictions, limited job and educational opportunities, and an ongoing societal lie that cast them as a singular racial entity, that set them apart and, defensively, united them. The Negro was more a social and political category, carefully designed by nonblacks for their own benefit, than a meaningful genetic or racial classification; the Negro course, it seemed to me, was only peripherally addressing the real issue. Colgate might have more productively offered a course in "white paranoia" or "Caucasian myopia" and examined why white America had so insistently affirmed racial designations and America's caste system.

After being released from the infirmary in mid-March and told that I shouldn't participate in competitive sports again, I returned to classes. The doctors' warning, while it didn't keep me off the bas-ketball courts, did demolish that faint but still alluring temptation to try my hand at professional baseball. Now I was determined to push toward a writing career.

Since I was far behind in all of my classes, I struggled during the remainder of the semester. Nearly all my time was spent studying and trying to catch up. Despite my efforts, I finished the term with the lowest grade average I'd gotten since my freshman year. None of my classes were as disappointing as the American Negro course, however; I finished the course with a C. Now, this was partly because of my absence and the fact that Professor Sio was one of the most demanding teachers at Colgate. But it also reflected our conflicting views of the Negro problem. I was more inclined to side with Malcolm X and the assertiveness urged by the Muslims and, later, by the SNCC than with the passive resistance Martin Luther King Jr. advocated. It was an unpopular position to hold and defend in an integrated setting during the early sixties. So, too, was my inability to accept the characterization of black culture as being the contorted, near-pathological reaction that many of our class readings suggested. Angry, disruptive responses and curtailed ambition, self-defeating as they might be, to my mind were not abnormal reactions in a society where one's self-worth was challenged and aspirations suppressed on a daily basis. Moreover, black life to me was as diverse as mainstream life, had in fact spawned a culture that was richer than any other in America. Still, it was a frustrating and ironic experience, particularly since I was the only black person in the class.

Finally, however, it only strengthened my resolve to celebrate the culture that had grown from a disenfranchised and repressed community and to ridicule racism. I didn't know where the path would take me, but it seemed the only realistic choice.

I did allow myself two diversions that spring. One was to get away to Syracuse on a few occasions. Most often, on those trips, I saw Pat. And by the end of the term we had started dating. The relationship didn't truly warm up until the following summer, but it was during the last few months of my senior year that the attraction began. And in the summer of 1963, just after she graduated, we were married. Our daughter Kim was born the following year.

I also amused myself, whenever time and the pressure of cramming allowed, with further contemplation of a parody that I'd begun while laid up in the infirmary. It kept me laughing and deflected some of my growing frustration with the Negro course. Partially inspired by George Schuyler and Jonathan Swift, it was set in a tiny mythical country whose chief export was wild berries. The problem was, fewer and fewer people were drawn to fruit gathering as a career. To resolve the quandary, the nation's leaders had established a caste system; they arbitrarily designated all short people—anyone under five feet, four and three-quarter inches—as Runties. Being closer to the ground, the logic went, they were ideal for the task of picking berries. The dimensions that would define the group and funnel its members into field work were selected because the nation's ruler was five feet, five inches tall.

Forced to work in the berry fields, denied access to other pursuits, and ostracized because they were somewhat odd and much too down-to-earth, they became pariahs; Squat Laws were passed to keep them in their place. Soon, although Elevated people seemed to enjoy patting Runties on the head for good luck whenever they looked down and saw one, the isolation was complete. They were forced to live in Bantamtown since all mainstream houses were built with extra-large steps, high-placed doorknobs, and cabinets and bathroom fixtures that were just beyond the reach of those in the lower class. Chairs and tables as well as bars in restaurants were heightened to ensure that any Runtie who tried to integrate would find it practically impossible to eat or drink comfortably. The children of Runties were taught in special schools that had smaller books, which, of necessity had less information. An underground petite market quickly developed among the Runties, and unscrupulous capitalists began selling them stools, oversized books, stretching devices, instant-growth vitamins, and shoe lifts at elevated prices. When it was discovered that many Runties were passing by using the outlawed shoe lifts and sneaking into Elevated facilities, further measures were taken. Even Italian and soul food restaurants, following the Japanese lead, demanded that customers take off their shoes before entering. Although a few Runties passed over into the mainstream, Elevated population, by and large the restrictions worked.

Soon, however, locked out of Elevated society, the Runties accepted their situation and began developing their own low-down culture. Their speech began to assume a colorful, doubled-edged piquancy. Faced with the obviously sardonic greeting "What's up?" for instance, they'd laugh quizzically and reply, "Livin' *Mi-noot*, Homes!" or, "Down in the dumps!"—which to those in the inner circle meant they were getting over. Since, ironically, their voices were generally an octave higher than Elevated people's, they sang with a uniquely soulful falsetto tone; moreover, with shorter legs and smaller feet, they were extremely spry and nimble footed on the dance floor. And while obviously earthier and less upstanding than their loftier countrymen—despite their own limited stature and the size of the hurdles they faced—they still demonstrated a remarkable ability to flourish and get over.

Most surprisingly, despite being ostracized from high society, they developed a seemingly carefree recreational and social life. Elevated people were astounded and perplexed. They couldn't understand why Runties were always smiling, laughing, dancing, and singing in that ebullient high-pitched tone. Finding an explanation became a national obsession and reams of esoteric, pseudoscientific but inconclusive sociological studies were turned out by high-minded academicians in the country's most highly regarded universities. Meanwhile, notwithstanding lofty mainstream critics' insistence that the culture was of little or no value, curious, free-spirited Elevated people began sneaking downtown in hopes that they too might loosen up and get down with it. Mixed Short and Tall cabarets sprung up all over Bantamtown, and Elevated folks swarmed in to get a taste of the action. Mystified by the attraction, Elevated leaders dispatched musicologists to eavesdrop and study Runtie music. When the low-down tunes were recorded and released, they soared up the charts and became the national rage. Not without a sense of spritelike, if underhanded, mischievousness, Runties devised new dances—the Stoop, Get Down, and Hunch—to accompany their music and watched with amused detachment as Elevated folks scrunched and contorted themselves in a most often vain attempt to emulate them.

The Runtie craze quickly reached its apex, or nadir, depending on where you stood on the issue. There were, after all, some nettling repercussions to the infatuation. Some Elevated women, for instance, abandoned high heels and developed a taste for lowly pursuits and undercover Bantamtown intrigues. Elevated children began mimicking the distinctive Bantamtown posture and sprightly strut—began walking with hunched, short-gaited strides and a curious dip in their hips. Many Elevated orthopedics panicked and predicted a breakdown of proper social bearing. Linguists were equally miffed, since those same children were adopting shorthand, colloquial phrases such as "down and dirty"; a few of the more rebellious took to wearing the popular Runtie T-shirt that proudly proclaimed, STUNT YOUR GROWTH.

Despite the objections of the Big-Its Society (a conservative, well-heeled, separatist group), the most talented Runties were increasingly invited uptown to Elevated soirees. In some parts of the country, the ban was lifted on shoe lifts and more and more Runties disappeared into the larger population. The newfound popularity, however, along with the increased desertion of celebrity Runties, began to divide the community.

Two factions evolved. Runtie integrationists, who advocated buying stools and lifts and disappearing into the Elevated world, opened their own businesses or joined large corporations, where many climbed up the corporate ladder by marketing products for Runt people. On the other hand, Runtie nationalists urged their followers to marry low and buy short; they roused street-corner gatherings with calls to "hold on to the short end of the stick" and brandished placards that urged supporters to adhere to the popular slogan STUNT YOUR GROWTH or asked HOW LOW CAN YOU GO?

The burlesque helped lighten my mood and entertained some of the basement denizens during the last weeks of school. And up until final exams, toying with its inherent ironies provided a much-needed break from the brutal regime of cramming to which I'd subjected myself in an attempt to make up for the lost weeks in the infirmary.

### III

I was ambivalent about graduation. The elaborate ceremony and rituals struck me as overwrought, superfluous, and somehow only vaguely connected to the real experience of having spent four years at Colgate. I didn't purchase a class ring for similar reasons. If my presence didn't reflect enough change to demonstrate that I'd made the journey, I reasoned, then the symbolic jewelry was mere show. Moreover, I knew that with or without a ring, to most mainstream Americans, as the Screaming Niggers' guitarist had laughingly reminded me, I'd remain an outsider. No, for me it had been a subjective journey; and I hoped that I would walk away from it free from many of the binds that had been externally imposed as well as those I'd unconsciously foisted on myself.

At the torch-lit procession around Taylor Lake the night before the graduation ceremony, however, I began to feel the impact of the pageantry. My cynical attitude wilted somewhat as the senior class marched down the hill to the lake. Still, standing along its edges, we all breathed a collective sigh of relief as the torchlight shimmered across the lake's surface and we finished singing the alma mater. It was impressive, but all the while I reminded myself that it would soon be over.

My parents and sisters, along with my sister-in-law Julia and her sister Wilhelmina, had arrived earlier in the evening; they were among the crowd that had gathered on Whitnall Field to watch the procession. After the elaborate proceedings had ended, we had dinner at the Bluebird Restaurant and I showed them a bit of the campus before they retired to a freshman dorm, where sleeping arrangements had been made for visiting families. Back at our rooms, Walt and I and the rest of the crew had one last nightcap in Andrews basement before retiring.

After breakfast at the Inn, I spent the next morning showing my family around the rest of the campus. Again, my mother beamed. It had been a long journey from the cotton fields of Tunica, Mississippi, to the ivy halls of Hamilton, an expanse that, despite my effort, I knew I could never fully appreciate. I did realize on that afternoon, however, that she and my father had, at least in spirit, traveled every step with me. Tennessee even momentarily relinquished the wary grin that, unless he was gambling and winning, was his most enthusiastic concession to enjoyment; he flashed a broad, unrestrained smile as I passed them on my way to the stage where I received my diploma. The cap and gown that I wore that day and the graduation ceremony itself were probably more of a triumph for them than it was for me. Black-and-white photographs taken with them that afternoon, some of which my sister Doris preserved, recall some of my favorite memories of Katie and Tennessee.

Just after midday, the graduation ceremonies began. And although all the seniors were uncomfortable on that sweltering June day, we sat quietly through rousing speeches that a few months ago we would have cynically ridiculed. It was, at least to me, my family's day, not mine. After the diplomas had been distributed and our caps tossed into the humid afternoon air, there was a wild celebration in the Quad. When the uproar subsided, I found my family and moved away from the crowd for a last good-bye. They were driving back to Ohio that afternoon and wanted to leave immediately, so our celebration was brief. Less than a half hour later, they were on their way out of Hamilton.

I had packed the day before, and shortly after saying good-bye to a few of my classmates, I began the drive to New York City. I had arranged to rent a room in St. Albans, Queens, with a friend of Pat's family. Those living arrangements and my anticipation of a closer relationship with Pat were the only concrete plans I had made. Everything else was unsettled.

I was excited and optimistic about moving to New York. But I was uncertain about what I'd do. I certainly had no idea that during the coming years I would meet, hang out with, interview, or review the books of many of the black writers whose works I'd read in high school and college (among them, Gwendolyn Brooks, Langston Hughes, Ellison, and Baldwin), as well as nearly all of the late sixties and early seventies rising literary stars (from Nikki Giovanni, Ishmael Reed, Claude Brown, and Alice Walker to Albert Murray, Alex Haley, John Updike, and Toni Morrison). Nor could I imagine that within eight years, as a writer and editor at the *New York Times Book Review* as well as the editor of a short-lived paperback literary magazine, I'd be actively involved in the ferment of the seventies' black arts movement.

As I sped down Route 20 toward New York, however, I did feel an overwhelming sense of exultation and liberation. I was determined to study and celebrate the cultural riches that had flowered from the so-called Negro's resilient spirit and bizarre American experiences. Mainstream denial and its mostly whitewashed representation notwithstanding, that culture—its comedy, dance, and music, at least—as far as I could see, had quietly shaped America's popular culture for decades. It would loom even more influentially in years to come.

If I was fortunate, I mused on that hot June day, the celebration might unearth an answer to the most tantalizing question Miss Aggie had ever posed for me.

Who knows, I smiled, perhaps I could, at least figuratively, " 'count *for where Bojangles's daddy came from.*"

The dance had only begun.